The Moroccan Soul

France Overseas
Studies in Empire and Decolonization

SERIES EDITORS:
A. J. B. Johnston
James D. Le Sueur
Tyler Stovall

The Moroccan Soul

French Education, Colonial Ethnology, and Muslim Resistance, 1912–1956

Spencer D. Segalla

UNIVERSITY OF NEBRASKA PRESS
LINCOLN AND LONDON

© 2009 by the
Board of Regents of
the University of Nebraska
All rights reserved
Manufactured in the
United States of America
∞
Library of Congress
Cataloging-in-Publication Data
Segalla, Spencer D.
The Moroccan soul:
French education,
colonial ethnology, and
Muslim resistance, 1912–1956 /
Spencer D. Segalla.
   p. cm. — (France overseas)
Includes bibliographical
references and index.
ISBN 978-0-8032-1778-2
(cloth: alk. paper)
ISBN 978-1-4962-0214-7
(paper: alk. paper)
1. Education — Morocco —
   History — 20th century.
2. French — Morocco — History
   — 20th century.
3. Education and state —
   Morocco.
4. Islamic religious education —
   Morocco.
I. Title.
LA1941.S44 2009
370.964 — dc22
2008036636

Set in Galliard.
Designed by R. W. Boeche.

For Ryan David

Contents

Preface	ix
Acknowledgments	xiii
Note on Arabic Spellings	xv
List of Abbreviations Used in the Text	xvii
1. Empire and Education	1
2. An Uncertain Beginning	33
3. The West African Connection	61
4. A New Pedagogy for Morocco?	89
5. A Psychological Ethnology	115
6. "A Worker Proletariat with a Dangerous Mentality"	151
7. Elite Demands	177
8. Nests of Nationalism	203
9. Legacies and Reversals	237
Notes	265
Bibliography	291
Index	309

Preface

This book is about French education in Morocco during the "protectorate," that is, the period of colonial rule, from 1912 to 1956. I am neither French nor Moroccan, yet I cannot pretend to be a disinterested observer in the matters discussed herein. As a former teacher at the Casablanca American School, I was for years a participant in a contested project of Western education in the Kingdom of Morocco. I say contested because it was not always clear whose agenda or agendas I and my colleagues were serving there: that of the U.S. Department of State, which provided a modicum of funding and had helped found the school; that of the Europe-based International Baccalaureate, which provided the curricular guidelines; or those of the mostly wealthy, mostly Moroccan parents for whom we were hired help, charged with the task of preparing their sons and daughters for a future in the Moroccan elite. I did not feel like a colonizer there. Not always.

As an academic historian, I have striven to keep my history tightly bound to the footnotes, tying my descriptions, narratives, analyses, and conclusions to a close reading of the documentary evidence. However, I acknowledge two prejudices that pervade this book. The present study focuses on French imaginings of Moroccanness as a static, natural, and neatly bounded identity. The reader will readily note my distaste for such concepts. It was at the Casablanca American

School that I developed this aversion, along with my interest in the history of Morocco. It made me uncomfortable when friends (Moroccan or Western) told me that my students were "not really Moroccan" because they spoke too much English or too much French. It made me uncomfortable to hear the native-born population of the kingdom described as a mixture of "Moroccans" and "Jews," and to know that my Moroccan-born students of south Asian descent would grow up to be excluded from the dominant conception of Moroccan nationhood. In my position as an "international educator" and as a scholar of Western imperialism, I could not help but wonder how ideas about the "Real Moroccan" were entangled in Europe's history of empire building, nation building, and school building. The West has devoted much energy to producing and propagating bounded descriptions and categorizations of conquered populations. The focus here is on Western pedagogical constructions of Moroccanness, and their practical consequences.

The second prejudice that I acknowledge concerns those who claim to prioritize action over intellect. When I left Casablanca in 2001 I returned to a United States gripped by a spasm of anti-intellectualism, in which talk-show hosts and political activists routinely denounced academics and intellectuals as, at best, effete and irrelevant, and at worst, treasonous. The most sophisticated sources of information and analysis were maligned as untrustworthy, while the population increasingly turned to the purveyors of flashy graphics, short sentences, and lowest common denominators. Political leaders and pseudo-intellectuals turned a lack of erudition into a point of pride and put forward the most inane and simplistic renditions of the world's affairs. Decisive action ("leadership") was meant to substitute for careful consideration and informed consent. Returning home after researching in the dusty tomes and files of protectorate Morocco, I was struck by a sense of déjà vu. The culture of Morocco's colonizers had been dominated by a similar fashion for muscular, masculine anti-intellectualism. Alongside French imaginings of the native "Moroccan Soul" was the ideal of the European male who through vigorous colonizing action had shed his soft metropolitan habits and had become a robust, hearty "Marocain." This notion, conceived in opposition to metropolitan intellectualism, bureaucracy, and democracy, became an ideal for Morocco's French policy makers. The results, as I argue, were infelicitous for all concerned.

History provides us with "things to think with," but it should not be turned into parable. The interactions among ethnology, pedagogy, psychology, politics and policy that occurred within French Morocco's colonial educational system were complex enough to prevent any reduction to a roman à clef.

Acknowledgments

This work, although composed mainly of my own analysis of archival and published sources from the colonial era, is built upon the work of other scholars, far too numerous to be named here. Some, however, require special acknowledgment.

On matters concerning French colonialism and anticolonial resistance in Morocco, I have found the work of Edmund Burke III, John Halstead, William Hoisington, C. R. Pennell, and Daniel Rivet particularly invaluable. My discussion of West Africa is heavily indebted to the work of Denise Bouche, Alice Conklin, James Genova, and G. Wesley Johnson. There are also several authors who have dealt specifically and extensively with colonial education in Morocco and to whom I am greatly in debt. These include Roger Gaudefroy-Demombynes, whose 1928 doctoral thesis was informed by his access to the protectorate's teachers and educational administrators, but who provides a perspective not found in official publications. A more comprehensive history of protectorate education is provided by Lucien Paye, who was the head of Muslim Education from 1939 through the early 1940s and was critical of the approach taken by his predecessors. More recently, excellent studies of particular aspects of colonial education in Morocco have been produced by Abdelqader Baina, Michael Laskier, Mekki Merrouni, and Pierre Vermeren.

I am also grateful to many other scholars whose suggestions, guidance, theories, and examples have shaped this book. First and foremost I thank my dissertation director, Herman Lebovics, for his practical, intellectual, and moral guidance over the years, and for the models that his writing and scholarship have provided. Input on this project was also provided by Amanda Bruce (my historian spouse), Osama Abi-Mershed, Frank Anshen, Ruth Bottigheimer, Julia Clancy-Smith, Frederick Cooper, Troy Duster, Yvonne Fabella, Ruth Ginio, Jonathan Katz, Daniel Monk, Ann Morning, Martin Thomas, Emmanuelle Saada, Madani Saïd, Olufemi Vaughan, Gary Wilder, and John Williams; I thank all of these individuals for the time, effort, and insight they have generously donated to support and improve this project. I also thank Karl Bottigheimer, Richard Kuisel, Joel Rosenthal, Wolf Schäfer, Fred Weinstein, and Kathleen Wilson for their tutelage and support.

I am extremely grateful to Heather Lundine, Sabrina Stellrecht, and their colleagues at the University of Nebraska Press, and to copyeditor Jonathan Lawrence. This book would also have been impossible without the knowledgeable assistance of the archivists and staff at the Archives nationales de France, the Centre des archives diplomatiques de Nantes, the Centre des archives d'outre-mer, the Fondation du Roi Abdul-Aziz Al Saoud pour les études islamiques et les sciences humaines, and the Bibliothèque générale et archives du Maroc. Many thanks are also due to Alicia Sanchez at the Nassau Community College Interlibrary Loan office.

My preliminary research in Morocco was made possible by my employment at the Casablanca American School; funding for the writing of my doctoral dissertation was provided by a Spencer Foundation Dissertation Fellowship for Research Related to Education. I am grateful to *French Colonial History* and the *Journal of North African Studies* for publishing my early efforts on this topic; although those early articles differ from the material that follows in organization and content, input from the journals' editors and reviewers played an important role in shaping the present volume.

Of course, all the shortcomings of this book come from me alone.

Note on Arabic Spellings

When spelling Arabic words, I have aimed for legibility and transparency rather than strict formal transliteration. In some cases I have chosen the more commonly used English spelling (e.g., Fez, ulema). Otherwise, I have generally preferred a simplified version of the transliteration recommended by the *International Journal of Middle East Studies*. Hamza and ʿayn are usually omitted. However, I have also tried to promote consistency between the text and the references by adopting, where it seemed appropriate, the French spellings used in the works I have cited. The reader will kindly forgive the inconsistencies that inevitably result.

Abbreviations Used in the Text

AEMNAF	Association des étudiants musulmans nord-africains en France (Association of North African Muslim Students in France)
AIU	Alliance israélite universelle (Universal Jewish Alliance)
AOF	Afrique occidentale française (French West Africa)
CESM	Certificat d'études secondaire musulmanes (Certificate of Secondary Muslim Studies)
DESM	Diplôme d'études secondaire musulmanes (Diploma of Secondary Muslim Studies)
DIP	Direction de l'instruction publique, des beaux-arts et des antiquités (Direction of Public Instruction, Fine Arts, and Antiquities)
ESLADB	École supérieure de langue arabe et de dialectes berbères (Advanced School of Arabic Language and Berber Dialects)
IHEM	Institut des hautes études marocaines (Institute of Higher Moroccan Studies)

The Moroccan Soul

1. Empire and Education

> *What I dream of, what many of you dream of along with me, is that among all these disorders that are shaking the world to the point that one asks when and how it will ever regain its equilibrium, in Morocco a solid edifice will be built, orderly and harmonious; that it will offer the sight of a group of humanity where men of such diverse origins, habits, professions and races, pursue, without abdicating any of their individual conceptions, a search for a common ideal and a common rationale of life. Yes, I have dreamed that Morocco would appear one of the most solid bastions of order against the sea of anarchy.* | Resident-General Louis-Hubert Lyautey, 1921

Situated at the northwest corner of Africa, Morocco has long been a crossroads, a place of interaction where merchants, soldiers, preachers, and teachers from Europe, Africa, and Arabia practiced their trades and worked out strategies of survival, domination, and resistance. Phoenicians from the Levant, Romans and Vandals from the north, Arabs from the east, and the local Berber-speaking populations all found in Morocco a site of contestation. The powerful among them sought, through various means, to dominate the culture and discourses of the areas they controlled, in order to maximize their own political and social influence. Meanwhile, the weak pursued strategies of survival and self-advancement, while "deflecting, appropriating, or re-interpreting the teachings and preachings thrust upon them."[1]

In the early twentieth century it was the French who invaded; they would rule Morocco, under the guise of a "protectorate," from 1912 until 1956.

Geographically, Morocco bears a general resemblance to California. Steep cliffs abut a palm-lined western oceanfront; coastal plains yield to foothills, then to mountains. In the south, and to the east of the mountains, lie stony deserts. The human geography of Morocco is likewise diverse. In the colonial period, Arabic dialects were spoken mainly in the cities and parts of the coastal plain, both by the Muslim majority and the Jewish minority. Elsewhere, the tribal people spoke dialects of Berber: Tarifat in the Rif Mountains of the north, Tashlehait in the arid south, and Tamazight in the Atlas Mountains. In these Berber-speaking areas, classical Arabic, the sacred language of the Quran, was used by Muslims for religious purposes, but most had little comprehension of the language.

The pages that follow explore, within the context of French colonialism, the development of certain ideas about "the Moroccan" and the "Moroccan soul," and the effect of these ideas on pedagogy, policy making, and politics. The historical analysis is constructed around three intertwined narratives. The first is the institutional and intellectual history of the French colonial educational system in Morocco, from the founding of the protectorate through independence and the creation of a Moroccan national education system. The second narrative follows the career and ideas of colonial administrator Georges Hardy, from French West Africa, where he served as director of education from 1912 to 1919, to Morocco, where he was director of Public Instruction from 1920 to 1926, and finally to his later career in Algeria and France. The third narrative traces the changing strategies of resistance and contestation employed by both elite and non-elite Moroccan Muslims, culminating in the rise of the Moroccan nationalist movement. The colonial school system is thus examined as a site of interaction among colonial authorities and Moroccan Muslims, exploring how the responses of the colonized shaped the ideas and policies of French colonial education, and how French ideas and policies shaped Moroccan strategies and discourses of accommodation and resistance.

Long before the French conquest, education played an important role in Moroccan society as a means of cultural reproduction and as a form of cultural capital that defined a person's social position. Traditional Moroccan education was primarily religious and legal in character. Most Muslim communities supported a local *msid*, where a *fqih* (religious teacher) taught young boys to memorize the Quran. At this level, education was primarily oral-aural and mnemonic. Even for native speakers of Arabic dialects, Quranic Arabic was quite foreign, but there was little explicit explanation of the texts, and no discussion. The intellectual discipline fostered by such an education was seen as a fundamental part of a proper Muslim upbringing; it facilitated the development of reason, "conceived as man's ability to discipline his nature in order to act in accord with the arbitrary code of conduct laid down by God and epitomized by such acts of communal obedience as the fast of Ramadan."[2] A similar approach to education characterized traditional Jewish schools. A few Moroccan Muslims received a more extensive education through private tutoring in reading and writing and by continuing their education at urban *madaris* and, in rural areas, at the *zawaya* of Sufi brotherhoods. At the top level of Moroccan Islamic education were two mosque-universities – the Qarawiyyin in Fez and the Yusufiyya in Marrakesh – where Islamic scholars, teachers, and judges were trained in Islamic law and theology.

European-style schooling in Morocco predated the protectorate by more than half a century, but on a tiny scale. In the mid-nineteenth century, anxieties about growing European power had led Sultan Moulay Abderrahmane (r. 1822–59) to create an engineering school in Fez and a school of "language, mathematics, and military science" in Tangiers. His successors Sidi Mohammed (1859–73) and Moulay Hassan (1873–94) began sending students to Egypt, Britain, France, Italy, and Spain, where they studied military science, architecture, chemistry, and law. The effect of this educational outreach was minimal, however. In sharp contrast to their counterparts in the Ottoman Empire, the Moroccan students who studied in Europe returned to find their skills underutilized, and men with traditional Islamic training continued to dominate the Moroccan state.[3]

Meanwhile, European teachers began to arrive in Morocco in pursuit of their own agendas. The first European-run schools were established in Morocco by the Paris-based Alliance israélite universelle (AIU), which was founded in Paris in 1860 by a group of Jewish Frenchmen including the politician Adolphe Crémieux. Although the AIU initially focused on the emancipation and gallicization of European Jews, most notably in Serbia and Romania, the AIU opened a school in Tetuan in 1862 and soon administered a network of French-style schools throughout North Africa and in the Ottoman Middle East. In Morocco the AIU gradually gained the support of local Jewish communities, although some traditionalists viewed the AIU teachers as dangerous atheists. By 1912 the AIU schools in Morocco had enrolled more than thirty-two hundred boys (including a few Muslims) and eighteen hundred girls.[4]

The Alliance israélite was soon followed by Spanish Franciscans and English and American Protestant groups, who opened small missionary schools that sought to convert the local Muslims and Jews. French Catholic missions were established in the port towns, although they ministered largely to Europeans. Meanwhile, the secular French state also began to take an interest in education in Morocco. In 1894 the private Alliance française, funded by the colonial administration in Algeria, began to offer classes in Tangiers. French consulates supported the opening of schools for Europeans and for the children of Moroccan consular employees and others with protégé status.

The development of European schooling in the decades preceding the French conquest was accompanied by growing European economic and political influence in Morocco, influence that progressively disrupted the power of the Moroccan sultan's state, or *makhzan*. In 1856 the British had negotiated a trade agreement that opened Morocco to European imports, while limiting the customs duties that the sultan could collect. European imports meant disaster for many of Morocco's urban crafts, especially textiles, shoemaking, soap, and pottery. The restrictions on revenue collection, combined with a Spanish invasion of the north in 1859, also brought fiscal disaster to the Moroccan state. Spanish forces withdrew in exchange for territorial concessions, but the *makhzan* was required to pay war reparations. This soon set in motion a process of *makhzan* decline that paralleled developments in the Ottoman Empire, Egypt, and China. The *makhzan*'s inability to pay its indemnity to Spain forced the Moroccan government to allow its customs services to submit to supervision by European officials. In hopes of alleviating Morocco's weakness relative to Europe, the sultan initiated reforms of the state and the army, but such reforms, especially the upgrading of military technology, increased the *makhzan*'s reliance on foreign loans. In exchange, Morocco was forced to accept still more European influence. After the 1904 Anglo-French Entente Cordiale, this influence was increasingly French. The French government took over the supervision of *makhzan* finances, French individuals bought up land, and French companies expanded their share of the Moroccan economy.[5]

French influence undermined the legitimacy of the reigning sultan, Moulay Abdelaziz (1894–1908), and precipitated the collapse of the Moroccan state. Public hostility to the foreigners created opportunities for Abdelaziz's Moroccan rivals, who denounced the sultan as an agent of the infidels. The more unstable the sultan's position became, the more dependent he became on French support, and the more susceptible to accusations of incompetence and collaboration. In 1907, riots and attacks on Europeans prompted the French to occupy Oujda in the northeast and then to bombard and occupy Casablanca. When Abdelaziz was unable to respond, a coalition of tribes and regional strongmen rebelled. By the end of the year, Abdelaziz's brother, Abdelhafid, was proclaimed sultan by the *ulema* (Islamic scholars) of Fez, on the condition that he eradicate foreign influence from Morocco. This, however, proved impossible. When Abdelhafid turned to the foreign powers for the loans he needed to establish a functioning state, he was forced to accept new concessions, and the tribes around Fez and Meknes rebelled against him in 1911. When the rebels attacked, the French intervened, occupying Meknes and Fez. Abdelhafid was saved, but he became dependent on the French, who began the military and political takeover of the country. This alarmed the Spanish and the Germans, but Madrid's interests were soon satisfied by French agreement to a separate Spanish protectorate in northern Morocco, and Berlin was consoled by a French cession of Congo River territory to Germany.[6]

The 1912 Treaty of Fez established the structure of the French protectorate in Morocco. The Moroccan state would continue to exist, headed by the sultan and his grand vizier, under the supervision of a parallel French administration headed by a resident-general in Rabat. In theory, the French "Residency" would assist the sultan's *makhzan* in the creation of European-style administrative and legal structures that would exert central control over the lives of Moroccans in a way that the previous regime had not. In practice, however, the authority of the *makhzan* was progressively eroded, as the French state took over crucial government functions. In the initial chaos of 1912 the French resorted to playing kingmaker, forcing the uncooperative Sultan Abdelhafid to abdicate the throne in favor of his brother, Moulay Youssef. Between 1912 and 1914 the *makhzan* dissolved its ministries of Foreign Affairs, War, Finance, and Administrative Appeals. The *makhzan* retained authority over traditional legal and religious functions under the grand vizier and through the new ministries of Justice and Hubus (charitable religious foundations).[7]

This arrangement proved very useful for the new colonial regime. The illusion of Moroccan sovereignty facilitated governance of the Moroccan population and sheltered the colonial regime from the meddling of the metropolitan Republic. The protectorate arrangement also allowed France to establish control over Morocco's economic resources despite the treaties of Madrid and Algeciras, which guaranteed equal access to the various European powers. Legally speaking, it was the Moroccan *makhzan*, not France, that took control of Morocco's mineral resources, water supplies, and arable land, but it was the French who benefited.[8] However, the great benefits of this arrangement for France gave the *makhzan* some leverage; the will of the sultan and his viziers could not be disregarded altogether, lest the illusion of the protectorate become inconveniently conspicuous.

Education, Assimilation, and Association

Although the *makhzan* retained its authority over traditional Islamic education, the French soon established a separate colonial school system. Colonial educational systems are particularly interesting subjects for historians because they were sites of close interactions between colonizing and colonized populations, loci of cultural contact that illustrate "the dynamics and inner conflicts of colonial societies; the social spaces that served as zones of both contact and separation between colonial and colonized societies; the borders between groups and the question of how those borders are constructed."[9] The reproduction of cultures, the definition of social roles, the categorization of individuals, and the transmission of ideas are central functions of all modern schools. In colonial situations, however, these functions demanded extra attention. As Frederick Cooper has argued, a central problem of empire building was that "colonial rulers needed to co-opt old elites and generate new collaborators, but such ties might soften the colonizer-colonized distinction."[10] Colonial schools aimed to produce willing collaborators among the colonized, but schools also created intimate contact between colonizing and colonized populations, producing the possibility that boundaries between colonizer and colonized might blur. Consequently, colonial states devoted much energy to the policing and definition of these boundaries within the schools, and school systems became places where the relationship between colonizer and colonized produced explicitly articulated theorizations about the nature of colonialism, of the colonizer, and of the colonized.

In Morocco, French-run schools were supposed to reinforce French hegemony by convincing the locals that it was in their best interest to comply with the French colonial agenda. As described by Antonio Gramsci, hegemony consists of "the 'spontaneous' consent given by the great masses of the population to the general direction imposed on social life by the dominant fundamental group; this consent is 'historically' caused by the prestige (and consequent confidence) which the dominant group enjoys because of its position and function in the world of production."[11] In the early decades of French rule in Morocco, however, the prestige of the colonizers had only the shallowest of roots. Yet the protectorate's leaders needed to minimize the overt use of coercion, if only because coercive power and resources were in fact limited. This made educators all the more important as the salesmen of empire. Schooling was intended to minimize conflict by promoting the consent of the colonized.

This proved difficult, of course. There were conflicting interests and agendas among the colonizers and the colonized, and such conflicts could not be resolved through pedagogy. The political and economic inequities of colonialism produced resistance throughout the European empires, and Morocco's French schools for Muslims, rather than functioning as centers of cultural hegemony and political collaboration, became focal points of contestation. The prominent and disproportionate role that graduates of the colonial schools played in anticolonial political movements highlights the frictions produced by colonial schools, but organized political movements represent only one strategy of struggle employed by students, former students, and their families. Moreover, colonial contestation was not limited to a Manichaean struggle between a monolithic imperial project and a unified colonized victim; various groups and individuals in Moroccan society had differing goals, ideals, and strategies.

There was considerable friction among European approaches to colonial theory and policy. Temporally, the Moroccan protectorate was formed late in the trajectory of European colonialism; it was thus a site of dissonance between French colonial discourses of "assimilationism" and the discourses of a supposedly new, better, and modern colonialism based on "association."[12] Assimilationism reflected the habits of French Jacobin republicanism: a pronounced faith in the ability of reason to prescribe a universal civilized way of life, and a commitment to universal equality, even if this latter ideal was never quite realized in the colonies. Associationalism, in contrast, affirmed the differences between colonizer and colonized and advocated that the French dominate colonized societies in "association" with native strongmen, without illusions about the applicability of French rights among the non-French. As analytic categories, assimilationism and associationism must be used with caution, however, for there was much overlap and ambiguity among the theories and policies associated with each. Policies of association often produced assimilating effects, while assimilationist theories were carefully circumscribed in practice.

Marie-Paule Ha has argued that assimilationism was generally a fiction and that "the belief that French colonial policy sought to transform 'natives' into 'Frenchmen' through pedagogic acculturation is an enduring myth, one that continues to inform the writings of many a contemporary Western postcolonial critic."[13] However, this myth, like many others, had roots in historical reality. In the nineteenth century there had been much French rhetoric, especially in pedagogical circles, about transforming natives into Frenchmen, and such rhetoric was not always empty. Since the Jules Ferry education laws of the 1880s, the Third Republic had sought to use schools in France to assimilate a polyglot and Catholic population to a universal and secular French civilization (turning "peasants into Frenchmen"). This pedagogical war against diversity became central to French republicanism and to the culture of the French teaching corps.[14] French teachers in the colonies often found it difficult to deviate from this pattern, regardless of the official policy. Moreover, assimilationist pedagogy was officially revived after World War II, leaving an enduring impression on popular memory. Yet it is true that French education assimilated very few colonial subjects to the point that they affirmed a French cultural identity; French law assimilated fewer still to French rights and citizenship. Exclusion and racism were intrinsic to colonialism.

Consequently, "assimilationism" was often a phantom — a fantasy of metropolitan republicans and a bogeyman for colonial conservatives and anticolonial nationalists. Yet assimilation was taken seriously by certain colonial subjects who saw it as a means to acquire power and dignity within the colonial situation, even as they hoped to retain their own cultural distinctiveness. Attempts by the colonized to demand inclusion using European discourses of universalism, rights, and political participation were as old as the French and Haitian revolutions.[15] However, such universalist demands were multiplied by the spread of these European discourses via colonial education in the nineteenth century. As Jean Suret-Canale has noted, it was precisely to counter these demands for inclusion that, in the early twentieth century, "the alleged 'assimilationism' was condemned as demagoguery and incapable of being realized."[16] Challenged by French-speaking colonial subjects demanding the rights of Frenchmen, colonial policy makers and especially colonial educators were then charged with the task of shepherding, preserving, and controlling the cultures and self-understandings of colonized peoples in order to prevent or stifle assimilationist demands.

Gary Wilder has argued convincingly that the rejection of assimilation was neither a failure nor a contradiction of the republican ideal. The delineation of reason and civilization and the very creation of a republic required the delineation of the irrational, the uncivilized, those unworthy of active citizenship, and those outside the republic. Rejection of assimilationism did not necessarily mean the rejection of republican values.[17]

This realization should not, however, obscure the fact that many French imperialists did indeed reject the values of the Republic. In the early twentieth century, France remained a divided society, as it had been since the Revolution of 1789. By the early 1900s most French conservatives had conceded "that some accommodation of the Republic was necessary,"[18] but this accommodation was grudging and, as the events of 1940 would eventually demonstrate, temporary. The divisions between republicans and anti-republicans in France took on new life and new forms in the colonial empire, producing "heated arguments between Frenchmen deeply divided over *what France stood for* in the world."[19] For traditionalists and Catholics alienated by the ascendance of republicans and Dreyfusards in France, the colonies offered an opportunity for redemption and resurgence. Morocco, in particular, was to become the model for a modern society rooted in a conservative respect for authoritarian hierarchies and traditional institutions, an antidote to what French conservatives saw as the rootlessness of the Third Republic.

Lyautey and Lyautism
Abdallah Laroui has written that colonial Morocco was cursed with "geographers with brilliant ideas, functionaries with scientific pretensions, soldiers proud of their learning, and art historians who refuse to specialize."[20] Colonial education was particularly susceptible to the aspirations and pretensions of functionaries who fancied themselves scientists or philosophers. Director of Public Instruction Georges Hardy, the central character in the present study, certainly fits Laroui's description. However, all such aspirations among Morocco's colonizers were shaped by the example of Resident-General Lyautey, a soldier who had made his name as a social theorist and yet expressed a deep disdain for intellectualism and theory.

Lyautey was a disciple of Joseph Gallieni, under whom he had served in Indochina and Madagascar. Gallieni's doctrine might be described as the doctrine of having no doctrine, of adapting policy to local conditions. But Lyautey's approach to colonialism went beyond Gallieni's pragmatism. Lyautey sought the rejuvenation of a France that he saw as mired in republican dogmatism, abstract intellectualism, and stifling bureaucracy. This rejuvenation was to occur through the creation of a new colonial man, a man of flexible action and exaggerated masculinity. The Moroccan protectorate was an attempt to do colonialism differently, to learn from the perceived mistakes of the past, and to respect difference in order to forge a more benevolent relationship between colonizer and colonized. Lyautey's protectorate was also an attempt to rejuvenate the agenda of the French Right, fusing nostalgic conservatism with the romanticism of a forward-looking modernist project.

At the heart of Lyautey's colonial philosophy was his loathing of the culture and politics of the metropole. After many years of military service in the colonies, Lyautey had developed disdain for republican France, which he found alien, decadent, and "unhealthy, fatal to will and confidence."[21] "Sick" republican France, in global decline, was contrasted to the vigorous British empire. Britain's strength, according to Lyautey, was rooted in its "serious grasp of social duties, of family, of functions, and respect for one's interlocutor" and in its aristocratic and undemocratic characteristics:

> Above all, they have a government, institutions – and it is not a matter here of the form a regime, which means little, but of fixed parts of their machine, aristocratic in the broadest sense of the word, which assure the permanence of programs, the fixity of methods, the security of persons, the scope of conceptions, and, above all, the hauteur of political views – all this [is] incompatible with the electoral lottery, the ephemeral and arbitrary attribution of functions, the universal incompetence that characterizes our regime.[22]

For Lyautey, the remedy to Parisian decadence could only come from the periphery, from the aristocratic traditions of provincial France and from the colonies, where the rigors and privations of life would purge the French character of weakness. Lyautey repeated Vicompte de Vogue's statement that "the only hope lies in us, the colonials, who remake for ourselves, on a veritable field of action, far from political intrigues, a head, a heart, muscles."²³ Morocco was therefore to be more than just a colony or protectorate – it was to be the birthplace of a new France.

Lyautey despised bureaucratic regulations and argued that colonial administration was chiefly a matter of putting "the right man in the right place" (a phrase he expressed in English).²⁴ He also displayed contempt for academic theoreticians. At the beginning of the protectorate, he had declared: "In order to attend to the difficult birth of this country, I don't want to be assisted by any Molière-type doctors in pointed caps speaking Latin, but by sturdy practitioners who roll up their sleeves and get down to work."²⁵ Applying this muscular philosophy often proved difficult, however. Valuing action and vigor over bureaucratization and contemplation was a challenge for colonial administrators, who were, after all, intellectuals and bureaucrats. But Lyautey's vision of national renewal resonated in conservative circles throughout the empire and in the metropole. After his retirement, Lyautey would be seen as the savior of the French nation. A 1930 scout song would celebrate Morocco's former resident-general:

> Il nous a sortis d' pétrin
> Par lui France est marocaine. . . .
> Sonne, fifre et tambourin
> Il se f . . . des mandarins.²⁶

> [He got us out of a jam
> Thanks to him France is Moroccan. . . .
> Sound the fife and drum
> He doesn't give a d— for mandarins.]

For Lyautey's followers, "marocain" became the antonym of the despised intellectual "mandarin"; the "Moroccan" was a Frenchman who embodied the vigor of Lyautey's new man, forged in the colonies.

Regarding the French relationship with actual Moroccans – the natives of Morocco—Lyautey also had definite opinions. His approach to colonized populations was shaped by Gallieni's *politique des races*, which sought to tailor colonial policy to the needs of particular ethnic groups, and by the "Lyautey method" of colonial conquest. This method, also derived from Gallieni's example, sought to spread French power like a *tache de huile* (oil stain) through the political collaboration of traditional elites, with minimal use of coercive force. In Morocco, Lyautey endeavored to provide

> to the conquered people, among whom one has preserved the integrity of their traditional structures, habits, law — the illusion of their independence. This is the only regime that has a chance to attach itself, really, truly, to the peoples upon whom we impose domination. It is the only regime that truly rests upon the association, the collaboration of two races. These lands must be able to preserve themselves, and consequently see the regime that we bring them as truly preferable, because at the same time as it gives them more security, more wealth, more order and more justice, it safeguards all the things that constitute the soul of this people, her traditions, her customs, her mores, her hierarchy, her religion.[27]

This was not just a vision of indirect rule, but an expression of Lyautey's attachment to the values of conservatism. Of course, these goals were subordinate to the overarching need to preserve French domination. Nevertheless, in twentieth-century Morocco, safeguarding the culture and "soul" of the Moroccan people and preserving the collaboration of the Moroccan elite became policy priorities for the colonial state. These priorities were particularly noticeable in urban planning and in education. In both, the modern goal of rational control over populations was fused with the conservative desire to preserve an attachment to the past and to promote the separation of cultures and classes.[28] In urban planning, the result was the creation of new European districts adjacent to the Moroccan city centers, a system that produced inequalities so appalling that historian Janet

Abu-Lughod has compared it to South Africa's apartheid. To Lyautey, however, this urban segregation was a remedy to the ills common to colonial cities, in which "the indigenous city is polluted, sabotaged; all of its charm is gone, and the elite of the population has left."[29] Lyautey was untroubled by the inequality between European districts with modern amenities and Moroccan districts with "charm."

Segregation of Moroccans from Europeans would also characterize education in Morocco, as would gross inequalities of resources and opportunities. For Lyautey, however, inequality was not a social ill: he equated equality and integration with social disintegration and decline. Accordingly, segregation was not merely an administrative convenience or a tool to facilitate exploitation; it was seen to be the essence of a healthy society, and therefore a fundamental obligation of the modern state. Lyautey's commitment to preserving Moroccan culture, and to preserving Islam, was an explicit rejection of republican assimilationism, but it was also a departure from the Catholic evangelism that had been republicanism's chief rival (and occasional collaborator) in the colonies during the nineteenth century. The commitment to preserve Islam made a virtue out of necessity; Catholic missionaries had largely despaired of converting North Africa's Arabic-speaking Muslim populations, although they had achieved some success among Algeria's Kabyle Berbers.[30]

Lyautey's desire to preserve difference also reflected the long-standing European fear of miscegenation and *métissage*, of course. In the nineteenth century this fear had manifested itself in biological terms; the offspring of mixed parentage was seen as "an abnormal, monstrous being."[31] However, biological theories of race were merely one incarnation of the tendency to condemn hybridity in order to preserve and define European dominance. In Lyautey's Morocco, the pursuit of purity would be expressed primarily in terms of culture and psychology. This made schooling as important as breeding: schools for Moroccan Muslims were intended to prevent cultural, social, and psychological miscegenation.

Ethnology and Pedagogy

The charge to preserve ethnic difference ("the soul of this people") meant that colonial education became imbricated with the discourse of colonial ethnology. Policy makers hoped that ethnology would provide the knowledge about Moroccan society necessary to adapt policy to ethnic traits and to tell educators just what it was that they were supposed to be preserving.

As Edmund Burke III has noted, ethnology at the dawn of the Moroccan protectorate was still not represented by chairs or programs in the French university system. The Société d'ethnographie de Paris had been founded in 1859, and the study of Muslim societies was pursued in the École des langues orientales and the Collège de France. Much early ethnography had been produced by colonial officials, such as the officers of the French army's Bureaux arabes in nineteenth-century Algeria; former Bureaux arabes officer Alfred Le Chatelier became the first chair of Muslim sociology at the Collège de France in 1903. Meanwhile, a rival center of ethnographic study developed at the University of Algiers, where a group of orientalists, including Edmond Doutté and René Basset, began to break from orientalism's philological tradition by conducting observational research. The colonial authorities were quick to embrace the practical potential that such research held for the French imperial state.[32]

Ethnology was thus a product of empire; yet the relation of the two was ambiguous. There were, as Alice Conklin has argued, "degrees of complicity."[33] The French state sponsored Chatelier's Tangiers-based Mission scientifique du Maroc (established 1903) and its publication, *Archives Marocaines*, in hopes that the knowledge produced would facilitate the eventual colonial conquest and rule of Morocco. Meanwhile, however, the very newness of the ethnological field – the paradigmatic and institutional fluidity of a field that was neither philological orientalism nor physical anthropology, and had no established home in the French *facultés* – produced "a momentary openness to the historicity and variety of the Muslim peoples."[34] Ethnographic research therefore had the potential to challenge, rather than support, colonial ideologies.

This seems to have been recognized within the culture of colonial administration. Although by 1913 the Société d'ethnographie de Paris had attracted support from a former colonial minister and several high-level colonial officials, rank-and-file colonial officials who took too careful an interest in the lives of the colonized often encountered skepticism and apathy. Administrator-ethnographers were sometimes criticized by their less inquisitive colleagues and superiors for having "gone native"; those colonial governors who did encourage their subordinates to write ethnographic reports were underwhelmed by the response.[35]

Soon, however, the rising popularity of associationalism led colonial governments to lend more official support to ethnology. This was evident in Lyautey's creation of the Institut des hautes études marocaines in 1920 and, in French West Africa, by Governor-General Joseph Clozel's 1915 creation of the Comité des études historiques et scientifiques and his appointment of ethnographer Maurice Delafosse as head of Affaires indigènes. For these administrators, ethnological knowledge was required for managing native populations in a way that would preserve their ethnic particularity and thus preserve the distance between ruler and ruled. In this view, "knowledge is an affair of State, and there is no division of labor between scholarly research and military action."[36] This meant the end of the "momentary openness" within the ethnography of Morocco; political imperatives left little room for alternative thinking. Burke has described the closing off of French ethnological thinking about Morocco that began as the long-expected French takeover became imminent. Those ethnographers, such as Alfred Le Chatelier, who persisted in promoting a more "open and pluralistic vision of the Muslim world . . . became increasingly marginalized both politically and intellectually."[37]

Meanwhile, however, ethnology's growing prestige in the colonies also facilitated the development of new institutions in the metropole.

The Institut d'ethnologie, created in 1925, was supported by funds from the colonial ministry. The institute had an ambivalent relation with colonial rule, however, which has sparked some disagreement among historians. Gary Wilder has stressed its role as a "node in the reformist network" that aimed to use ethnology to better develop and control the subjects of empire.[38] Alice Conklin, in contrast, has argued that Marcel Mauss, Lucien Lévy-Bruhl, and Paul Rivet, the institute's founders, cared little for the problems of colonial administration. They wanted to support more field research, however, in order to distinguish ethnology from the text-based methods of orientalism and from physical anthropology (i.e., from biological theories of race), and this was expensive. Conklin has argued that although these men lobbied for government funds by promising that ethnology would yield practical guidance for colonial policy, they were motivated by an interest in pure science and by their own "professionalizing ambition"; consequently, they made no effort to tailor research projects to serve the particular needs of colonial administration.[39]

Questions of motivation and culpability are inherently murky. What is clear, however, is that ethnologists deliberately fostered the hope, however illusory, that correct knowledge about colonized cultures could produce a more humane and more efficient colonial policy. This was a most dangerous optimism, and it had grave consequences in Morocco. If academic ethnology avoided becoming the "handmaiden of colonialism,"[40] colonial administrators nevertheless continued to generate their own ethnological discourses, which they believed to be the key to successful colonial rule. These ad hoc (hack) ethnologies of the periphery, rather than the new centers of academic ethnology, became central to the history of colonial education in Morocco.

French Schoolmasters and the Moroccan Soul

The foundational educational policies of French Morocco were developed under the leadership of Directors of Public Instruction Gaston Loth (1912–19) and Georges Hardy (1919–26) and Head of Muslim Education Louis Brunot (1920–39). Their mandate was to use education as a tool for maintaining Moroccan traditions and social hierarchies and as a means to avert the dangers associated with uncontrolled modernization. French education for Moroccan Muslims was intended to maintain social stability and to protect the elites upon whose collaboration the French depended. Schools were supposed to facilitate the economic modernization of Morocco while resisting the cultural changes prompted by the transformation of economic life, warding off the dreaded specters of social disintegration and Bolshevization.

Hardy and Brunot were committed to the principle of adaptation to ethnic difference, and colonial education became the center of a distinct ethnological discourse that reflected the presuppositions and intuitions of the educational leadership. These presuppositions in turn reflected broader discourses of European imperialism, orientalism, and racialism, but the ethnological thinking of these administrators borrowed only selectively from the work of ethnographers. This was neither an accident nor a mean-spirited and cynical corruption of pure science. Empirical ethnological research could provide little guidance for pedagogy. The urgency of administrative challenges and the pressing need to formulate policy often undermined the attempt to ground colonial administration and education in empirical research. In Morocco this urgency was exacerbated by Lyautey's glorification of action and his ideological hostility to intellectualism. "Adaptation" was the slogan of the protectorate administration, but colonial policy and discourse often reflected the culture of the colonizers rather than successful adaptation to the characteristics of Moroccan societies, cultures, or politics.

It was not that information was lacking about the colonized population. To the contrary — colonial educators found that ethnology produced a cumbersome abundance of information. As Timothy Mitchell has noted in his discussion of British Egypt, the complexities of scholarly discourse were often ill-suited to the needs of day-to-day colonial administration: "What was needed was a way of moving quickly from these empirical particulars to the abstraction of an Oriental mentality."⁴¹ Hardy and Brunot found a solution to this problem by fusing ethnological discourse with that of psychology. Psychology provided them with a scientific discourse within which to pinpoint the fundamental characteristics of the Moroccan *âme* (soul or mind). Psychological intuition allowed them to overcome the inconveniently messy particulars of ethnology and to assert the existence of abstractions that transcended the particulars. The resulting abstractions were then used in educational policy making and propagated through the press of the *Bulletin de l'Enseignement Public du Maroc* and through the teacher-training institutions of the protectorate.

Such abstractions were not unique to the colonies. Like the contemporaneous discourses about French national identity described by Herman Lebovics, the colonizers' description of the Moroccan soul utilized "the essentialist, determinist language of a lost or hidden authenticity that, once uncovered, yields a single, immutable national identity. The idea . . . it consecrates is profoundly static and ahistorical, indeed antihistorical, for despite all the vicissitudes of history . . . a vital core persists to infuse everything and everyone with the undying if seriously threatened national character."⁴²

In Morocco, the colonial image of "the Moroccan" facilitated policy making, and therefore the control of the Muslim population. However, it also restricted the options of the policy makers, and sometimes it became a discursive straitjacket that limited the ability of the colonizer to respond to the agency of the colonized. As Burke has written, colonial ethnology can be seen as a "systematic intelligence failure" because of the "inability of researchers to pierce the cloud of orientalist stereotypes that occluded their vision, preventing them from seeing Moroccan society as it then was."⁴³

The complicated relationship between ethnology and policy making may be seen in terms of what James C. Scott has called "seeing like a state": "a state's attempt to make a society legible, to arrange the population in ways that simplified the classic state functions," including, in this case, education, administrative policy making, and the maintenance of power. Like the "high-modernist episodes" examined by Scott, the narrative presented here is a story of failure, a story of how the "tunnel vision" produced in the attempt to know-in-order-to-control, combined with an overly optimistic view of the epistemic and governmental capabilities of the state and its intellectuals, produced unforeseen and undesired consequences.[44] The leading antagonists in this story of colonial education – colonial administrators and nationalist dissidents – were dedicated to preserving aspects of perceived traditions and to resisting the transformations of culture and society brought about by capitalist modernization in Europe and cultural exchange in Africa. However, to act as a privileged knower and to identify the traditional and authentic characteristics of a population, and to use educational institutions to hold them in stasis or to allow only controlled change in a period of chaotic, tumultuous social and cultural metamorphosis – this was simply beyond the capacity of the twentieth-century colonial state.

Precedents

It has been argued that colonial policy, including educational policy, was determined by particular local conditions, not by colonial theories expounded in metropolitan capitals or by the ideals of colonial governors. Denise Bouche has stated that "it is not in Paris, but in Saint-Louis and in Dakar that educational policy is defined. The local authorities are not determined according to principles. They obey necessity."[45] William Zartman's statement about postcolonial Morocco could be applied here to the colonial period: "pedagogical doctrine was an obsession, but *ad hoc* solutions were a habit."[46] However, local authorities are never isolated from the politics and discourses of the global imperial project they take part in, and their perceptions of necessity and their apparently ad hoc solutions are always profoundly shaped by prevailing assumptions of the imperial culture. Lyautey's educational administrators certainly intended to tailor colonial policy to suit the specific necessities of the Moroccan situation. However, the very uniqueness of the Moroccan situation made it confusing and disorienting, prompting administrators to resort to familiar colonial discourses and ideas imported from other contexts.

The global culture of imperialism was far from homogeneous; as Nicholas Thomas and others have pointed out, there was not one such culture, but many.[47] Or perhaps it is more accurate to say that while there was a culture of modern European colonialism, this culture, like culture in general, was variegated and borderless. Consequently, colonial situations must be examined for their particulars (i.e., historically), not for an "essence of being colonized independent of what anybody did in a colony."[48]

Nevertheless, there are obvious commonalities among colonial situations, especially within the empire of a particular colonial power, in this case the French. Some of these commonalities result from structural similarities. Gross inequities of power, wealth, and technology in the relationship between colonizing states and colonized peoples produced similar results in many disparate cases. Other similarities among colonial situations result from cultural habits and beliefs shared by colonizers throughout an empire and the adoption or co-optation of these habits and beliefs by the colonized. These shared cultural habits and beliefs included, for example, the organizational habits of colonial governance, "orientalist" discursive patterns of describing colonized societies, and the notion of the nation-state.

The colonizers could learn these habits in the metropole formally or informally, by studying at the École coloniale in Paris (although only a fraction of colonial officials studied there) or by reading popular novels or in a thousand other ways. But the culture of French colonialism was not merely a projection from the center to the periphery. The colonizers also developed cultures of colonialism that emerged from experiences in the colonies and which were distinct from the culture of the metropole. Because colonial soldiers and administrators moved from colony to colony, because they interacted with each other, and because they read each other's writings, experiences from different colonial situations became bound together in the lives and minds of the colonizers.

The British empire provided a general (and idealized) model for French associationalist colonialism, but the most direct influences on policy in Morocco were France's own imperial experiences. Lyautey had cut his teeth as a colonial authority while serving in Indochina (1894–96) and Madagascar (1897–1902). He referred to Madagascar as a model for Morocco's *écoles de fortune* (ad hoc frontier schools at military posts, where soldiers taught French to interested locals).[49] Indochina also provided some useful examples. As in Annam before 1906, the educational service in Morocco allowed the traditional educational system to continue relatively unmolested. Schools for interpreters had been created in Cochinchina in 1861 and Tonkin in 1886, and in Morocco Lyautey immediately founded a language school to train Frenchmen to be interpreters and bilingual administrators.

However, colonial education in prewar Indochina was largely unsuitable as a model for Lyautey's Morocco. French schools there had been founded to serve the French population and followed metropolitan programs and principles. Indochinese who could pass the entrance examinations were admitted, and by the early 1900s, significant numbers of children of Vietnamese elites were attending French schools and going on to compete with French colonists for positions in the colonial administration. In 1906 the colonial state founded the Indochinese University, where Indochinese could study medicine, administration, and law. This prompted fears among the *colons* that "Vietnamese trained at a university would demand equality and a right to rule the country."[50] Such fears produced a backlash against educational integration. However, it would not be until 1917 that the colonial state would create a segregated system for the colonized population, and curricula designed to encourage the maintenance of tradition and difference would not be introduced until 1924. When the administration then introduced new textbooks and curricula extolling "the 'great men' of the Vietnamese past" and the virtues of traditional Confucian society, Indochina's French rulers were following the anti-assimilationist trend in colonial education that had been exemplified in Lyautey's Morocco since 1912.[51]

Algeria, the most important of the French overseas possessions, was obviously relevant to the Moroccan project, because the native Algerian population was primarily Muslim and made up of Arabic speakers and Berber speakers. Beginning in the 1830s, the French had eviscerated the precolonial Algerian educational institutions by weakening the religious brotherhoods and by seizing the property of the *hubus* (religious endowments) that funded the traditional Muslim teachers. Seeking to remedy this situation, the Second Republic began the development of French-sponsored education intended to reflect the culture and traditions of the Muslim Algerian population. Beginning in 1850, the French began opening Franco-Arab schools that offered bilingual education: Quranic Arabic in the morning and French in the afternoon (explained in Arabic translation). Higher-level instruction was also offered to the sons of chiefs and notables at *collèges arabes-français* in Algiers and Constantine. The colonial government revived several Islamic *madaris* as French-run *médersas* to train judges for Muslim courts of law.[52] The colonial school system in Morocco would reflect these precedents from the Second Republic and Second Empire in Algeria.

Under the Third Republic, however, French rule in Algeria took a very different turn. After the republicans had consolidated their control, the Parisian government had attempted to support an assimilationist educational policy in Algeria, modeled after the 1881–82 Ferry Laws in France. This policy had two basic educational goals: the first was to undermine traditional education; the second was to educate Algerian Muslims into Frenchmen. However, the assimilation of Algerians remained largely a fantasy, and "native politics were strangled by the presence of a minority of white colonists."[53] The European settlers opposed French-style schooling for Muslims, and settler influence in the Chamber of Deputies and settler control of local governments allowed them to block funding for new schools. From 1884 to 1914 attempts to expand French-style primary education were frustrated by these *colons*, who in theory advocated very basic vocational training for Muslims but in fact resisted this too. Muslim enrollment in the French-run primary schools did increase threefold to more than thirty-three thousand by 1908, but this still amounted to only 4.3 percent of the school-age population. Meanwhile, the bilingual and bicultural Franco-Arab schools and *collèges* were closed, and the *médersas* were neglected.[54]

Lyautey shared the Algerian settlers' objections to educational assimilationism. Like them, he disapproved of the small number of French-educated Algerians who actually sought civic assimilation – the "Young Algerians" who in the early 1900s lobbied for the rights of Frenchmen. However, Lyautey did not share the *colon* hostility to Muslim institutions. He was a firm believer in traditional institutions, whether French or Muslim, and had little sympathy for low-born settlers who wanted to destroy established indigenous traditions and transform stratified native populations into a featureless proletariat. To Lyautey, Algeria had become a foreshadowing of what leveling democracy might produce in France: an atomized society, *"une véritable poussière*, [with] no constituted state, no solid social organization upon which we can rest."[55] The putatively assimilationist model of republican Algeria was seen as the antithesis of Lyautey's conservative principles. In Morocco, it would have to be done differently.

Tunisia was a potential model for Morocco: like Morocco and Algeria, it was Arabo-Berber and mostly Muslim. Unlike Algeria, Tunisia was a protectorate, and secondary education therefore aimed to prepare the Tunisian elite for collaboration with the French. However, the Tunisian educational system had a legacy of cultural hybridity that was at odds with Lyautey's goals for Morocco. Elite education in Tunisia was strongly influenced by the Ottoman Tanzimat-era reforms of Khair al-Din al-Tunisi. Khair al-Din al-Tunisi's desire to incorporate European knowledge into Tunisian society had inspired the 1875 creation of the Collège Sadiqi, where students combined French-language coursework with traditional studies in Arabic. After the French took control of Sadiqi in 1882, it continued to function as a center of bicultural learning. This role was supplemented by Franco-Arab primary schools and, for the elites, the Collège Alaoui, a secondary institution. Under Director of Public Instruction Louis Macheul (1883–1908), the goal of colonial education was assimilation and integration: the bilingual Franco-Arab schools were open not only to Muslim Tunisians but also to Jewish Tunisians and European settlers, and 20 percent of the students at the Collège Alaoui were Europeans.[56]

At the turn of the century, however, a conservative backlash against this assimilationist policy emerged in Tunisia, bringing Tunisian education closer to what Lyautey had in mind for Morocco. A settler lobby persuaded the French foreign ministry to cut back funding for the education of Tunisians, and after 1907 primary schools for Europeans and Muslims became increasingly segregated, with a vocational emphasis for the Muslim masses. This trend led to Lyautey's appointment of Gaston Loth, director of the Collège Alaoui, as French Morocco's first director of education, although Loth was not Lyautey's first choice for the position. As head of education in Morocco through 1919, Loth followed the pattern established in Tunisia after 1907, developing education for Europeans and Muslims in distinct and generally (but not completely) segregated institutions.[57]

The colonial educational system of French West Africa would be a particularly important model for Morocco, especially after West Africa's former educational director, Georges Hardy, replaced Gaston Loth as head of Moroccan education in 1919. L'Afrique occidentale française (the AOF) had long offered intermittent examples of indirect rule through West African chiefs, and it had educational institutions that aimed to support, rather than level, existing hierarchies. In West Africa, Governor-General Ernest Roume (1902–7) had ordered the organization of a two-tier system that offered rudimentary primary and vocational (or "professional") education for the average African, as well as regional schools to provide the sons of African chiefs with an education that was more advanced but which nevertheless was not equivalent to that provided in the French *lycée*. Thus the West African school system preserved the distinction between colonizer and colonized while reifying the authority of the collaborating native elite.

The colonial state in French West Africa had also sought to co-opt the Islamic educational tradition, recognizing both the potential of Islamic education as a political tool and the impossibility and political folly of repressing Islamic instruction altogether. Although the Third Republic had mandated the secularization of West Africa's Catholic schools in 1903, this secularization did not apply to the French relationship with Islam. The administration adopted the Algerian model, creating French-run *médersas* to train a bilingual Muslim elite who would collaborate with the French administration. The administration hoped that these schools would give the French the ability to promote an enlightened and moderate (i.e., pro-French) form of Islam within the federation, to counter the influence of Sufi *marabouts* (holy men), who were seen as hostile to the French.[58]

The attempt to establish French-run Islamic schools designed to produce a collaborationist Muslim elite made the West African example appealing to Lyautey. So did the emphasis on vocational education as a means to promote economic development. However, there was another side to the West African example. The universalist policies of the First, Second, and Third Republics had produced a new class of Africans in the Four Communes of Dakar, Gorée, Saint-Louis, and Rufisque. The inhabitants of the Four Communes, called *originaires*, had French citizenship and voted for representatives to the French Chamber of Deputies. The rights possessed by the *originaires* were under attack in the early twentieth century and were never extended to the inhabitants of the rest of French West Africa. Nevertheless, the status and political influence of the *originaires* represented the sort of egalitarian assimilation that Lyautey despised.

Moreover, from 1908 to 1915, French West Africa was ruled by Roume's successor, Governor-General William Ponty, a republican whose relative hostility to traditional political leaders and indigenous cultures contrasted sharply with Lyautey's desire to preserve native elites and their traditions. Ponty died in 1915, however, just as West Africa's colonial authorities were mobilizing a reaction against African demands for French citizenship and educational assimilation. West Africa's educational director at the time was Georges Hardy, who joined in this anti-assimilationist reaction. Hardy's efforts to suppress Senegalese aspirations to equality outraged Senegal's French-speaking African activists and led to his dismissal in 1919. Later that year, however, Lyautey chose Hardy to become Morocco's new director of Public Instruction. Through Hardy, French experiences in West Africa would make a deep imprint on schooling in Morocco.

Resistance and Accommodation

The beliefs, experiences, and desires of the colonizers would not alone determine the shape of colonial education in Morocco, of course. Moroccan resistance to French agendas was ever present, forcing colonial authorities to repeatedly recraft the imperial educational agenda in a "constant negotiation of power relationships and identities."[59] Yet Moroccan resistance occurred within the context of widespread accommodation and overt acceptance of French rule.

It was not evident in 1912 that French rule in Morocco would last a mere forty-four years. Prior to the rise of the nationalist movement, rural revolts and working-class urban insurrections periodically lashed out against French rule, but prolonged defiance was generally limited to the mountain hinterlands, where the French continued to wage wars of "pacification" until 1934. Most Moroccans had no choice but to accept French rule. Many, from sultans to shepherds, had much to gain through collaboration and everything to lose from overt defiance. Often, "there was no point in aiming for and sticking to a minimum level of compromise."[60] While many collaborated for the sake of personal power or gain, or mere survival, others collaborated out of conviction, believing that the French could bring about a long-sought-after modernization. As Jonathan Katz has argued, the historian of anticolonial resistance must also attend to these "transcripts of acceptance."[61]

Distinguishing acceptance from resistance is often difficult, however. Every Moroccan official who retained his position after 1912 did so only by accommodating the protectorate, and every Moroccan family that sent a child to a French school was actively demonstrating fealty to their imperial masters. Yet the agendas of these officials and families, whether ideological or self-serving, were never identical to those of the French, and consequently their interactions with the French were always subversive. Moreover, French colonial agendas were themselves woven from the tangled discourses of republican assimilationists and Lyautist advocates of difference and separation. Consequently, Moroccan Muslims often found themselves resisting the assimilationists by accommodating the Lyautists – or vice versa.

Because the French school system for Moroccan Muslims was divided into distinct tracks for social elites and for common people, two parallel patterns of resistance and accommodation emerged. Before nationalism spread to the masses, resistance in the primary and professional schools for the average Muslim was most often inarticulate, consisting of what Scott has referred to as the "everyday" or "normal" forms of resistance: "the ordinary weapons of relatively powerless groups: foot dragging, dissimulation, false compliance.... They require little or no coordination or planning; they often represent a form of individual self-help; and they typically avoid any direct symbolic confrontation with authority or with elite norms."[62] For the first decade and a half of the protectorate, this resistance mainly took the form of rejection and avoidance: non-enrollment, truancy, and dropping out. Eventually, economic hardships led poor families to become more accommodating of French educational efforts. Yet, even as they sent their children to colonial schools, parents simultaneously resisted the Lyautist agenda by stubbornly persisting in the attempt to use the schools as a means of upward mobility, in defiance of the schools' mission to preserve the social status quo.

Among the Moroccan elite, avoidance was also a popular early tactic, although a few *makhzan* officials actively embraced French education as a tool for strengthening the Moroccan state. Once the sons of the Moroccan elite were enrolled in the colonial schools, however, resistance soon became organized and explicitly articulated. Just as the colonizers were connected to a global network of imperialism, colonized elites from around the world encountered each other as fellow students, exiles, or writers, and shared ideas, sometimes in the European metropole but also in the schools, newsstands, and salons of the imperial periphery. In Morocco, elite students and former students lobbied colonial authorities for increased access to political power, social mobility, and French educational and professional opportunities. They also expressed their commitment to a culture rooted in the Arabic language and the Islamic religion. Beginning in the 1930s, these grievances and commitments became part of the platform of the nationalist movement, a movement dominated to a considerable extent by the French-educated Muslim elite. The frustrations and cultural priorities of the masses and the nationalists converged sufficiently for elite nationalists to rally the support of the common people beginning (slowly) in 1930, and eventually to win Moroccan independence in 1956 under Sultan Mohammed ben Youssef, redesignated King Mohammed V. This political victory over French rule could not undo four and a half decades of colonialism, however. The intimacy of the relationship between colonizer and colonized meant that the discourses of anticolonial resistance and postcolonial politics were intricately connected to the history and culture of the colonial rulers.[63]

Although Moroccans had resisted French attempts to use colonial schools to enforce economic and social boundaries between colonizer and colonized, Moroccan nationalists had been quick to co-opt and subvert the discourses of cultural essentialism, authenticity, tradition, and difference that had become endemic under French rule, reformulating the colonial discourse about the fundamental characteristics of the "Moroccan soul." The colonial educational project of using schools to define ethnic traditions and identities would live on in the postcolonial attempt to "arabize" Morocco's diverse cultures and institutions. Like the imperial knowledge produced by the colonial state and taught in the colonial schools, "the terrible simplifications of the nationalist ideologues" would serve the agendas of the new ruling elite only imperfectly, and would maintain hegemony after independence only with the aid of much coercion.[64] The hope of averting alienation and anomie by maintaining purportedly bounded and traditional cultures proved vain in both the colonial and the postcolonial periods. Yet the attempts by imperialists and their subjects to use education in order to define and promote such cultural boundaries shaped the formation of new self-understandings and new social and political realities in both colonial and postcolonial Morocco.

2. An Uncertain Beginning

> *It is knowledge of the French language that will allow you to preserve your prosperity and wealth, in contrast to what happened to your brothers in Algeria. It is also by this knowledge that you will defend your rights.* | Mohammed al-Hajoui, 1913

> *Let us state very clearly, our Moroccan school does not propose the assimilation pure and simple of the indigenous element and does not aim for European-style education. It knows to consider heredity and the characteristics of race and the environment.* | Gaston Loth, 1917

Article 1 of the 1912 Treaty of Fez included education in the French mandate to "reform" Morocco, but to General Lyautey the education of Moroccan Muslims was more than a treaty obligation. Lyautey saw schools as a means to establish collaboration with local elites and to maintain the traditional culture and hierarchy upon which their elite status was based. In the words of Lyautey's first educational director, Gaston Loth, the role of schooling was "to establish between the Muslims and ourselves the moral understanding that will consecrate the material conquest."[1] Education was to persuade the Moroccan elites that Lyautey intended to keep them in power, albeit as clients of the French colonial state. Education was also a means to promote economic modernization, which would not only profit the French but also, it was hoped, bring benefits to Moroccans and thus give them further reason to cooperate with their French overlords.

Administration of traditional Islamic education remained the purview of the sultan's government (the *makhzan*), but the French quickly set about building a new colonial school system. In 1912 the Residency commissioned a study of educational needs and placed existing European-run schools under the supervision of the Residency's Service économiques, headed by René LeClerc. Soon, however, Gaston Loth was brought in to lead a newly created Service de l'enseignement public. This organization would become the Direction de l'enseignement in 1915 and then the Direction de l'instruction public, des beaux-arts et des antiquités (DIP) in 1920. The new educational administration was charged with two enormous tasks: educating a wave of European settlers and promoting political, economic, and linguistic liaisons between the French and the Moroccans. Soon, however, educational institutions were called upon to assume additional functions involving research and the dissemination of ethnological knowledge, in order to provide guidance to the country's new conquerors, rulers, and administrators.

The colonial educational service immediately began to expand French schooling for Muslims. Although many families hesitated to send their children to French-run schools on religious or political grounds, enrollment in the primary schools increased steadily. Some *qaïds* (rural governors), in order to demonstrate their loyalty to the new regime, began forcing their subjects to send children to the French schools, although the administration discouraged such coercive tactics. The use of Muslim teachers from Tunisia and Algeria facilitated recruitment, as did support from the *makhzan* leadership. In Fez, schoolmaster Alfred Bel made his school more palatable to the Moroccan elite by arranging for some of his older students to study law and theology at the Qarawiyyin mosque-university, although this practice was soon abandoned in the face of Qarawiyyin complaints that the French-schooled students lacked the necessary preparation and motivation.

Muslim enrollment figures at French-run schools rose from 794 in 1912–13 to 2,300 by 1914. The outbreak of war in Europe threatened this expanding educational project, and indeed the entire colonial project in Morocco. Schoolteachers became scarce as current staff and prospective recruits were called up for military service. The prospects of opening for a fall term in 1914 seemed uncertain. The entire protectorate was in a precarious position. If Moroccans hostile to French rule sensed weakness and organized a revolt, no reinforcements could be expected from the metropole. For Lyautey, however, this only increased his commitment to colonial education: French rule depended more than ever on persuading Moroccan populations to cooperate. Maintaining such hegemony in 1914 was not primarily a matter of curricular content or pedagogy per se. Central to Lyautey's endeavor was a show of strength. Success required the demonstration that, despite the war, the French were firmly in control. Schools may have been instruments for the control of young minds, but they were also another way to demonstrate the vitality of the new colonial regime. In this moment of crisis, what was taught in the schools was less important than keeping them open, and the administration's energy was focused on the practical requirements of opening schools and meeting staffing needs. Female instructors were recruited (twelve in Casablanca alone) to teach European boys, and twenty-one *moniteurs* (teaching assistants) were assigned to teach classes for Muslim boys. In addition, fifty-eight soldiers from the French army were assigned to work as schoolteachers. World War I stretched the colonial state's resources to the limit, but 1914–18 was nevertheless a period of growth for French education of Muslims, with official enrollment rising to 3,500 by the end of the war.[2]

Loth stressed that the schools for Muslims were not to be imitations of European schools, that French language instruction was to be "elementary," and that much of the emphasis was on practical agronomy, domestic skills, hygiene, and basic science.³ This echoed his declaration in Tunis in 1907 that "the great mass of native schoolchildren should receive a rudimentary French education, having an eminently practical goal, and whenever possible a vocational character."⁴ According to Loth, primary education for Muslims "is destined to make customers ready for our commerce and our industry, feeling the need to improve their existence, aiding the economic transformation of the country which is the necessary condition of moral evolution."⁵ This vision of primary education accorded with Lyautey's desire to modernize the Moroccan economy without revolutionizing Moroccan culture or disrupting the social order; it also served to assuage the fears of European colonists who feared that the education of Muslims would create rootless, *déclassé* malcontents but who nevertheless needed employees and customers.

Meanwhile, however, Lyautey was defending his vision of colonialism against pressures from outside Morocco. Lyautey's anti-universalist and anti-egalitarian convictions were not yet dominant in the Third Republic, still divided by the legacy of the French Revolution. Throughout the French empire, the desperate French need to recruit and conscript colonial troops during World War I provided leverage to French-speaking colonized elites and Parisian republican universalists who demanded that French citizenship be given to soldiers from the colonies in exchange for their service to France. Lyautey believed that giving French citizenship to veterans would be a threat to Moroccan social hierarchies, and thus to French rule, leading to the kind of social disintegration that was so widely condemned in Algeria. He successfully persuaded the Parisian government not to extend the naturalization of soldiers to Morocco, arguing that removing Moroccans from the authority of the sultan, and removing Muslims from Islamic law, would constitute a violation of not only the Treaty of Fez but also the Treaty of Madrid.⁶

Lyautey's best defense against assimilationist pressures from the metropole, and against the possibility that Moroccans, like Algerians and West Africans, might someday demand the rights of Frenchmen, was Morocco's status as a protectorate. Lyautey did not wish to see his much-vaunted strategy of collaboration erode into a mere facade. It was hoped that the existence of the sultan and his *makhzan* government as a partner in the Treaty of Fez would keep French assimilationists at bay, while ensuring against the emergence of demands for rights and citizenship among Moroccan Muslims. It was crucial, therefore, that the French develop a true partnership with the *makhzan*. The problem was, of course, that the *makhzan*'s desires were not always compatible with French interests and agendas. This was the perennial problem of indirect rule. Although Sultan Moulay Youssef was more compliant than his dethroned brother, Lyautey recognized that conflicts with the *makhzan* were likely to persist.

Creating a Collaborationist Elite

As Lyautey saw it, the French policy of association with the *makhzan* could only succeed if a new generation of Moroccan rulers could be created who understood the French approach to administration and were willing and able to collaborate with the French. If the French could gain control over the education of the next generation of *makhzan* administrators, then harmonious collaboration would be assured. In 1914 the French therefore attempted to administer a reform of the Qarawiyyin mosque-university in Fez, the traditional educational institution for *makhzan* administrators and magistrates. This strategy met resistance, however.

With the help of Mohammed al-Hajoui, the sultan's delegate for education, the French established a *majlis* (administrative council) of *ulema* (Muslim professors) elected by their peers and proposed a reorganization of the Qarawiyyin teaching faculty, standardizing appointments and salaries. Such reforms sought to make the Qarawiyyin faculty more transparent and easier for the French to control, undermining the traditional networks of scholars who established expectations for scholarly learning and conferred recognition of the status of *ulema*. Once the colonial state gained influence over faculty appointments and made the Qarawiyyin faculty dependent on French-subsidized salaries, the French planned to reform curriculum and pedagogy.

Hajoui was an advocate of Salafiyya, an Islamic reformism that aimed to modernize Islamic education while purging it of heterodox corruption; he and a faction among the *ulema* hoped to co-opt the French reforms and use the *majlis* to put forward their own reform project. The French reforms were opposed, however, by another faction, led by Justice Minister Bouchaib Doukkali and Abdelhay al-Kittani. The reasons for their opposition were various; it was not merely a matter of "traditional" *ulema* resisting "modern" reforms, although the French showed little awareness of this. Doukkali, like Hajoui, was an advocate of Salafi reformism. Kittani, in contrast, was head of one of Morocco's most powerful Sufi brotherhoods and as such was an enemy of the Salafis; he would prove a reliable ally for the French. Both, however, had much to lose by letting the French impinge upon their spheres of influence in the Qarawiyyin.

The French did not insist. Because maintaining the prestige of the Moroccan political and religious elite was central to Lyautey's vision of the protectorate, the French were fearful of offending *ulema* or the *makhzan*. In addition, the budget crisis occasioned by World War I made the planned subsidies impossible. A second push for reform in 1918 did lead to some regularization of compensation for *ulema*, but the rest of the French reform project became a "dead letter."[7] The new *majlis* became impotent, and further French reform efforts were abandoned until the early 1930s.

The French, meanwhile, altered their tactics. As the French administration saw it, the problem with the *makhzan* was that its ministers and functionaries lacked an education compatible with modern ideas and were therefore incapable of recognizing the needs of Morocco in the modern world. If the Qarawiyyin could not be reformed, then French schools would have to educate the new generation of *makhzan* leaders. In October 1915, Lyautey called a series of meetings intended to orient educational policy toward the preservation of traditional Moroccan hierarchies and cultural identities, strengthening the Residency-*makhzan* partnership. French schools were to provide a new generation of elite Muslims with "instruction and education which, without rendering them strangers to their traditions and to the characteristics of their race, will prepare their intellects to open to all the modern conceptions compatible with the necessities of the evolution that their country is called to accomplish under the tutelage of France."[8]

A plan was therefore drawn up for the creation of elite schools, the *collèges arabes*. These schools, soon renamed *collèges musulmans*, were to prepare future *"pashas, khalifas,* indigenous financial agents . . . judges, etc."[9] A school in Fez that had been operating since 1914 was converted into the Collège Moulay Idriss, and the Collège Moulay Youssef opened in Rabat in February 1916. The Fez school served 150 students (114 in the elementary grades, 36 at the secondary level) by 1917, mostly children of *makhzan* administrators and wealthy merchants. The Rabat school was smaller, with only 96 students; a dormitory housed 20, so that the school might also serve the sons of nearby rural leaders.[10] A different sort of school was opened in Meknes in 1919: a military academy. This school was also intended for the sons of the Moroccan elite, although it had difficulty recruiting young men from elite families.

The dangers that education posed to colonial rule were well known. Creating a new elite of diploma-bearing functionaries could threaten French interests, either directly, should this educated elite adopt European notions of republicanism or socialism, or indirectly, should the old class of Moroccan notables start to feel menaced by lower-class Moroccans pursuing social mobility through French education. The French leadership sought to avoid these hazards by segregating the social classes throughout the educational system and by rooting the curriculum of the schools, especially the schools for elites, in arabophone Muslim culture. It was resolved that *écoles des fils de notables* (Schools for the Sons of Notables) were to be distinguished from non-elite primary schools, a policy that Lyautey had long advocated but which had received little attention in the initial scramble to open schools and recruit students. Class segregation was to be ensured by charging tuition fees at the elite schools. Existing primary schools for Muslims in Fez and Casablanca were designated *écoles des fils de notables*; four more would be added, in Marrakesh (1919), Rabat (1921), Salé (1921), and Meknes (1929). These schools were to provide a recruitment pool for the *collèges* (and the Marrakesh school would be upgraded to a *collège* in 1936).[11]

In order to ensure that instruction at the *collèges musulmans* in Fez and Rabat remain safely rooted in Moroccan and Muslim tradition, the administration put the *collèges* under the supervision of a high-level consultative committee composed of *makhzan* officials and Moroccan educational authorities, including the grand vizier and the ministers of Justice and Hubus. In keeping with Lyautey's policy of making schools local centers for interaction with Moroccan elites, in Fez the *collège* held public conferences in Arabic where Fezi intellectuals could gather to hear speeches by prominent Muslim scholars and *makhzan* notables like Bouchaib Doukkali.[12]

The *collèges musulmans* were to provide Morocco's future *makhzan* leaders with an education that was "Moroccan and Muslim, and not a European *culture* that neither their instincts nor their traditions prepared them to really understand or assimilate to." The primary language of instruction was to be Arabic, although students were also to acquire "a complete knowledge of the French language."[13] Arabic-language specialists were chosen to head the colleges: the Rabat school was placed under the direction of J. Neigel, and the Fez school was given to Louis Brunot. Students were to learn French as a second language, for use as an "instrument," and were to acquire "exact and complete notions of European civilization," but they were not to be immersed in French, since they were not to become part of French civilization themselves.[14] Six hours per day were to be spent in Arabic-medium instruction, including both "Sciences" and "Letters." The "Letters" classes were to consist of Quranic studies, Islamic theology, Arabic grammar and syntax, logic, Arabic literature, rhetoric, and Islamic law. "Sciences" were to include mathematics, natural history, physics, chemistry, and geography. Only one hour per day was to be devoted to French.[15] Moroccan Muslims who desired a fully French education could apply for admission to the French *lycées*, but the future *makhzan* leaders trained in the *collèges* were to remain "entirely Muslim."[16]

The purpose of the Meknes military academy was quite different from that of the *collèges* in Fez and Rabat. The academy was placed under the control of the army, not the Direction of Public Instruction. The school was to train Moroccans to become junior officers in the colonial army, with the rank of *sous-lieutenant indigène*. There was a much stronger focus on French language skills than was planned for the *collèges*, and less Arabic and religious instruction. Although it was hoped that, after retirement, these Moroccan officers might be useful as French-appointed rural *qaïds*, the focus was on military discipline and on achieving sufficient assimilation to allow graduates to function as part of the French officer corps. Perhaps as a result, the Meknes school would not become a center of anti-French activity in the late 1920s and 1930s. Although there were some incidents of insubordination, the Meknes school was largely successful in creating a loyal corps of Moroccan officers.[17] The French attempt to use the *collèges* in Fez and Rabat to create a loyal corps of *makhzan* ministers would be less successful.

Moroccan Agency Undermines Lyautism

Lyautey's vision for the *collèges musulmans* was soon subverted by the agency of Moroccan elites. Neither the *makhzan* nor the *collège* students wanted the French schools to provide a pseudo-traditional Arabic and Islamic education. While Lyautey saw the Arabic and Islamic curricula of the schools as essential to the preservation of the *makhzan* under French rule, the *makhzan* leadership saw knowledge of French as the key to maintaining the economic and political power of the traditional elite in the new colonial context. Al-Hajoui had publicly encouraged Moroccan Muslims to learn French.[18] Grand Vizier El Mokri also wanted the French schools to provide a Western education sufficient to allow Moroccan elites access to power within French social and economic hierarchies, without allowing French-educated Moroccans to gain influence over Morocco's traditional institutions.[19] Meanwhile, the students reportedly neglected their Arabic and pressured their frustrated school directors for more French courses. The new schools represented a nontraditional route to success through a close relationship with the French and access to Western knowledge, and for this the French language was crucial. Families who did not place a high priority on the French language tended to avoid the French-run schools altogether. The parents of *collège* students did want their sons to get a solid Arabic and Islamic education, but they wanted an equal amount of time to be spent on French studies. A second hour of French was added to the secondary program for the 1916–17 school year.[20]

In 1917, hoping to preserve the original mission of the *collèges* in the face of opposition from students and the *makhzan*, Lyautey appointed a commission to study the problem. The commission consisted of Loth, Neigel, and Brunot along with two of the protectorate's top officials: Raoul Marc, Conseilleur du gouvernement chérifien, and Colonel Henri Berriau, head of the Cabinet politique at the military Service des renseignements (Intelligence Service, known also as Indigenous Affairs). Of these five men, only Brunot and Neigel, the *collège* directors, seem to have been truly committed to Lyautey's plan for the *collèges*. Lyautey insisted that the *collèges* were to remain small and devoted exclusively to the education of "the part of the elite destined to remain and evolve within the Muslim norm, and to recruit especially for offices and employment of a Muslim character: the *makhzan*, the *ulema*, functionaries of the administrative and judicial type, and, finally, individuals who, without seeking paid employment, desire a higher education without losing any of their Muslim character."[21] Lyautey stated that he did not want to close off all Moroccan access to careers of a European sort ("quite to the contrary, since the whole conception of the Protectorate rests upon the close association of the two races"), but he feared the creation of "malcontents" and insisted that if some Moroccan Muslims had to be given a more European-style education, this should occur in institutions other than the *collèges*. Lyautey, however, was preoccupied with the ongoing military pacification of the Moroccan hinterlands and had little time for educational matters. Over the course of the next two years, the commission gradually gave in to Moroccan demands.

On 17 September 1917 the commission met to discuss the need to accommodate the *collège* programs to student desires. At this meeting, Loth described three groups of students at these schools, each with different goals. The first consisted of students who wanted a wholly French education in order to go into French careers such as law and medicine. The second group better fit Lyautey's vision for the colleges, aspiring to careers in the *makhzan* or among the religious elite; these students desired a rigorous Arabic and Islamic education, with merely "sufficient" French. Loth argued that there were only a few students in each of these groups. The "great majority" of students, according to Loth, fell into a third category; these students desired "a sufficient Muslim education but, at the same time, to acquire a French education developed enough to permit them access to lucrative employment in the [French] Administration, and in industry."[22] The committee decided that, while the most French-oriented students could best pursue their goals in the French *lycées*, the other two groups could be accommodated by the creation of separate secondary sections within the *collèges*, one French-oriented, and one Arabic-oriented. This was a major step away from Lyautey's principle that Arabic was to be the primary language within these elite schools. The commission asked Neigel and Brunot to discuss the matter with the parents, who agreed. Some of the Rabat families suggested that a commercial section be added as well. In 1918 a proposal was presented to the sultan for a six-year program, divided into two cycles of four and two years. For the last two years, students would have a choice of three sections: French language, Muslim law, or commerce.[23]

The proposed French and commercial sections were accepted by the *makhzan*, but the section for Muslim law encountered opposition. In 1918, Grand Vizier El Mokri demanded that Islamic education be provided exclusively in mosques, by *ulema*. Arabic-language instruction in the *collèges* was to be limited to *belles-lettres* and grammar. This would shield the training of Islamic judges and scholars from the French, ending French hopes of using the *collèges* to infiltrate the traditional institutions of Morocco. Mokri also asked that the French-medium instruction in the *collèges* conform to metropolitan programs and that the *collège* diploma be made equivalent to the French baccalaureate, in order to allow access into French higher education and to the liberal professions.[24] The *makhzan* thus followed the pattern established in the nineteenth century by the Ottoman Tanzimat and the Egypt of Muhammed Ali: the state encouraged the acquisition of Western knowledge through new educational tracks, in hopes of strengthening its position vis-à-vis the European powers, without reforming traditional institutions dominated by entrenched interests. Meanwhile, the French were made dependent on the *makhzan* by Lyautey's hope for real collaboration and his desire not to upset social hierarchies.

The commission immediately made concessions to the *makhzan* position. The new *collège* programs did declare that students were to be instructed "according to the same principle of maintaining students in their social habits." Law and theology were excluded from the Arabic-language curriculum, however, and the idea of separate Arabic and French sections was dropped. A single "general" secondary section would prepare students to work in the French administration or in liberal professions. The mission of the *collèges* was reoriented "to create an educated middle class exercising, all differences of milieu maintained, professions of commerce, agriculture, industry, as well as most liberal professions."²⁵ A third of the instruction would be in Arabic, with the remainder spent in French language and literature and in other subjects taught in French, including history, geography, and mathematics. Furthermore, the commission agreed that, it being desirable to develop French education as much as possible, the *collège* diploma would be developed into an equivalent to the French baccalaureate, possibly with the aid of the Faculty of Bordeaux.²⁶ This was a stunning surrender of the Lyautist vision, much to the frustration of Louis Brunot, director of the Fez *collège*. He embraced Lyautey's original concept of the *collèges* as preparatory schools for future magistrates, and had hoped that the Fez *collège*, as a feeder school for the Qarawiyyin, would provide the French with a means to influence and control the mosque-university. Brunot lamented the lack of cooperation between the *collèges* and the Qarawiyyin, brought on by the decision to eliminate the teaching of Muslim law from the *collèges* in response to *makhzan* pressure. He predicted that the new French orientation of these schools would create a division within the Moroccan elite, so that "a blunder, a political crisis, could create conflicts, then struggle, between the old turbans and the young Moroccans."²⁷ Thus far, however, the old turbans and the young *collège* students were united in their desire to see the French schools focus on the French language.

The *makhzan* and the students had been aided in their efforts to reshape the *collèges* by the inherent pedagogical, political, and personnel difficulties involved in creating a modern Arabic-medium program that would include the physical and social sciences. The French lacked staff and materials for such instruction. Arabic grammar and literature could be taught by French Arabists like Louis Brunot or by arabophone Muslim Algerians, but such teachers were in short supply, and Moroccan families tended to be suspicious of infidels teaching Arabic; even Muslim Algerians were widely seen as "in-betweens," the "subaltern companions of the Christians."²⁸ The French, for their part, had little respect for the methods of the *foqya* (sing. *fqih*, traditional Moroccan teachers), whose emphasis on memorization was extraordinary, even for the Islamic world.[29] To the French, these rote methods were a worthless remnant of a decayed cultural tradition. Nevertheless, a lack of Arabic-speaking personnel forced the educational administration to concede that traditional teachers could be retained to teach written Arabic to younger students. But neither the *foqya*, nor the French, nor the Algerians were accustomed to teaching math, science, and history in Arabic, and appropriate printed materials were lacking in Morocco. During the 1916–17 school year, history and part of the geography curriculum were reportedly taught in Arabic, but mathematics and natural sciences were taught in French. Rabat director Neigel proposed the obvious solution to this problem: bring in instructors and materials from Egypt, Tunisia, or Syria.[30] However, the administration and Fez director Louis Brunot feared that such instructors might bring anticolonial political ideologies to the *collèges*.[31] A secondary motivation for the creation of the *collèges* had been to prevent Moroccan elites from sending their children to school abroad, where they might be infected with undesirable ideas; bringing foreign Arabic teachers to Morocco was therefore an unacceptable solution.

Meanwhile, even among Lyautey's top officials there was a strong tendency to fall back on assimilationist habits. A memo from Indigenous Affairs called for programs that would demonstrate to students "the genius of our [French] civilization" and stated that although the *collèges* ought "to produce young Moroccans of good Muslim bearing," a primarily Arabic education would "canton the indigene in the profoundly xenophobic mentality which is proper to the Moroccan race."[32] The educational service lacked the personnel and, in some quarters, the political will necessary for a fully Arabic-based program, and the *makhzan* prevented the French schools from preparing students for prestigious careers within the traditional hierarchy. It was therefore easy for the commission to give in to the demands of Muslim students and their families for a more French-intensive program in the 1910s, despite the misgivings of Brunot and, as would soon become evident, of Lyautey himself. A few years later, when Moroccan elites would begin to demand more education in Arabic, it would be much harder for the French to meet their demands.

The Berber Policy
Not all Moroccans were arabophone, however. Berber dialects were spoken in the north and south and in the Atlas Mountains. In recognition of this fact, a 1912 report on educational policy proposed that "two groups of schools for natives will therefore co-exist in the country: one where French-language instruction will be given in parallel with an education in the Arabic language, another where they will study a Berber dialect. The first will be situated in the cities; the others will be instituted for the Berbers, devoted to agriculture or animal husbandry."[33]

This idea of distinguishing between schools for Berbers and Arabs was much more than just a practical response to Morocco's linguistic diversity, however. It was part of a larger policy that aimed to prevent the "arabization" of the Middle Atlas. The French Berber policy had its origins in French racialist discourse about Algeria that emphasized a dichotomous antagonism between Arabs and Berbers. In Algeria the French had developed an idealized view of the Algerian Berbers, and particularly the Kabyles. The "Kabyle myth" held that the Kabyles had European ancestry (Roman, Gaul, or Vandal) and were "only superficially Islamicized and the hereditary enemies of the Arabs."[34] As a result, they were considered more easily assimilated to European laws and even to Christianity. As Patricia Lorcin has argued, this favorable view of Algeria's Berbers had its roots in the experiences of the French army during the conquest of Algeria in the 1830s, and developed as a counterpoint to negative French views of Islam and of Algeria's nomadic arabophone groups. This discourse of "bad Arabs" and "good Berbers" soon spread to medical and ethnographic circles, although the "Kabyle myth" of the "good Berber" never became a basis for policy in Algeria.[35] In Morocco, however, maintaining divisions between

Arabs and Berbers became a major policy goal. This Berber policy would reach its apex with the famous "Berber *dahir*" of 16 May 1930, a decree that provoked a wave of protest in French Morocco's arabophone cities and marked the beginning of Moroccan nationalism as a mass movement.

As Edmund Burke III has argued, French ethnographers and military officers had initially recognized the complex and heterogeneous character of the various groups who spoke Berber dialects. However, French discourse had by 1912 developed a clear distinction between the *blad al-makhzan* (land of government) and the *blad al-siba* (land of dissidence), the latter being territory controlled by tribes not in submission to the sultan's state. Increasingly, the *siba* became associated with Berbers, although the categories were not precisely coterminous. The French struggle to subdue the Tamazight-speaking Middle Atlas tribes after 1912 created a demand for more knowledge about Middle Atlas society. In 1913 a Berber "study center" was created in Meknes, and publication of the *Archives Berbères* began in 1915. However, as was so often the case, a basis for French policy in Morocco had to be found sooner rather than later, and French policy makers fell back on familiar tropes — in this case, the principle of the bad Arab and the good Berber, imported from Algeria.[36]

Colonel Paul Henrys, who led the 1914 "pacification" campaign in the Middle Atlas, cautioned against using local Arab families as collaborators in the mountains and against imposing the authority of the *makhzan*. Believing in a dichotomy between Berbers and Arabs, Henrys sought to identify and collaborate with an authentic Berber culture divorced from elements he considered "Arab" intrusions. In a policy echoing that of contemporary French West Africa, Henrys recognized only the *jemaa* (local tribal or village councils) and "customary law" as indigenous institutions, rejecting the complex (and potentially threatening) ties between Berbers and the *makhzan*, as well as the regional alliances among Berber tribes. As was so often the case, the French policy of associating with existing elites degenerated into the handpicking of a loyalist local leadership. The local French authorities became the arbiters of Berber tradition, and had direct oversight of the Berber *jemaa*, which were given judicial authority.[37]

In contrast to Algeria's settled Kabyles, most Middle Atlas Tamazight were semi-nomadic transhumants, but French descriptions of these Middle Atlas Berbers nevertheless soon came to resemble the (imagined) Algerian Kabyle: a kind of noble savage, only superficially Islamic, hostile to the *makhzan* and preferring their own customary law to the *sharia* (Islamic law). The dichotomy was often expressed in racial terms: in contrast to Arabs, the Middle Atlas Berbers were whites, virtually uncorrupted by outside influences. Racial differences were correlated with moral distinctions: the Berbers were said to be honest and brave, "of very democratic mores," without the Arabs' troublesome devotion to Islamic doctrine.[38] Morocco's Berbers were one of the "Latin races"; they had been Christian and Roman before they had become Muslim; they were the people of Augustine and Tertullian.[39] The French desire to maintain and encourage separation between Arabs and Berbers was made official with a *dahir* (edict) issued on 11 September 1914, stating that "the tribes said to be of Berber custom are and will remain regulated and administered according to their laws and their own customs under the control of the authorities."[40]

The planned distinction between Arab and Berber schools was intended to support the legal and political aspects of the Berber policy by helping to maintain the cultural and linguistic divisions between the *blad al-makhzan*, portrayed as arabophone and urban, and the *blad al-siba*, seen as rural and Berber. Proscribing Arabic-language instruction from the schools for Berbers would, it was hoped, reduce the danger of the arabization of the *siba*. However, although the creation of distinct *écoles franco-berbères* had been planned since the beginning of the protectorate, unrest in the Middle Atlas and the disruption of World War I prevented the development of a distinct educational structure for Berbers during Loth's administration. A few schools were set up in Berber-speaking Middle Atlas towns such as El Hajeb, Azrou, and Agourai, but these were still little more than ad hoc *écoles de fortune* run by the military; at El Hajeb, class was conducted in the *qaïd*'s house.[41] Because the few schools in berberophone regions were under the control of the army's Indigenous Affairs service, Loth's educational service focused on social rather than ethnic distinctions among Muslims: *notable* and commoner, urban and rural. The idea of a parallel system of schools designed to suit the ethnic characteristics of the Berbers would be revived in 1923. However, the discourse of the Berber-Arab dichotomy in Morocco would never be accepted by the protectorate's second educational director, Georges Hardy, and colonial pedagogical discourse would be at odds with the Berber policy throughout the 1920s.

Schooling Muslim Girls

Regarding the education of Muslim girls, French conservatism dovetailed with traditional Moroccan attitudes toward girls' education. There was much resistance in Moroccan society to the idea of sending girls to any school, much less a French one, and fear of local hostility made the French very cautious about getting involved in the education of Muslim girls. Throughout North Africa the French had been more than willing to acquiesce to Muslim opinion, for Muslim concepts of feminine honor and propriety were not at all alien to the French. Even in "assimilationist" Algeria, administrators had feared that the education of girls would lead to deracination and immorality.[42]

In Morocco, French timidity toward female education accorded smoothly with Lyautey's governing philosophy. Unlike republican colonizing projects, the goals of colonial rule in Morocco did not highlight the liberation of the colonized from traditional forms of oppression, and consequently there was little dissonance where girls were concerned. Despite the hypermasculinity of Lyautey's conception of the "colonial man," educational discourse in French Morocco was characterized by little of the eroticization of Arab women so common in colonial discourse elsewhere, nor the desire to rescue them.

French ideas about the masculinization of the colonial man through the weakness and subjugation of the colonized did raise concerns among the male colonial leadership that the colonial experience might erode the feminine domesticity of settler women.[43] But the administration had little interest in sensationalizing the oppression of the Moroccan woman, and traditional Moroccan gender norms remained strong enough to preclude the need for the French to reinforce them through pedagogy.

When schools were established for Muslim girls, instruction was shaped by local sensibilities. Rather than begin by creating a new, alternative educational system, as was done with Muslim boys, the French decided to begin with existing institutions. As they had done in Algeria and Tunisia, the French in Morocco sought to establish "handicrafts schools" modeled on the traditional *dar al-muallimat*, where a local *maalma* taught girls of the urban bourgeois embroidery, needlework, and "social and moral values."[44]

In Morocco, the administration described most of the existing "schools" for girls as little more than sweatshops, where poor girls toiled for long hours. However, in October 1913 the educational service commissioned the study of an embroidery workshop in Salé that seemed to fit the model of a respectable *dar al-muallimat*, run by a local Muslim woman named Slimana who recruited among the daughters of the local political and commercial elite. Louise Bouillot, a graduate of the École des langues orientales who spoke fluent Arabic, was assigned to inspect this workshop, "to study the feminine society of this city, its character, its aspirations, and to deduce from these aspirations what might be done for it."[45] Exercising a caution that would become typical of the French approach to girls' education, the administration first took on the role of student, collecting knowledge about Moroccan society, before taking on the task of instruction.

Gradually, the French took control of the Salé institution. As Hamid Irbouh has argued, Bouillot reshaped the *dar al-muallimat* into a school that reflected a Western vision of discipline, rationality, and hygiene. The workspace was reorganized and then moved to a new location in 1913. Running water was introduced and assistant instructors were hired, creating a hierarchy of director, employees, and students. Bouillot officially took over as director in 1915. Despite this transformation, however, she strove to follow Lyautey's colonial philosophy, advocating "evolution and not revolution" and stressing the importance of preserving the "mentality" of Moroccan women.[46] In sharp contrast to the schools for boys, no French language instruction was introduced in the Salé girls school until 1916, and then only orally; the school remained mainly a workshop. Instruction remained limited to embroidery and domestic skills, including the preparation of the bridal trousseau, and Bouillot sought to teach the instructors and students the importance of preserving the traditional characteristics of their work, not only because these "picturesque features" made them salable to European customers but also because of the inherent importance of preserving Moroccan culture.

In 1914 Bouillot helped to found a similar French-run embroidery workshop in Rabat. In Rabat, argued Bouillot, the crafts instruction provided by the *maalma* was already of high quality, and therefore it was time to take the step of introducing French and Arabic instruction. In Fez, Bouillot's work was imitated in an institution created under the supervision of Alfred Bel. Bel's school included French and Arabic instruction along with Islamic instruction provided by a local *fqiha*, within the context of a primarily manual curriculum. In Fez, as in Salé and Rabat, the French director identified authentic and traditional crafts specimens which they designated as models for their Moroccan instructors and pupils to imitate.[47]

During 1917 the French attempted to further expand schooling for Muslim girls, opening new schools in the coastal cities of Mogador (Essaouira), Mazagan, and Safi. Moroccan interest in these schools was limited, however. By 1917 there were already 450 Muslim girls in French-run schools, but this number would not rise until the mid-

1920s. The French found it particularly difficult to persuade upper-class families to enroll their daughters. Unlike the schools in Rabat and Salé, which grew out of existing institutions already serving local elites, the new schools were only able to attract students from the lowest classes, frustrating the French desire to use the schools to create contacts with the Moroccan elite. Apparently, affluent families had little interest in risking their reputations by sending their daughters to a foreign school to learn embroidery and tailoring techniques, although it was a reasonable strategy for some poor families.

Louise Bouillot envisioned vocational training as a step toward the economic liberation of Muslim girls from poverty, if not from "the prejudice to which she is a slave."[48] She hoped that vocational training was merely a first step toward the provision of a more academic sort of education, stating that "Muslim girls will never enter into school until they have first crossed the threshold of the workshop."[49] For the male French leadership, however, the mission of the school was primarily political; the education of the girls themselves was of minor importance. Loth, Bel, and Brunot focused on the schools for girls as tools to acclimatize the Moroccan elite to interactions with the French, overcoming the anti-French attitudes among elite Moroccan women, which were assumed to be the result of ignorance. Education was to lead these women to welcome French supervision; their influence was to persuade Morocco's ruling-class men to embrace the protectorate. The actual education provided to the girls was of little importance, and the tendency toward more academic instruction begun by Bouillot and Bel would later be reversed under the leadership of Georges Hardy beginning in December 1919.

The Other Others
Although the present study focuses on the education of Moroccan Muslims in French schools, any attempt to describe the Franco-Muslim relationship would be incomplete without an acknowledgment that similar processes of ethnological definition through pedagogy were at work in the education of Europeans and Moroccan Jews. Although

the colonial state initially left the education of Jewish Moroccans to the Alliance Israélite Universelle, World War I produced a financial crisis for the AIU and provided the colonial state an opportunity to take on a more active role. Although the protectorate agreed to subsidize the AIU schools, this agreement was "largely ignored."[50] Loth's educational service took over the administration of several AIU schools and began creating a rival system, the *écoles franco-israélites*. By 1918–19 there were almost sixteen hundred students in these schools, and AIU enrollment had dropped by more than 50 percent, to about two thousand.[51] This created considerable resentment among AIU leaders, who objected that the government-run schools lacked the AIU's commitment to Jewish culture and aimed to assimilate Moroccan Jews into the settler population. Meanwhile, envy of the French-style *écoles franco-israélites* provoked resentment among Muslims. In 1924 Hardy would reverse Loth's policies and return the administration of Jewish schools in Morocco to the AIU, including those established by the colonial state, in order to "delay as much as possible Moroccan crises of anti-semitism and the dangerous pressures of semitism."[52] Thus the AIU school system survived in Morocco, complementing the work of the colonial state by promoting French-style education without full integration into the European system.

A higher priority for the Direction de l'enseignement was the education of Morocco's European population. The arrival of almost thirty thousand European settlers overwhelmed the colonial state's material and human resources, and school enrollments jumped from 350 to more than 1,400 by June 1913.[53] Sometimes more than a hundred new students were enrolled in a single week. While the scale of this system paled in comparison to the mass education handled by the Ministry of Public Instruction in the metropole, the rate of growth of the colonial system presented staggering challenges as the educational service raced to stay ahead of settler immigration.[54]

The French school system for Europeans in Morocco served a mixture of European nationalities, most notably Spanish and Italian.

Educational policy aimed to eliminate this ethnic pluralism. This was an enormous task of cultural assimilation. The unity of "Europeans" in Morocco was a goal of the educational system, not a presupposition, and it was a goal that consumed a great deal of energy. There was an explicit attempt to engineer social harmony through history pedagogy: schoolteachers were encouraged to emphasize historical cooperation among France, Italy, and Spain and to downplay points of conflict. Thus lines of identity dividing Europeans were deliberately effaced, seeming unimportant compared with the differences between Muslim, Jew, and European in Morocco.[55]

Weighing the French Commitment to Muslim Schooling

In the 1918–19 school year, official enrollment in the colonial schools for Moroccan Muslims had reached 3,189, plus 342 in the *collèges*. By then, however, enrollment at the schools for Europeans had reached 9,764 (including about a hundred Muslims of unspecified origin). The colonial school system for Moroccan Muslims would grow over the ensuing decades, enrolling almost 12,000 students in 1930 and almost 33,000 in 1944. However, schools for Muslims typically received only a fifth of the protectorate's educational budget (15 million out of 70 million francs in 1930, e.g.). Moroccan Muslim enrollment would grow rapidly after World War I, surpassing 100,000 students in 1950, but the French would never educate more than a fraction of Moroccan schoolchildren (about 13 percent at independence in 1956).[56]

These figures indicate that the challenge of educating an ethnically and nationally diverse wave of European colonists became an institutional priority, taking precedence over the education of the colonized population. Loth was quite aware that the "Franco-Muslim" school system for boys and girls served only a tiny proportion of the Muslim population of Morocco, but he argued that this was understandable considering the limited resources and the short time span. His desire to expand Muslim enrollment was also tempered by his desire for high professional standards for educators and his concern with hygiene and sanitation in schools.

The French leadership was sincere in its desire to provide educational services for Muslims, but within the context of the Treaty of Fez this was seen as foreign aid or diplomacy – a form of beneficence or a political tactic. Although it was considered desirable to "create enough schools to receive all the indigenous children whom parents are willing entrust to our teachers," this did not imply establishing parity with metropolitan services.[57] Regarding the European colonists, the underlying assumption was that their needs had to be met, insofar as was possible, at a level meeting metropolitan standards of quantity as well as quality. Despite Lyautey's reported statement that Europeans could send their children to school in Europe,[58] there was little serious doubt in the Direction de l'enseignement public that its duty was to accommodate the children of these "immigrants debarking in throngs."[59] Muslim education was part of the diplomatic and colonial mission of the educational service, but the primary education of French citizens was the sine qua non of an educational system under the Third Republic, committed to universal education for French citizens, a commitment which in Morocco was extended to the entire European population.

When considering enrollment figures, one must keep in mind the fact that there was considerable Muslim resistance to French schooling in the early years of the protectorate, while the ever-growing numbers of European settlers flooded the schools with requests for admission. Nevertheless, enrollment patterns reflected the underlying assumptions of the colonizers. French schools for Muslims were intended to exist alongside indigenous education, not replace it. Schools for Muslims were important to the colonial leadership, but under Lyautey there was no intention of ever providing universal education for the Moroccan population. Unlike earlier colonizers in Algeria, the French did not deliberately attempt to weaken Islamic education in Morocco (although the French presence would inevitably undermine the utility and prestige of the Moroccan institutions). The French did not consider the education of Muslims to be wholly a French responsibility: it was expected that the French would take a leading role, but it was hoped that support would also come from the *makhzan* and from Muslim community leaders.

One must also take into consideration the initial lack of basic infrastructure and resources. Materials had to be imported, and maintaining communication with schools was difficult. In 1917, when the educational service began regular inspections of the schools, the rudimentary transportation infrastructure proved exasperating: Rabat, Casablanca, and Berrechid were by this time connected by light rail and trolley, but heavy rains often rendered the road to Meknes impassable, and even Settat could be still be reached only by mule.[60] Any assessment of French educational accomplishments in the early years of the protectorate must not underestimate the daunting challenges that had to be overcome in order to accomplish the simplest of tasks. These difficulties also meant that the metropolitan model of pedagogy was the norm: the physical demands of building and running a school system took precedence over the elaboration of a new pedagogical model. Considering the rapid growth of the European population, it might be argued that under Loth's direction (1912–19) the colonial state achieved impressive results in the development of Muslim education, during a time when the colonial budget was stretched thin by military priorities. Lyautey, however, did not agree.

The Sacking of Gaston Loth

Lyautey was displeased with the development of education for Muslims, and in mid-1919 he abruptly dismissed Loth. According to Lyautey, Loth had fine organizational skills and was well suited to be an administrator of schools for Europeans. However, Lyautey felt that Loth was not committed to Lyautey's vision for Muslim schooling, and had failed to make Muslim schools a priority. The resident-general declared that the schools for Muslims were "developing neither in quality nor in quantity" and suffered from "a lack of direction, of impulsion, and in sum, communication." He also accused Loth of being too preoccupied with his own local business ventures and those of his family members.⁶¹

Loth's educational administration in Morocco was characterized by improvised responses to the challenges of understaffing, underfunding, immigration, and war. In a time of rapid expansion and scarce resources, Loth was necessarily preoccupied with the material and personnel needs of the school system. This was in keeping with Lyautey's preference for action and adaptation over policy and theory. Loth's writing exhibited an accord with Lyautey's anti-assimilationist philosophy, stressing the importance of useful, vocationally oriented education that was tailored to the perceived racial characteristics of Moroccan Muslims. However, there is little evidence that Loth's talk of practical, adapted education had much impact in the schools. The teaching staff was accustomed to the norms of metropolitan general education. Few specific curricular guidelines were established, and the limitations of communication and staffing meant that teachers were not closely supervised.⁶² Moreover, the first director of the schools in Fez, Bel, complained that his independent efforts to establish vocational schooling in 1914 were not supported by Loth's administration. As always, resources were limited and the colonists were taken care of first, resulting in limited vocational training for Muslims during Loth's tenure.⁶³

But what irked Lyautey the most were the *collèges musulmans*. Regarding these *collèges*, Lyautey felt that Loth presented "a real inertia and a notorious incomprehension of the goal to be attained." According to Lyautey, "Mr. Loth has remained an '*Inspecteur d'Académie*,' and this is a totally different mentality than what is needed."⁶⁴ This implied that Loth was too assimilationist or too bureaucratic, or both. At any rate, he lacked the drive to give the schools the direction and "impulsion" needed to overcome *makhzan* resistance, *collège* student pressure, and French republican habits.

Lyautey found the drive, ideological commitment, and charisma he was looking for in the person of a talented colonial administrator named Georges Hardy, "a man of broad mind, generous inspiration, and high culture, in service of communicative activity and conviction."[65] Hardy was a prolific writer who as a child had dreamed of becoming a Catholic missionary, but who instead became a *lycée* professor, *agrégé* in history and geography from the Faculty of Lille. In France he had published pedagogical and scholarly works on ecclesiastical history and French geography. In 1912 Hardy had gone to Senegal to become the head of colonial education for French West Africa. After arriving in West Africa, he began to study the colonial ethnology of Africa and penned works such as *Géographie de l'Afrique occidentale française*, and *Une conquête morale: L'enseignement en A.O.F.*

Hardy's tremendous energy, his Catholic background, and his interest in ethnology and ethnic difference made him a kindred spirit to Lyautey. In April 1919 Hardy had been dismissed from his post in West Africa after losing a political battle with Senegal's pro-assimilation African elite. Hardy's zeal for the maintenance of colonial segregation and cultural difference would eventually lead him to become one of North Africa's leading spokesmen for Marshal Pétain's Vichy regime in 1940, but first it brought him to Lyautey's Rabat at the end of 1919, where he became the new director of education.

During his seven years as head of colonial education in French West Africa, Hardy developed the approach that became the foundation of educational policy in Morocco from 1920 through the 1930s. This approach included an emphasis on ethnology and preservation of ethnic difference, defined in the most general terms; the French language as a tool of economic modernization; a restricted pedagogy; a distrust of educated natives; a rigid and generalized view of native capabilities; and the practice of using the pedagogical bulletin and the teacher-training institute as tools to disseminate ethnological views. In French Morocco, Hardy's pedagogy would be subtly transformed by a different institutional and political context, by Lyautey's philosophy of colonial action, and by a new metropolitan reformism, but the West African precedent would remain strong. Under Hardy, French educational efforts would continue to be shaped by Moroccan responses, but the pedagogical and ethnological discourses fostered by Hardy would have a profound effect on the future of colonial schooling and the Franco-Moroccan relationship.

3. The West African Connection

The ethnic differences, as deep as they are, don't preclude there being a clearly recognizable archetype of the black student. | Georges Hardy, 1917

One realizes, reading Mr. Hardy's book, that this man, who so often claims to, does not know the soul of the indigene at all. | Amadou l'Artilleur, 1919

No colonial situation exists in isolation. The culture and policies of colonial education in interwar French Morocco were shaped not only by the patterns established in Morocco in the early years of the protectorate but also by the politics and culture of French West Africa (l'Afrique occidentale française, the AOF) during this period. The most direct catalyst for this influence was Lyautey's decision in 1919 to bring to Morocco the AOF's former educational director, Georges Hardy.

Even without Hardy, Morocco would have felt the shock waves of the momentous events in Senegal during World War I. There had emerged in urban Senegal a political movement in which colonized Africans used republican language and politics to wrest concessions of political and civic equality from an imperial France momentarily made vulnerable by the war.[1] This threat to colonial power exposed the danger of the universalist, liberatory ideas about the *mission civilisatrice* (civilizing mission) that had long been used to justify French conquest and rule around the world, ideas that remained popular in Paris, if not among the colonists. The emergence of the Young Senegalese, along with the emergence of the Young Algerians north of the Sahara, seemed to validate Lyautey's philosophy of maintaining difference, tradition, and hierarchy.

However, Hardy's personal itinerary meant that French West Africa had a particularly direct impact on Morocco. Hardy's approach to colonial education was shaped by three individuals whom he encountered during his time in the AOF. Governor-General William Ponty, Deputy Blaise Diagne, and ethnographer Maurice Delafosse were mutual rivals, but each left his imprint on Morocco's future educational director. Of the three, Diagne was most pivotal, for it was the backlash against this African politician that would transform Hardy from a protégé of Ponty into a student of Delafosse, an enemy of the Young Senegalese, and finally into a disciple of Lyautey. An excursion into the history of French West Africa is therefore indispensable to an understanding of French colonial education in Morocco.

Politics and Pedagogy under William Ponty, 1908–1915

In 1912, Governor-General Ponty had appointed Hardy, a twenty-eight-year-old with no prior colonial experience, as head of education for all of French West Africa. Ponty, like Lyautey, was a military officer who had served under Gallieni in Madagascar. Ponty's method of administration, like Lyautey's, was derived from Gallieni's *politique des races*: the attempt to govern in accord with the differing needs and traditions of colonized ethnic groups, relying on the collaboration of native elites. Ponty, however, was a republican with an aversion to African political hierarchies. While Lyautey romanticized the Moroccan aristocracy, Ponty contrasted the despotism of African rulers to the civilization offered by the French; he considered African regional rulers to be "parasites living off the population."[2] French rule, as Ponty saw it, would bring an end to traditional African tyranny and "destroy all hegemony of one race over another, or one ethnic group over another."[3] "Association" with these rulers had been a practical necessity during the period of conquest, but Ponty believed it was time to turn toward a new phase of liberating colonialism. Yet it would be misleading to portray a stark dichotomy between Lyautey and an "assimilationist" Ponty. Ponty referred to his native policy as *apprivoisement* (domestication), which became a policy of asymptotic assimilationism—Africans could approach Frenchness but never merge with it.[4] His educational policies did not promote individual assimilation; rather, they aimed to bring African society ("the entire race," as Ponty put it) closer to French civilization while respecting indigenous traditions insofar as was possible.[5] Ponty's philosophy of liberating Africans from tyranny was approached as a matter of ethnic self-determination; individualism would come only in the distant future, and assimilation would never be more than partial.[6] Yet his policies were justified in republican language that would have been alien to Lyautey ("the obligatory force that we wish to recognize in customary rules derives solely from the consent of the populations").[7] Although Ponty agreed with Lyautey that French policy ought to be adapted to the existing ethnic characteristics of the colonized populations, Ponty believed that the goal of French rule, and the task of French colonial education, was to reduce and minimize ethnic difference.

Toward this end, Ponty had initiated an expansion of colonial schooling when he became governor-general in 1908, and the administration claimed to have doubled the number of students enrolled in the colonial schools to twenty thousand by 1914.[8] The first years of Ponty's administration were years of stagnation, however, at the several small, specialized schools in Senegal that became known, perhaps ironically, as West Africa's *grandes écoles*. These included the École supérieure professionnelle Pinet-Laprade, the École normale (later renamed the École William Ponty), and the École des pupilles mécaniciens de la marine, which trained engine mechanics. Enrollment in these *grandes écoles* was tiny, and it fell during the first years of Ponty's administration: at the professional Pinet-Laprade school, enrollment in the entering class declined from twenty-seven in 1907 to ten in 1910, and by 1912 the entering class of the École normale had declined from thirty-seven to ten.⁹ Hardy, it was hoped, would reinvigorate these specialized schools as well as improve the instruction and curricula at the rural village primary schools, regional schools, and urban primaries.

Upon arriving in West Africa, Hardy declared his intention to develop texts and programs "adapted to the *habitudes d'esprit*" of West African students.¹⁰ Hardy moved quickly to accomplish this, and in 1913 he authored a geography text, *Géographie de l'Afrique occidentale française*, which appeared along with a history of French West Africa by André Léguillette, an instructor at the École normale. In 1914 Hardy produced a set of curricular programs for village and regional schools throughout the federation. In 1916 the new programs for village schools were incorporated into a comprehensive reader by Louis Sonolet and A. Pérès.¹¹

Hardy's 1914 programs reflected Ponty's vision of colonial education; Hardy and Ponty declared that the colonial schools were to have "a double goal: on the one hand, to be practical, to serve directly the economic development of the Colonies of the group and direct our populations in the sense of agricultural and industrial progress; on the other hand, to be the most effective instrument of our civilizing work, to impose upon the indigenes this idea that they can and should ameliorate their conditions of existence, to awaken the desire for betterment [mieux-être] and give them the means to achieve it."¹²

Despite their interest in economic development, Ponty and Hardy made it clear that primary schooling for Africans was not to consist of apprenticeships, although urban schools were to prepare students for subsequent placement as apprentices. Several hours per week were to be spent working the school garden or in simple woodworking or metalworking crafts, but this pre-apprenticeship constituted only one part of the program. Throughout his career in colonial education, Hardy consistently emphasized the importance of general education and "moral" instruction, which emphasized the benevolent nature of

French colonization, in order that the African worker might become appreciative and compliant as well as productive. The three-year program of the village schools included five hours per week of oral language instruction, plus five hours of reading, five hours of arithmetic, two and a half hours of written exercises, and two and a half hours of drawing.

In addition to these village primary schools, the French had also established regional schools throughout the West African federation, in order to prepare the sons of chiefs and the best students from the region's village schools to act as intermediaries for the French: to work for the administration or for French companies, or go on to more specialized training at the colony's upper primary school or the *grandes écoles* of the federation. The academic goals of the regional program were quite modest. Students were to be able to read fluently, but teachers were to foster a distrust of book learning, because "the indigenes have a great tendency to believe that everything written or printed implies truth, and the absolute confidence in the virtue of the book can lead to grave errors."[13] History was to be primarily local, focusing on the benefits of French colonialism in the AOF: "the profound difference . . . between the past of their country, unstable and bloody, and the present, peaceful and fertile." Writing was to be limited to business letters, inventory reports, and the like. Intellectual experimentation was to be discouraged; the 1914 programs stated: "It is recommended to teachers to take care that the students only employ words or formulas that they perfectly understand the sense of, and that they attach themselves to the simplicity of style, clarity, and sincerity."[14] In order to maintain political compliance, learning was to be carefully limited.

Urban schools were a somewhat different case. These schools, unlike the regional schools, were not to be selective; all children and adolescents were to be welcomed, lest they become juvenile delinquents instead. Hardy recognized that the introductory programs of the village schools were inappropriate for children already familiar with French ways, "children already awakened [éveillés], sometimes too awakened." The urban schools segregated African students from European ones, with some exceptions (those with native-like fluency in French at a very early age). However, Hardy allowed that the urban programs for Africans might need to be similar to the metropolitan programs, because "it is not useful, in an urban school, that the school repeat what the city has already taught to the student."[15] There were limits to Hardy's openness to cultural hybridization among colonized urbanites, however. Elsewhere he complained about what he saw as arrogance among educated Senegalese, "into whom a malicious destiny has injected foreign ideas, incoherent pretensions, perfectly unjustified seeds of resistances and revolts."[16] The events of the following years would only increase this hostility toward overly assimilated natives.

French nevertheless remained the language of education. Ponty declared in 1910 that French language instruction was "the primordial condition of our success and its longevity," by which the colonizers' "influence will insinuate itself among the masses, penetrate and envelop them like a thin web of new affinities."[17] He also mandated the use of French in all courts for natives and in all administrative acts, effectively prohibiting Arabic as a language of official business.[18] Hardy would later distance himself from some of Ponty's policies, but the younger man firmly adopted this belief in the central role of the French language.

However, Ponty and Hardy stressed that French was merely a practical tool, not an end in itself: it was the language of instruction merely because the AOF was too linguistically diverse to allow instruction in indigenous languages. Ponty claimed that the language used was irrelevant, because the goal was not to turn natives into Frenchmen but rather to improve African societies within their own setting. Students at the village schools would probably forget their French anyway, but that was not the point: "The words will pass away perhaps; the ideas will remain, and these ideas, which are ours, and the use of which constitutes our moral, social, and economic superiority, will transform the barbarians of yesterday bit by bit into disciples and auxiliaries."[19] Ponty's introduction to the 1914 programs stated that "these are no longer lessons of words, these are lessons of things [leçons des choses]."[20]

The use of *leçons des choses* was a form of the "direct method" of foreign-language pedagogy. Real objects were to be presented to the class so that, instead of learning through translation or rote memorization, students would learn to associate signifiers directly with the objects and actions signified. The objects chosen were to be locally obtained and relevant to the students' lives. This hands-on approach to beginning language instruction allowed the integration of French with other subjects. The two-year program of the village schools included eight topics that were to be introduced sequentially and repeated each year: the school, the human body, food, clothing, housing, the family, the village, and travel. No classroom time was allotted to agronomy at the village schools, but agricultural topics were integrated into the oral language curriculum and were to be reinforced through hands-on work in the school garden. The prescribed topics included "physical conditions" (the sun, water, seasons, agricultural tools), cultivated plants, and the care of plants, forest products, and animals. The 1914 programs stressed that "by virtue of the principle that all language lessons are to be based on a demonstration, lessons about agricultural work ought to be given in the open air, in the garden, if the school has one, or in the neighboring fields."[21] In regions near ports or industrial operations, the second-year language lessons might address other topics such as fishing and boat engines, or local industries. In the *Bulletin de l'Enseignement*, Hardy advised teachers in the village schools to be flexible and sensible in following the official programs. Although metropolitan French history and geography were excluded from the programs, teachers were not to avoid all discussion of France. On the contrary, "France, its spirit, its beauty, its power of radiance, this is the very air and light of our classes."[22] AOF schools were to attend to moral hegemony, not just economic utility.

Ponty and Hardy promoted a version of the *mission civilisatrice* that was to be transforming but only asymptotically assimilationist. The goal of colonial education was not equality or integration but rather "to attach them to us by prolonged contact and to reinforce with a broader culture the social utility that we expect of them."[23] The *Bulletin* declared in 1913 that the French would "lead these populations to make men, in the economic and moral sense of the word, and we will thus obtain the most appreciable result that a colonizing race could, in its heart, hope to achieve."[24] This hoped-for result fell somewhat short of Frenchness. As Alice Conklin has pointed out, there was a sharp distinction between making Frenchmen and making "useful men."[25]

Blaise Diagne and the African Frenchmen of Senegal

A pivotal moment in Hardy's career—and, more broadly, in the history of French colonialism—was the sudden rise in the political power of the French-speaking *originaires* and "*évolués*" of Senegal. The former were Senegalese born in the Four Communes of Gorée, Saint-Louis, Dakar, and Rufisque; they had acquired French citizenship under the July Monarchy. Their citizenship had been reaffirmed by the Second Republic in 1848 and the Third Republic in 1871, although by 1912 their political and legal rights had been circumscribed by the stipulation that these rights were not portable and could only be exercised or inherited within the geographic limits of the Four Communes. The so-called *évolués* ("evolved ones") included, in addition to the *originaires*, literate French-speaking Africans who lacked the quasi-citizenship of the *originaires*. The *évolué* group included many Muslims, who had often attended Catholic or secular French schools; they commonly worked as clerks or translators for French businesses or the administration.[26]

In the nineteenth century, electoral democracy in the Communes had been dominated by wealthy families of mixed descent and by the influence of French trading companies. In the early twentieth century, however, groups of *originaires* and *évolués*, like their contemporaries the Young Algerians, began to make political and moral claims based on French discourses of assimilationism, citizenship, and universal rights. As G. Wesley Johnson Jr. has pointed out, "the African quest for assimilation was not a quest for total assimilation into French culture.... For the overwhelming majority of Senegalese *originaires*, and for those who aspired to *originaire* status, the goal was political parity with the French: political and civic rights, combined with enough Western education and skills to allow participation in an urban market economy."[27] To their French critics, however, this focus on civic and economic integration was evidence of avarice and insincerity, a corruption of the civilizing mission that revealed the dangerous futility of assimilationist policies and republican idealism.

The rise of the *originaires* began with the 1909 election of Galandou Diouf, a Catholic-educated Muslim Wolof, to the municipal council of Rufisque. In 1912, French-speaking Africans in Saint-Louis organized a group called the Young Senegalese, and soon they began expressing sharp criticisms of French policy in the pages of *La Démocratie du Sénégal*, published in Dakar. This set the stage for the 1914 election of Blaise Diagne as the Four Communes' representative to the French Chamber of Deputies, a seat previously monopolized by prominent *métis* (mixed-descent) families. Diagne was a "black" African, born on the island of Gorée, who had made a name for himself by championing the rights of Africans, both in the metropolitan press and in the performance of his duties as a customs officer throughout the French empire. His campaign stressed his commitment to full citizenship rights for the *originaires*, while insisting that the traditions and customs of Africans, Muslim and non-Muslim, should be respected. Diagne presented himself as a "citizen of the empire" who was representative of a cosmopolitan French society: "I am black, my wife is white, and my children are mixed. What better guarantee of my interest in representing all our population?"[28] He owed his victory, however, to the relatively united support of black voters, while French and *métis* voters split their votes among multiple candidates.

In the Chamber of Deputies, Diagne worked to expand the rights of the *originaires*. His bargaining power was enhanced by France's need for African troops. In July 1915 he persuaded the legislature to allow *originaires* to join the regular French army rather than the segregated colonial troops. Military eligibility became a stepping-stone to political rights, and the Chamber of Deputies passed laws in 1915 and 1916 affirming the full citizenship and attendant military obligations of *originaires*, despite opposition from the Government General in Dakar. This citizenship was also extended to the descendants of those born in the Four Communes. Of course, the population of *originaires* was insufficient to meet the recruitment needs of France during World War I. In 1918, in need of more soldiers, Clemenceau asked Diagne to lead a massive recruiting drive throughout the AOF for the colonial army. In exchange for his recruiting efforts, Diagne obtained decrees facilitating the access of African veterans to French naturalization, along with promises to improve the legal and material status of Africans after the war.[29] Meanwhile, the colonial press attacked Diagne vociferously for "his hatred of all that which is white."[30]

Diagne's accomplishments signaled that a new political force had emerged from the most assimilated urban segment of African society. This urban elite was no longer a mere corps of clerks who facilitated French rule; the clerks had become political players who sought to turn Paris against the Government General in Dakar. The election of Diagne put the French republican doctrines of liberty and equality to the test. Ponty, and France, had now come to a crossroads in the history of colonialism: would the French, for the first time since 1871, expand and deepen African membership in the fraternity of the Republic?

The rise of Diagne and the Young Senegalese produced an immediate reaction, as the colonial state attempted to counter the new African power in Paris. This anti-assimilationist backlash within the colonial administration was facilitated by Ponty's death in June 1915. Ponty's successors did not share his vision of colonialism. Ponty, however, had himself been alarmed by the election of Diagne, which he described as "a dangerous situation for the future of white men in Africa."³¹ Therefore it is perhaps unwise to speculate that things might have been different had Ponty lived. Throughout the French empire, what remained of the assimilationist impulse was giving way to the advocates of separation and difference. In any case, the AOF's political shift was reflected in educational policy, and Hardy became part of a regime that emphasized ethnic difference and association with traditional elites. This would eventually make Hardy a fine candidate for the top spot in Lyautey's educational system.

Hardy's new boss in 1915, François-Joseph Clozel, had never agreed with Ponty's methods of rule, and as lieutenant governor of Côte d'Ivoire and Haut-Senegal-Niger he had resisted Ponty's policies as much as possible by upholding the power of African rulers who collaborated with the French. Clozel blamed Ponty for a series of revolts in early 1915 that had broken out as a response to French wartime conscription. Clozel used the revolts to justify the rejection of Ponty's version of the *mission civilisatrice*, advocating a return to a policy of rule through African overlords.³² In 1916, Clozel, in ill health, was replaced briefly by the lieutenant governor of Côte d'Ivoire, Gabriel Angoulvant, and then by Joost Van Vollenhoven in 1917. Van Vollenhoven took Clozel's political method a step further by suggesting that where authentic overlords did not exist, they should be invented so that French interests might be better served. This was an utter reversal of Ponty's policies.

The colonial administration's new ideological slant would have a strong influence on Hardy's thinking and career, affecting his later work in Morocco. Called for military service in 1914, Hardy served for ten months until he was wounded in 1915. Upon his return to West Africa he had little difficulty adjusting to the new colonial leadership. There is little in his background or writing to suggest that he had ever shared Ponty's deep distrust of tradition or aristocracy, and the shift in the AOF toward a more conservative and less republican native policy was soon reflected in Hardy's apologetics.

Clozel set forth his approach to AOF education in no uncertain terms. He referred to Africans as "primitives" and mocked educated Africans, dismissing their intellectual accomplishments (and implicitly their political aspirations) as "a pompous and ridiculous verbalism" that was nothing more than a "new fetishism" that had created a class of "vain, incompetent, and malcontented simpletons."[33] Therefore he pushed for greater restriction of education and advocated a curriculum that would provide linguistic and professional skills as well as basic hygiene, without awakening political discontent. He warned against exaggerating the opportunities that would be available to graduates of primary schools, and instructed that professional schools should focus on educating workers and should eliminate classes for typists and telegraphers. If nurses were to be trained, they needed no instruction in natural history, physiology, or botany, but only practical skills.[34]

Clozel's crude hostility was complemented, however, by the more sophisticated influence of Maurice Delafosse, who became a major inspiration for young Georges Hardy. Delafosse was a colonial administrator who had become a leading French scholar on West African history and society. He had served in West Africa in the 1890s and had a long-standing interest in education (he had taught the first French class offered in the interior of Côte d'Ivoire). Since 1900 he had been teaching at the École coloniale and the École des langues orientales vivantes in France, but Clozel was interested in ethnography and brought Delafosse back to Dakar to lead the bureau of Indigenous Affairs, a post that Delafosse retained under Van Vollenhoven.[35]

At the École coloniale, Delafosse had developed and taught a position that opposed both universalism and white supremacism. He criticized notions of innate African inferiority while stressing the importance of differences in "mentality" and social forms. Urging "respect" for non-European cultures, Delafosse criticized what in today's discourse would be called "ethnocentrism." He argued that those who insist that all humans are the same inevitably make their own society the yardstick for humanity; measured thus, other societies inevitably fall short. While Ponty had stressed the need to bring French influence to the "races of inferior civilization," Delafosse argued that African moral "barbarity" was no worse than the European record of slavery and torture and that African political institutions were no less stable than European ones.[36]

In the context of West African politics, Delafosse's ethnology became a critique of Ponty's administration. While Delafosse was in France, Ponty had criticized him for promoting ideas that contradicted current policy. Delafosse argued that Africans were not mere "primitives" but had their own complex political and moral institutions. This meant that Ponty had been wrong to undermine the power of African rulers; regional chiefs were the heads of authentic African states. Furthermore, Delafosse argued that the village chiefs through whom Ponty had wanted to rule were largely a creation of the French. The destruction of the larger political institutions produced alienation and resentment. Instead of breaking down the most advanced and complex African institutions, the French ought to strengthen them. Respect for indigenous institutions meant that the French ought to seek allies among African leaders.[37] Delafosse rejected Ponty's republican discourse of an African population that needed to be rescued from tyranny; he promoted instead a discourse, much like Lyautey's, of a traditional society that needed protection and preservation.

Conklin has argued convincingly that colonial officials used Delafosse's ideas only selectively. His approach was used to justify a conservative policy of supporting rural strongmen and resisting the new urban elite, but little was done to realize his desire that the French rule in true collaboration with traditional village councils, and for the material benefit of Africans.[38] The subtler aspects of Delafosse's thinking were also lost on Hardy, who was charged with the task of applying ethnological knowledge to educational policy.

Hardy followed Delafosse in opposing the notion that Africans were mere brutes, unsuitable for anything but manual labor, and agreed that Africans had social structures and cultural habits that had to be accounted for. African society was not formless clay that the French could shape as they chose. Hardy dismissed as irrelevant the question of whether Africans were innately inferior to Europeans or whether African civilization merely suffered from developmental retardation that might be overcome. Regardless, argued Hardy, educational policy must adapt to the current state of indigenous societies and to the needs of both natives and colonizers. Hardy would eventually come to see Delafosse's ethnography as more than a guide to pedagogy and colonial policy: for Hardy, Delafosse's ideas eventually became doctrines that would save European civilization. In the meantime, Hardy continued to develop the AOF's educational system, and his work in West Africa was shaped by Delafosse's work as well as by the new political priorities of the colonial administration.

As Delafosse saw it, French ignorance about African societies had led to bad policy, which was the primary cause of rebellion and social discontent in the AOF. He advised educators that metropolitan methods could not be imported to West Africa, because Africans possessed "intelligences which are assuredly awake, but which have processes of reasoning as different from those of our French children as the physique of the blacks differ from that of the whites."[39] Successful colonial education, like colonial political strategy, had to be based on careful study of indigenous groups. Toward this end, Hardy turned the *Bulletin de l'Enseignement*, which he had created in 1913, into a forum for ethnographic writing on the characteristics of "les races scolaires" (scholastic races) and for discussions of how ethnic characteristics (as well as regional geography and history) affected pedagogy. The ethnographic writings published in the *Bulletin* were not Hardy's alone. Hardy solicited the input of both African and European teachers, and he and Delafosse are credited with midwifing the birth of African ethnographic writing, which became a means for educated Africans to assert an intellectual status that set them apart from the "traditional" societies they wrote about.[40] Hardy's purpose, however, was to create, under his centralized control, a common intellectual approach to education in West Africa, one that would motivate and enable teachers to act independently, yet in accord with the desires of the administration: "to produce a strong moral unity among the African teaching corps."[41] This attempt to use the *Bulletin* and related publications to promote a preferred discourse about pedagogy and about the colonized population would become an important feature of Hardy's work in Morocco as well.

In his writing, Hardy became increasingly at ease with assertions of ethnic characteristics. In 1913 he had qualified discussions of ethnic traits with a disclaimer stressing the diversity of individuals: "we consecrate to the child of each race, not a portrait, but a gallery."[42] By 1917, however, he was more comfortable describing archetypical traits for an ethnic group, although he continued to avoid biological determinism. The Foulah were keenly intelligent but resistant to French influence and therefore became quite miserable and depressed in the classroom; the Malinka children were well behaved and hardworking, but slow learners; the Sénoufos were patient, docile, and good with their hands, but without curiosity or initiative. The Senegalese sought to use education to secure positions as functionaries or commercial employees, while other groups were attached to agriculture or husbandry. Hardy argued that successful pedagogy would have to take these ethnic characteristics and preferences into consideration.[43]

Yet Hardy also maintained his commitment to the educational principles developed under Ponty. As a result, his educational philosophy became a hybrid of contrasting discourses rather than, as he would later claim, a "perfect communion of ideas and of sympathies" with Delafosse.[44] Hardy accepted Clozel's emphasis on practical education but argued that the conservative emphasis on "utility" and social order ought not to stifle the "truly active elements" that developed the intellect and its powers of observation and reason.[45] Education for Africans was to be restricted, but it was not to be reduced to mere apprenticeship or vocational training. In accord with Clozel, Hardy criticized "les coloniaux en chambre," French legislators who had never left the hexagon and who sought to force republican principles upon the colonies. But Hardy was also critical of "l'esprit colon" (settler mentality), which despised the African and saw the education of natives as a threat.[46] His attitude was more optimistic, though no less racist: "The soul of the black is essentially affective; it is possible to modify it, happily, by the influence of work and the contagion of kindness."[47] Hardy's attempt to preserve Ponty's policy of educational *apprivoisement* received further support from Clozel's successor, Van Vollenhoven, who believed that although "the native of French West Africa is a child," education could still rescue the native from barbarism and "develop the spirit of the students without uprooting or deracinating them."[48]

Hardy warned that French schools must not be too rigid in their attempt to preserve authentic racial characteristics and social structures. French colonialism was transforming West Africa economically. Colonial policy ought to respect the indigenous social order, but it also had to allow for social change that would accommodate economic modernization, lest a social revolution result. This meant that curricula based entirely on current local occupations were therefore inappropriate; West Africa was changing, and Africans had to learn general skills that would allow them to work in new capacities. This argument upheld the importance of general education and justified the imposition of a common educational policy throughout the AOF.

Hardy also justified such standardization by arguing that despite the diversity of the AOF, some ethnic traits were common to all Africans: "The ethnic differences, as deep as they are, don't preclude there being a clearly recognizable archetype of the black student; there subsists a common pool of habits, preferences, and concepts that neatly separate the school for natives from the European school, but which permits the existence of a uniquely African education, valuable for all the AOF schools, and merely susceptible to variations in detail according to locations and races."[49]

This meant that AOF education could mimic the metropolitan model of a standardized, centrally administered educational system while still heeding the Delafosse doctrine of adapting policy to African society. A common educational policy was justified not only by the common need to adapt to colonial modernization but also by a preexisting commonality of cultural or racial traits. Hardy undertook to describe the characteristics of the students who were inducted into the French schools. Whatever their ethnicity or religion, African youths were allegedly accustomed to liberty and undisciplined by their parents; like African adults, they ascribed all causation to supernatural forces; they were predisposed to vanity, insolence, indolence, and uncomprehending memorization, or "verbalism." These were faults that AOF education aimed to counteract, but at the same time, pedagogy could make use of these traits: for example, African "vanity" could be used to motivate students to display their mastery of the material.[50]

This established an approach that Hardy would apply in Morocco as well. In theory, he followed Delafosse in affirming that indigenous society was different but not inferior. However, Hardy's description of the archetypical indigene was essentially negative and led to a highly restrictive pedagogy. Hardy invoked ethnography primarily in order to establish a clear difference between the European and the native. Yet he downplayed the importance of diversity in order to describe common characteristics that would provide clear guidance for a unified educational policy. This tendency would put Hardy at odds with the ideas behind the French Berber policy in Morocco, despite the Berber policy's similarity to Ponty's more particularistic approach to defining ethnic characteristics and customs.

The practical orientation and modest goals of the 1914 programs were well suited to the post-Ponty political agenda, and these were echoed in Hardy's more detailed 1917 guide for teachers, *Une conquête morale*. Language pedagogy was to be carefully restricted in both pacing and content. The pace of the curriculum should be slow, argued Hardy; to avoid "verbalism," it was essential that a perfect mastery of each lesson be achieved before moving on. Instruction was to consist exclusively of *leçons des choses*. Vocabulary was to be limited to nouns referring to everyday things; abstract nouns were to be carefully avoided. Recitations were to be used to correct pronunciation and to promote acquisition, but texts were to be limited to "bits of prose completely limpid, precise, and condensed." Writing tasks were to focus on business letters and reports. Advanced students were to be prevented from reading "literature of high value" and were to be steered toward authors who wrote "soberly, simply" (Jules Verne was specifically recommended).[51]

The strongly anti-assimilationist political climate after Ponty made it necessary for Hardy to defend the use of French as the language of instruction in the village schools (Gaston Loth was meanwhile engaging in very similar apologetics in Morocco). Hardy continued to insist on French, repeating the purely practical argument that he and Ponty had put forward in 1914: "the diversity of languages spoken in French West Africa renders instruction in the indigenous languages materially impossible."[52] This argument from necessity divorced the choice of instructional medium from republican ideology. In West Africa, colonial instruction had to be in French because there was no indigenous lingua franca.

Hardy hoped that careful control of student exposure to language would allow French education to promote the development of knowledge while preventing the emergence of undesired discourse among Africans. Yet neither he nor Clozel could admit that francophone Africans might fully understand French concepts of political rights and responsibilities and turn the political ideology of the colonizer to their own advantage by seeking full membership in the Republic. To admit such a possibility would have authenticated the political project of the Diagnists and their assimilationist allies in Paris. Instead, the danger was cast as African vanity and "verbalism." This mocked African social or political aspirations and implied that Africans were unsuited for equality within the French system. Colonial pedagogy was thus imagined not as repressive, but simply realistic.

The Expansion of Schooling and
Political Contestation, 1916–1919

Ethnological discourse and the threat to colonial power posed by Diagne and the Young Senegalese pushed the AOF administration to emphasize the maintenance of difference and the restriction of education. However, the manpower shortage caused by World War I necessitated an increased reliance on African personnel, both in the army and in the colonial bureaucracy. The government of the AOF had no choice but to give in to African demands for educational expansion and access to jobs in the administration. This concession was made more palatable by the success of Diagne's recruiting efforts. The performance of African soldiers in World War I persuaded some administrators that concessions to African aspirations might be appropriate. However, as the French-educated Africans' political and social leverage grew, so did the colonial backlash, and educational policy became increasingly controversial.

The wartime expansion of education began in 1916, when Clozel revived the defunct École Faidherbe as a school of "commercial and administrative apprenticeship" to train secretaries, typists, and bookkeepers. A medical school was soon created as an annex, to train doctors' assistants. In 1918 this expansion would be carried further, with a veterinary section and a midwifery course, and a school of agriculture and sylviculture. At first Hardy applauded this expansion of education, stating that such specialized schools would produce, "not people polished [frotté] with disparate knowledge, but technical agents," and only as many as were needed to meet personnel needs, "avoiding the danger of training *déclassés*."[53] Nevertheless, he still defended the importance of general education, insisting on a three-year program that would impress upon students the material, intellectual, moral, and social progress that the French had brought to West Africa: "the fight against disease," "the disappearance of slavery," and "justice."[54] In February 1918 Hardy pressed the administration to bring more European teachers to West Africa and to further expand enrollment at the École normale and the École Faidherbe to 100 students per class.⁵⁵ Few European teachers were available, but the enrollment goals were met and exceeded by the fall of 1918, when 100 students entered the École normale, a tenfold increase since 1912, and 150 new students were enrolled at Faidherbe.⁵⁶

The wartime expansion of education and the opening of low-level administrative posts to Africans provoked resentment among some colonial administrators, however. In 1914, Raphael Antonetti, the interim lieutenant governor of Senegal, accused the French schools of producing a cohort of political malcontents who were radicalizing the masses: "the illiterate population follows the direction of the literate part, and their association forms a block against which our persuasive action has no influence."⁵⁷ In mid-1918, Antonetti, by then lieutenant governor of Côte d'Ivoire and "an outright foe of the *originaires*," again targeted the educational service.⁵⁸ He attacked the École normale and its African graduates and criticized Hardy for expanding education too quickly, arguing that Hardy's attempt to "forge a common soul for all the educated indigenes of the AOF" had been "extraordinarily dangerous."⁵⁹ Antonetti declared that the École normale ought to be shut down for two years and "emptied of children without education, without character, and who are unusable." Its students were, in his opinion, "hardly more educated than our monitors, but, on the contrary, completely *désorbité* and mad with arrogance."⁶⁰

Hardy dismissed Antonetti's complaints as "manifestly invented," and Interim Governor-General Angoulvant defended the École normale and the African schoolteachers.⁶¹ This did not, however, end the complaints about the students at the *grandes écoles*, whom French officials found insufficiently deferent.⁶² These complaints were linked to larger anxieties within the French administration about the influence of the Young Senegalese. Feeling that he was caught in the middle, Hardy defended himself against "both extreme parties." Wartime changes in West African society should not entail a revolution in education, he maintained. The programs and goals proclaimed in 1914 had been put into practice, Hardy argued, and it would be "senseless" to throw them away after such a successful beginning.[63] By July 1918 Hardy was opposing further expansion at the École normale William Ponty and the École Faidherbe, citing the need to maintain quality control. He warned that the recent expansion, while a worthy achievement, posed a danger: "the danger, in this case, is that we get used to this heterogeneous recruitment, hasty, a bit disorganized, and that we take as the rule what should only be an exception, a revolutionary measure, a necessity in time of war." Hardy feared that students would desire to advance too quickly and that students entering the specialized schools lacked "a solidity, a depth that a few exam compositions cannot test."[64] He called upon teachers and administrators to carefully select the students who were allowed to enter the specialized schools.

While Hardy's 1918 emphasis on the restriction of educational opportunities may have been a response to critics such as Antonetti, it also accorded with his long-standing ambivalence toward exposure of Africans to French ideas. In 1916 Hardy had cautioned instructors at the École normale to stick to the programs established in 1914, to "defy words, which are perfidious friends" and to cultivate "veritable phobias: a phobia of high theoretical pedagogy, a phobia of sublime morality classes that do not ameliorate the individual, of beautiful literary language that impedes reflection," and of any instruction that went "over the heads of the students."[65] In 1917 he had argued that access to regional schools should be carefully controlled and had encouraged the expulsion of insolent or unruly students, lest the schools "create official anarchists and raise foxes in our hen-houses."[66] In 1918 Hardy again warned that "we will gravely compromise the future, if our schools each discard the role which was imparted to them by the May 1914 programs."[67] His fear of overly educated Africans was evident.

By the autumn of 1918 Hardy had begun to focus on exerting "moral" influence over those Africans who had already graduated and who were working for the French administration or teaching in the French schools. He produced a new book titled *Les deux routes: Conseils pratiques aux jeunes fonctionnaires indigènes*. Unlike *Une conquête morale*, which had been written mainly for European teachers, *Deux routes* was a handbook for French-educated Africans who were embarking on a career in public service.

Hardy began *Deux routes* by acknowledging that the time was coming when Africans would make up the majority of employees of the colonial government. Change was indeed inevitable. But there were two ways to approach this—the *Deux routes* of the book's title. One was patient and gradual; the other was "abrupt, arid, and dangerous." France, thus far, had taken the former route. The French had always intended to rule through "collaboration" with Africans, implied Hardy:

> But if France loves generosity and liberty, she is no less concerned about good sense. And it would have been proof of a singular lack of good sense to want to produce collaboration, equal or almost equal, out of elements who do not know each other well, who do not think in the same way . . . you don't use the same harness on an Arabian horse and an ox.
>
> It has therefore been absolutely necessary that collaboration be preceded by mutual accommodation.[68]

A new era had now begun, however, and things were changing quickly. But Hardy warned French-educated Africans not to get carried away, for the situation was precarious:

> This may be a success; it may be a disastrous failure. This will be a success if this elite realizes its real role and its real value, if it does not indulge in self-admiration, if it recognizes what it lacks and works to perfect itself intellectually and morally. . . .
>
> This may be a failure, if those who benefit from the new regime see it only as a personal victory, if they refuse to take into account the possible and the impossible, if they pursue excessive and in-

opportune demands, if they bring to these questions a clannish spirit which will foster general irritation and will risk provoking severe reactions.[69]

These introductory comments reflected Hardy's negative view of the most assimilated Africans as well as his racist beliefs about African tendencies toward vanity, selfishness, and clannishness. However, Hardy was not wrong to fear that the new role of African functionaries might provoke a backlash of "l'esprit colon." *Deux routes* was intended to serve the interests of (slow) African progress by preventing such a backlash.

Hardy's handbook went on to provide a wide variety of practical advice for the new African functionary. This advice included tips on living on a tight budget (take turns cooking; don't eat out), how to furnish one's home (make furniture from packing crates), what to read (geography and ethnology of West Africa; Pierre Loti), how to read (slowly, savoring each passage), and how to conduct married life (wear the pants). It also advised young Africans to interact humbly with Europeans and to avoid intellectual vanity. Hardy advised the reader to imagine the position of the Europeans, who had been accustomed to dealing with Africans solely as subordinates and who were nervous about the new reforms. Europeans, noted Hardy, were alarmed by Africans of bad character who "walk with arrogant airs, pretend to be indispensable, speak about their rights and their needs in a tone that permits no reply." To avoid offending Europeans and provoking a counterreaction, African functionaries must be "polite, deferent, amiable without familiarity."[70]

The French-educated Africans of Dakar and Gorée did not take kindly to Hardy's paternalistic advice or to the educational administration's long-standing emphasis on primary and practical education. Education was a flashpoint in the larger conflict, played out in the Senegalese press, between the Diagnist desire for the rapid assimilation of Africans to French rights and the desire of Delafosse and Hardy to preserve traditional societies and keep the *évolués* isolated from the rest of the population. Diagne's supporters were in no mood for Hardy's suggestions that they remain servile and humble and take care not to overstep their bounds. They also resented his recent attempts to abolish scholarships allowing African students to transfer into the Saint-Louis secondary classes, as well as his advice to teachers and administrators to stick to the 1914 curriculum and to pursue "the lightening of programs."[71]

In January 1919 *La Démocratie du Sénégal* began to print editorials attacking Hardy under the pseudonyms "Doctor" and "Amadou l'Artilleur." This campaign in the press inevitably spread to the schools of Dakar and Gorée, where students began to criticize the educational leadership. Hardy was denounced as unqualified, since he had been only a professor back in France, "not even a *primary* school inspector." Amadou l'Artilleur called for "a complete housecleaning" of the administration and claimed that Hardy had accomplished nothing except to lower the level of instruction in Senegal. On 9 February, Amadou l'Artilleur accused French politicians and businessmen of wartime profiteering and accused Hardy of "sabotage": "Instead of advancing, we regress, even in this century of secularization, of steam, and of electricity! This says: Negro! You are inferior to the European, and you will remain so, regardless of your capacities!"[72]

In March, Amadou l'Artilleur offered a review of Hardy's *Deux routes*, taking offense at Hardy's exhortations to Africans to be deferent and submissive in their dealings with Europeans. L'Artilleur argued that African veterans were not returning from the war in Europe only to perform menial tasks for Europeans, "but with a clearer sentiment of their dignity as men and as free citizens of republican France." Moreover, L'Artilleur took offense at Hardy's portrayals of Africans and his claims of ethnological knowledge, condemning the "foolish vanity of the European, when he pretends, like Mr. Hardy, to know the indigene profoundly."[73]

L'Artilleur's critique of *Deux routes* failed to shake Hardy's confidence in his ability to understand the African mentality. The press campaign against Hardy did, however, make him a political liability to the colonial regime.

The Sacking of Georges Hardy

Discontent with colonial education was not unique to French West Africa, and the AOF was not the only place where the resistance of the colonized was reshaping colonial policy. For example, the controversy in Senegal was soon echoed in faraway Indochina, where the Constitutionalist Party began a similar press campaign in 1920, denouncing new school programs that had been introduced in 1917–18.[74] However, the situation in the AOF was distinguished by the influence of Deputy Diagne and the Young Senegalese. The success of the campaign against Hardy was facilitated by the alliance Diagne had forged with Minister of Colonies Henri Simon. When word of the controversy reached Paris, the ministry took the opportunity to encourage a bit of housecleaning in Gorée and Dakar. In March 1919, Quincili, the director of the École normale, and Pariset, one of the instructors there, were both put on a three-month "congé de convalescence" (sick leave).[75] In April, Hardy, too, was sent on a leave that became permanent.

Paris then began to push for policy changes. In May, Simon declared that "the percentage of the population in our colonies receiving elementary education ought to be brought up to the normal number"—that is, to a figure comparable to the rate of education in the old colonies such as Martinique, if not to those of the metropole.[76] In June he declared that in West Africa "we encounter no obstacle to complete assimilation."[77] By October 1919 a proposal was developed for a bill that would require universal, obligatory, and free primary education throughout the AOF within ten years, and which would also require the development of secondary and higher education within each colony. In the Four Communes, Hardy's beloved 1914 programs were rejected, and in 1921 school programs in the Communes were made identical to those of the metropole, with equivalency for diplomas and teaching credentials.

This appeared to be a decisive victory for the Young Senegalese, but it proved to be temporary and partial. Almost immediately, budgetary calculations brought an end to the idea of requiring universal schooling, and the continued presence of anti-assimilationist colonial administrators undermined the reforms. At the École normale there was a purge of students accused of "insolences or rebellions."[78] Hardy's initial replacement, the director of the École Faidherbe, denounced the "ingratitude and insolence" of the students and vowed to continue "in the same spirit and the same method" that Hardy had set out in *Conquête morale* and *Deux routes*.[79] In 1921 Governor-General Merlin declared the failure of assimilationist educational policy, claiming that there was, "among those natives trained in our schools and abruptly separated from their environment, a different frame of mind and a marked tendency to elude the discipline which an evolved society has the right to expect from its members."[80]

Access to higher education, and to the *lycée* teaching corps (the *cadre supérieur*), were now theoretically possible for Africans, but most were excluded by selective admission policies that judged not only academic ability but also moral (or political) character. The number of graduates produced by the *grandes écoles* was sharply reduced. The École normale and the École Faidherbe were consolidated into a single institution, which kept the name École William Ponty. Although graduates earned degrees equivalent to those awarded in France, the entering class was restricted to forty-five. The École William Ponty would produce an elite that would play a vital leadership role in the West African colonies and postcolonial states, but it would be a tiny elite, carefully selected by the French authorities.[81]

As James Genova has shown, power was shifted away from the educated urban elite toward rural chiefs, who had much to gain from continued French rule. There was a new push to educate the sons of chiefs so that the rural elite would become the new educated intermediaries that the French needed. Thus Diagne and the Young Senegalese were outmaneuvered. Colonial education became increasingly oriented toward inculcating cultural difference, culminating in the late 1930s in a push to build "rural popular schools" that aimed to teach "ancestral morals" and African culture. However, the discourses of the urban African political class and the colonial administration increasingly converged in the late 1930s. French-speaking intellectuals like Leopold Senghor, working within the newly hegemonic discourse of cultural separation, hoped to use the rural popular schools to "cultivate difference" and encourage a new African response to colonialism, based on cultural identity.[82] Political and civic assimilationism had failed to free West Africans from French domination. The future of anticolonial resistance in French West Africa would belong to Negritude and nationalism. Meanwhile, the discourses of French colonialism were likewise dominated by the advocates of ethnic difference: Delafosse, Lyautey, and, increasingly, Hardy.

Conclusion

The culture of French colonialism was transformed by the rise of Blaise Diagne and the Young Senegalese, but not in the way that the Young Senegalese had hoped. The threat that these French-speaking Africans posed to European domination had invigorated an already-growing campaign against the colonial theory of assimilation. The reaction against Diagnism that had begun in Senegal would continue in Morocco. Hardy would bring to Morocco his commitment to restricted French-language instruction and general education as means of producing a politically compliant and economically productive population. He also brought with him a freshly aggravated disdain for French-educated elites and a new pessimism about the possibility, not only of assimilation, but even of *apprivoisement*. In Morocco, Hardy's efforts became increasingly focused on promoting an image of the "Moroccan soul" that could be used to guide pedagogy and that could prevent the sort of disruptions that had driven him out of West Africa.

4. A New Pedagogy for Morocco?

There is, therefore, in my view, an urgent task, and a task which is best founded, not on the hope of a progressive transformation, but on the fear of a rapid change in local habits and tendencies. | Georges Hardy, 1921

In West Africa, Georges Hardy had become committed to the principle that colonial policy needed to reflect the ethnic traits of colonized peoples. In Morocco his mandate was to put this colonial theory into practice within the educational system. Lyautey hoped that Hardy had the leadership and will to create an educational system that would preserve the fundamental characteristics of traditional Moroccan society and promote the collaboration of Moroccan elites. Hardy would be assisted in his efforts by Louis Brunot, promoted in 1920 from his position as director of the Fez *collège* to head a new Bureau de l'enseignement musulman within Hardy's Direction de l'enseignement. Later in 1920, three additional departments were put under Hardy's authority: the Service des arts indigènes, the Service des monuments historiques, and the Service des antiquités préislamiques. The Direction de l'enseignement was renamed the Direction de l'instruction publique, des beaux-arts et des antiquités (DIP).

Hardy brought an explicit commitment to the role of ethnology in colonial administration, and he placed greater emphasis than his predecessor on the principle that educational success required expert knowledge about the culture, mentality, and environment of the Moroccan population. In 1920 a vizierial edict created the Institut des hautes études marocaines. This new ethnological institute was placed under the educational administration so that the knowledge produced might be channeled into teaching. Hardy would personally play the dominant role in this process, overseeing the connections between the knowledge production of ethnological research and the knowledge dissemination of the colonial schools and educational publications. He became the sponsor and arbiter of an official pedagogical discourse about Morocco, and through his own prolific writing he became its leading voice until 1926, when his departure for the École coloniale would leave Brunot as the defender of the Hardy approach through the 1930s.

It proved much easier to declare that education should be "adapted" than to conceive a fresh approach to such adaptation. Educational policies had to be generated in a hurry; reform could not wait until all the research was in and the results compiled and debated. As a "man on the spot," Hardy, like his colleagues and predecessors, was forced to fall back on old patterns while waiting for new knowledge. Hardy's work during his first years in his new country reflected imported models more than the influence of ethnographic knowledge specific to Morocco. A man of the colonies and a student of human diversity, he nevertheless drew upon the precedents of metropolitan working-class education, borrowed elements from the contemporary movement for metropolitan educational reform, and fell back on orientalist and West African discourses and models. These early decisions would have an enduring effect on Moroccan education and on the way the French saw Morocco. Combined with the anti-intellectualism of Lyautey's philosophy of colonial action and Delafosse's principle of ethnic differentiation, the result in Morocco was a restrictive, paternalistic approach to instruction based on crude ethnological generalizations and an antipathy for rapidly changing Moroccan aspirations.

From Dakar to Rabat

Hardy avoided acknowledging his use of the West African model in Morocco. The philosophy of ethnic difference made such parallels problematic. He contrasted Moroccan "civilization" with the "barbarous social contracts of black Africa," thus ignoring Delafosse's argument that West Africans were not barbaric but merely different.[1] At the same time, Hardy transposed to Morocco Delafosse's respect for colonized cultures, stating that Morocco's Muslims had been shaped by centuries of history and a possessed a "civilization truly worthy of the name."[2] This assertion of Morocco's difference from Africa reflected the search for a specifically adapted Moroccan policy. However, tailoring policy to the characteristics of Moroccan civilization was a challenging goal, for it first required Hardy to explain to himself what Morocco was like and what role the French were to play there. New to Morocco, Hardy could offer few new insights into the Moroccan situation. In the absence of any clear guidance from ethnographic knowledge, he made broad use of West African and metropolitan models.

In Morocco, Hardy retained his faith that French-language instruction could promote economic development and political compliance without assimilating or deracinating the students or preparing them for political agency. This resulted in a weaker commitment to Arabic-language instruction than Lyautey had initially envisioned. As in West Africa, Hardy's French programs were infused with vocational vocabulary and content, and time was allotted for manual arts and gardening practice. Instruction was to center around *leçons des choses*. First, an object was to be presented to the students, along with the French noun modified by an adjective, preferably possessive. When this had been learned, linking verbs and predicate adjectives were introduced, to describe the object. In successive steps, other verbs and direct and indirect objects were introduced. The students were not to recite; instead, the teacher was to ask questions of each student (What is this? Whose is it? What does it do?). As the class became more fluent in French, the *leçons des choses* could become less structured. The goal was to avoid memorization without understanding, or "verbalism."[3]

The meaning and implications of this pedagogy must be understood within the context of an anti-assimilationist colonial culture and in the context of Hardy's antipathy to the educated Senegalese who had demanded the rights of Frenchmen. The Georges Hardy who arrived in Morocco in December 1919 was a different man from the one who had arrived in Dakar in 1912. The events of his final years in the AOF had profoundly affected his colonial philosophy. Influenced both by the experience of the war and by his political conflict with the educated Senegalese, Hardy grew more reactionary regarding the changes he saw taking place around him. He began to question whether it was possible to promote even the slow, asymptotic evolution of non-European peoples. In 1921, Hardy wrote:

> It seems well demonstrated today that in history, as in natural history, slow evolution, as conceived of by Lamarck and Darwin, does not exist: what we call evolution is nothing but a succession of *brusque variations*. For my part, I long believed the contrary; I thought that it was possible to make the indigenes of our colonies evolve within the plan of their traditional civilization and the habits of their milieu. I am persuaded today that one can at most retard the brusque variation and especially deflect, in some measure, its effects.[4]

If positive, gradual change was impossible, then the efforts of the colonizer had to be directed toward resisting social or cultural change, not promoting it. Any deviation from tradition within the colonized society was dangerous. Hardy was not consistent on this point — he would often speak favorably about slow evolution — but his intermittent pessimism contrasted sharply with his earlier faith in the *apprivoisement* advocated by William Ponty in West Africa.

At the end of Hardy's tenure in West Africa, his support of "the struggle against the teaching of words" had converged with the need to restrain the political ambitions of Diagnists and the desire to contradict the idealism of Parisian republicans.[5] In the colonial context, the "verbalism" widely condemned by educational administrators no longer referred merely to schoolchildren who memorized without understanding; it now conjured up images of Africans holding forth about republican principles in municipal council meetings and on the floor of the Chamber of Deputies.

Hardy's approach to education in Morocco was also affected by his reaction to World War I. Hardy concluded that the Germans had been partly right in proclaiming the decadence of France: "the omnipotence of the bureaucracy, the deep social troubles, the absence of strong intellectual direction, the tyranny of a low-level ideology." The war, however, had produced a "renaissance" of French strength and unity.[6] Hardy now phrased the mission of colonial education in martial terms. He called for an "assault" against "the funereal verbalism of great discourses" and urged teachers to "struggle against the invasion of memorization and the tyranny of the book; [to] decisively make the school a source of good sense and moral activity. . . . distrust words which do not lead to precise rules of action; ban discourses which are not the exposition of a neat and practical program; hate the speakers [of such words and discourses] as public enemies."[7] The military experience of the war also provided Hardy with a model for political organization: the unity of the troop and the authority of the leader were the keys to success; this was contrasted to individualism in the form of "sterilizing debates" motivated by "ambition."[8] World War I thus inclined Hardy toward Lyautey's (and later Pétain's) vision of French renewal through muscular authoritarianism.

Metropolitan Precedents

Colonial education in Morocco was influenced by the prior experiences of French colonizers throughout the empire, including Hardy's experiences in West Africa. However, French colonial education was everywhere infused with metropolitan patterns. As a result, it is fruitful to consider intersections between Hardy's educational policies and the educational discourse of metropolitan France.

The key to colonial harmony, in Hardy's view, was pedagogy properly adapted to the particular needs of Moroccans in particular social roles. As Hardy declared in his 1920 curriculum:

> The role of education is not to subject all children to the same program, to democratize a society whose roots are not well known, to teach our students with a view to an ideal future society where success comes only through pure merit. We must see men and things as they are and improve them by a slow evolution. The little peasant should, upon leaving school, return to the land; the son of an urban laborer should later become a laborer, the son of a merchant a merchant, of a functionary a functionary. . . . [T]he child of a particular social milieu should receive an instruction which is adapted to that milieu and which keeps him there, and makes him better able to serve his social role, however humble it might be.[9]

There was nothing distinctively colonial about this view of education. In the colonies, adaptation to the milieu differed from metropolitan social stratification in that colonial schooling was overtly differentiated along axes of ethnicity as well as class. However, the increased differentiation of the ethnic axis in the colonies was not accompanied by a paradigm shift in pedagogy. Hardy's reforms and doctrines worked to increase the degree of institutional and theoretical segregation between schools for Moroccan Muslims and those for Europeans. Nevertheless, despite the popularity of Delafosse's maxims about ethnic difference and the ubiquitous calls to "adapt" education to the characteristics of ethnicity, colonial ethnic differentiation tended to mimic metropolitan class differentiation.

Public education in the metropolitan Third Republic consisted of two parallel systems, the free primary system and the fee-paying secondary system: the former was for the working classes, the latter for the middle and upper classes. Both systems extended from classes for small children through higher education, but there was very little crossover from one system to another. A talented child in the primary system might go from an *école primaire* to an *école primaire supérieure* or even to an *école normale*, in order to become a teacher in the primary system. However, access to the *lycée*, and therefore to the university faculties and *grandes écoles*, was reserved for children coming up from the *lycées*' fee-paying elementary classes. In this parallel structure, one educational system prepared the future elite and the other prepared future subalterns. This dual system was itself paralleled at the lower levels by the schools for girls: girls, too, were segregated into elite and non-elite tracks, but the girls' *lycées* prepared their pupils for domesticity and marriage to educated men, not for access to higher education or professions.[10]

Although the division in Morocco between the elite track (*écoles des fils de notables* and *collège musulmans*) and the non-elite primary system imitated the metropolitan model, many elements of the metropolitan system were incompatible with the Lyautey-Hardy approach. The fundamentals of the Third Republic's primary system had been established in 1887 and were aimed at creating a common culture and consolidating support for the Republic against a traditionalist opposition. This was quite contrary to Lyautey's desire to maintain traditional Moroccan political and social structures and hierarchies. In the Third Republic, public schooling was to be universal, obligatory, and secular; in Morocco, universality would not become a policy goal until 1937, obligatory education would be attempted only after independence, and secularization, never. Moreover, the metropolitan primary's mission to promote republican values was anathema to the leaders of the protectorate.

In other respects, however, the metropolitan primary supplied the protectorate with a useful paradigm of how to educate those who were not to rule. The curriculum was "relentlessly utilitarian" and included French, morals and civics, *leçons des choses*, basic science and agriculture, arithmetic, the metric system, music, manual skills, and military-style physical training. Critics argued that the metropolitan primary schooling stressed "facts to the detriment of the need for explanation, contemplative observation to the detriment of the exercise of judgment."[11] The same could be said of Hardy's curricula for Muslims, which resembled the Third Republic's primary curricula, pared down and purged of republican ideology.

In some respects, Hardy's schools for Muslims – even the elite *collèges* – most closely resembled metropolitan *enseignement primaire supérieur* (upper primary education), with its more vocational emphasis. The *écoles primaires supérieures* were schools to prepare working-class and lower-middle-class students for skilled work, low-level clerical positions, or teacher training for the primary system. As one sympathetic observer put it, *enseignement primaire supérieur* "raises the level of instruction and of morality. . . . Opening to everyone access to all careers in which secondary studies are not necessary, it gives satisfaction to legitimate ambitions, without overexciting blind pretensions that are as disappointing to individuals as they are fatal to society."[12] The goal, like that of Morocco's colonial schools, was to produce the skilled labor necessary for economic growth without promoting social mobility.

In the late 1800s, reformers had argued that although working-class youths did not need the elite education offered in the *lycée*, they did have specific needs that ought to be addressed by the educational system through post-primary schooling. Reformers' concerns were defined around three issues: vocational training, adolescence, and gender. These concerns would be transfigured in colonial education. As Kathleen Alaimo has argued, the traditional apprenticeship system in late-nineteenth-century France seemed to be collapsing at a time when increased use of technology in industry was increasing the demand for skilled and semiskilled labor. Meanwhile, working-class movements were making the owning classes very nervous. *Enseignement primaire supérieur* offered a way to provide vocational training in a setting where "carefully guided socialization" could inculcate the values necessary to produce harmonious class relations. However, the attempt to produce social harmony through education depended on "the submission of popular culture to official directives," and this proved difficult in both metropole and colonies.[13] It was easier to teach technical skills.

The development of *enseignement primaire supérieur* was connected to the emergence of the concept of "adolescence" in psychological and pedagogical discourse. Adolescence became recognized as a stage of life with specific psychological characteristics; educational reformers argued that this psychological difference ought to be reflected in pedagogical methods and institutions. This was particularly important because adolescence was such an unstable and potentially rebellious phase of life. Without the proper education, youths might "go astray and lose themselves on that dangerous path that leads from the end of [primary] school age to the age of majority."[14] The recognition of adolescence in educational policy was a step away from the universalist ideal; it recognized physio-psychological difference as a reality that demanded pedagogical adaptation. If such a difference existed among age groups in the metropole, it was no great leap for colonial theorists to argue that the distinct psychological traits of colonized ethnic groups also required pedagogical differentiation.

Moreover, the connection between the psychology of age groups and of ethnic groups had become part of the discourse of child psychology. Comparisons between European children and "primitives" had been legitimated by child psychologists as "recapitulation theory," which held that the development of the (Western) child mirrored the evolutionary stages of human "races." Metropolitan psychologists like Edouard Claparède were primarily interested in this theory as a means of understanding child development, and they advocated tailoring pedagogy to the psychological traits of specific age groups.[15] In the colonies, however, ethnic characteristics were emphasized to the exclusion of age characteristics. Colonial pedagogical discourse paid little attention to age differentiation, because it followed from recapitulation theory that primitive adults had not passed beyond the stages reached by the Western child. The result was Hardy's contention that the Moroccan child and adult had identical psychological traits.[16]

The pedagogical adaptations to the "Moroccan soul" advocated by Hardy were not unique; they bore considerable resemblance to the metropolitan model, mimicking metropolitan adaptation based on age and class. Just as the metropolitan upper primary targeted a "different" and potentially dangerous group (adolescents from working-class and lower-middle-class backgrounds), so did the colonial schools for Muslims. The result, in Morocco as in the metropole, was the deliberate restriction, in the name of utility, of the knowledge to be conveyed. In the metropole, the *écoles primaires supérieures* restricted language instruction because it was believed that workers, "whether in offices, shops, or factories had little use for knowledge of the great writers or for sophisticated, literary writing skills. Teachers emphasized vocabulary building and clear expression of simple ideas."[17] Foreign language instruction was offered to metropolitan upper primary students, but only for commercial purposes such as writing letters and reports; literary studies were unnecessary. This approach was echoed in the approach to French instruction in the AOF and in Morocco. Things were not so different in the colonies after all.

Hardy's educational policy also reflected the influence of the Compagnons de l'université nouvelle, a movement for educational reform in France begun in 1917 by a group of educators-turned-officers under General Henri-Philippe Pétain. Perceived military shortcomings during the war had inspired a critical reexamination of the structure and content of metropolitan education, while the sense that the world had changed irrevocably encouraged a desire to break with the past.[18] Some elements of the Compagnons' proposal were incompatible with the goals of Lyautey and Hardy in Morocco, such as the Compagnons' call to replace the subaltern primary schools and the elite elementary classes with a single, meritocratic primary system, an *école unique*.[19]

In Morocco there was no question of creating a single, meritocratic school system, even for Europeans. The protectorate leadership, like metropolitan conservatives, feared that egalitarian schooling would disrupt society and create "rootless" proletarians and "unemployed intellectuals."[20]

However, there was another side to the Compagnons' call for educational reform. The Compagnons also aimed to promote practical vigor and social solidarity, in order to remedy what was perceived as archaic intellectualism. After the catastrophe of the war, the new schools were to create new men, "active men, of modern and practical spirit . . . knowing their own nature, loving their own life and that of their fellows, desirous of the general interest and the public good."[21] More than technical skills, French schools needed to cultivate "les forces morales" that had led to victory.[22]

The Compagnons held up German virility and Anglo-Saxon pragmatism as antidotes to sterile French intellectualism: "in Germany, the ideologues do not despise men of action, they go to them and work for them." Better yet were the examples of the British and Americans, with "their healthy realism and their confidence in life." The Compagnons proposed a school that would reflect the principles of William James and President Wilson. The new school was to provide not just intellectual exercises but "education of the body, education of the will, education of the spirit."[23] In this the Compagnons echoed prewar writings by psychologists like Claparède, who had declared in *Psychologie de l'enfant et pédagogie expérimentale* that schooling ought to promote "the education of the heart, the character, and the will" rather than focus on mere "instruction"; such education should "make of the child an honest and healthy man, independent in mind, and a lover of the good, the true, and the beautiful, and . . . his physical and intellectual potentialities should be developed with due regard to his personality."[24] As the Compagnons put it, "we must make men, not brains or machines."[25]

In terms of the metropolitan pedagogy proposed by the Compagnons, this meant a simplification of the curriculum ("few things and few books"), with more physical activity ("culture virile") and more relevance to real life.²⁶ It was argued that existing curricula burdened young minds with excessive, meaningless facts and subjected young bodies to long days of inactivity. Claparède had devoted an entire chapter to "intellectual fatigue." Accordingly, the Compagnons proposed that the *lycée*'s "general culture" curriculum should be lightened. But it was not just the quantity of work that was to change, but the type of work: at all levels, lessons should be of interest, and therefore practical, dispensing with rote learning and excessive abstraction, and book learning should be supplemented by physical education.²⁷ Following this trend, Henri Roorda in 1918 suggested that the ideal school would consist of two hours of basic reading, writing, and drawing, at a leisurely pace, in which the only "rules" learned by the children would be those they figured out for themselves, according to the principle, "the activity first, the formula later." Another hour would be left to the teacher for a lesson aimed at creating a "culture of enthusiasm," employing "all possible means to provoke the admiration of the students, to develop in them the desire to know, to undertake, to create."²⁸ The rest of the day would be devoted to physical exercise, hands-on crafts, and elective lessons in science and drawing. All of this was a response to what were accurately recognized as tedious and burdensome curricula and methods that had limited relevance to the demands of modern life.

In Morocco, these new critiques of arid pedantry and calls for a new generation of muscular, active men accorded with Lyautey's criticisms of metropolitan bureaucratic stagnation and his glorification of the rugged "colonial." The Compagnons seem to have seen the possibility that their ideas might catch on faster in the colonies, as they explicitly stated that their reforms were intended for "greater France." However, the protectorate leadership was very selective in its application of the ideas of the Compagnons. The protectorate administration would echo the cry that education should be adapted to the milieu of the student, but there would be no decentralization and little attention to individuals or even regions (the Berber-Arab distinction notwithstanding). The belief that the Muslim student population was characterized by homogeneous psychological traits and limited capabilities led the educational administration to disregard the need to tailor educational offerings to individual talents and to age groups, issues that were of fundamental importance to the metropolitan reformers.

However, Hardy was receptive to the muscular modernization proposed by the metropolitan reformers, and he advocated a simplification of curricula for both Europeans and Muslims. The Compagnons had recommended that curricula be lightened, not in order to limit the aspirations of the students, but to make it more accessible. A more active, hands-on program was intended to stimulate human potential, not to limit it. Nevertheless, the new reformism's call to produce a more virile, less intellectual generation of youth helped to justify the restrictive pedagogy that Hardy had favored in West Africa.

Adaptation in Morocco's Schools for Elite Muslims

Under Hardy, the call for a more modern pedagogy was combined with the ethnological assertion that Moroccan Muslims, like West Africans, had only limited mental potential. Hardy blamed recent unrest in West Africa and Indochina on assimilationist schools that trained natives to enter the French administration and liberal professions. He was particularly determined to prevent a recurrence in Morocco of what he now called "the xenophobia movement of Blaise Diagne."[29] In Morocco, Hardy felt that the principal danger lay with the Moroccan elite, and he arrived intent upon reversing the concessions that had been made to the *makhzan* and to the *collège* students under Gaston Loth. Lyautey had sent a clear message by firing Loth, and Hardy had little difficulty persuading the commission on the *collèges* to reverse the decisions they had made in 1918: "The members of the commission fell rapidly into agreement regarding the need to return without delay to the very foundations of 1917, considering the sudden collapse [coup de barre] of 1918 to be dangerous from a political point of view.

... leading, among other things, to the envisioned equivalence of the *collèges musulmans* with the French *lycée*'s baccalaureate."[30]

In reverting to the principles of 1917, however, Hardy did not revive the original (1915) idea of predominantly Arabic-medium curricula in the *collèges*. The French-based programs were a fait accompli, and the methods of the traditional Moroccan teachers were still considered too primitive and rote. Hardy also agreed with his new colleagues that bringing in Arabic teachers from Egypt or Tunis would infect Morocco with dangerous political notions; he even conducted a partial purge of Algerians and Tunisians already teaching in Morocco and suggested restricting the use of imported Arabic texts.[31] Hardy maintained his belief, developed in polyglot West Africa, that French could be taught as a practical "instrument" without alienating students from their native culture. In both elite and non-elite systems, French-medium instruction was to take up a large portion of the school day, for this was to be the basis of modernization and collaboration with the French. In the elite *écoles des fils de notables*, which served as feeder schools for the *collèges* and provided terminal education for many elite youth, five times as many hours were devoted to French-language classes as to Arabic in the first year, dropping to three times as much in the fourth year.[32] Nevertheless, the content of French-medium subjects was restricted, as it was in all the schools for Muslims.

Loth's dismissal in 1919 had coincided with a new 1919 edict on the *collèges* which had stated that Moroccans were "eminently practical people, who only want to understand a truth in terms of its useful application"; therefore, teaching "ought to be practical and founded essentially on useful notions."[33] French was not to become a vehicle for critical thought or political integration but merely an economic tool. These goals allowed Hardy to apply his restrictive West African pedagogy to Morocco's *collèges* and *écoles de fils de notables*. Elite Muslim boys were to learn to speak and write French correctly and well, but Hardy's 1920 programs declared that, at the *écoles de fils de notables*, "the study of the French language aims solely at the acquisition of an instrument, a means of accessing other knowledge for entering into relations with the French and doing commerce with them."[34] Much emphasis was placed on verb conjugation, although composition was introduced. The elementary French language course included comparative units on clothing, religions, and races, and the intermediate course addressed Moroccan political organization. Geography and history were to focus on French North Africa, stressing the benefits of colonialism. However, there was little guidance for the positive use of knowledge; instead, the emphasis was on what ought not to be taught. The section on Moroccan history consisted of the same vague outline found in the European program, little more than a list of dynasties. Regarding metropolitan history, Hardy declared that pre-1789 French history was "useless" for Muslims, and post-1789 history was "totally incomprehensible."[35] The curricula of the *écoles de fils de notables* generally resembled that used in West Africa's regional schools, beginning with local, mundane topics: school, clothing, housing, and so forth. Hardy instructed the *collège* directors to restrict the French curricula to only *usuel* (everyday) French, to eliminate *dissertations littéraires*, and to reduce instruction in natural science, history, and geography.[36] In practice these restrictive policies were tempered by the tendency of teachers to respond to the intellectual curiosity of their students. Nevertheless, Hardy's policies pushed *collège* instructors toward an anti-rationalist and anti-assimilationist pedagogy.[37]

Primary and Professional Schooling for Muslims

Hardy's prescriptions for primary and professional schooling for non-elite Muslims relied even more heavily on the West African model. Rather than invent a primary education tailored to Moroccan culture (What would that mean? Who could teach it?), Hardy cast Morocco's non-elite urban and rural schools in the image of the AOF's, retaining the curricular structure of general education, borrowed from the metropolitan primary, but with a vocational orientation that stopped short of real apprenticeship or job training.

In urban schools, boys were to grow up to do the work their fathers had done, only better: "We merely want society to benefit from the manual aptitudes of artisan's sons, for each child to do better and with more profit for everyone what he would have done without the school."[38] Nevertheless, as in West Africa, Hardy prevented the reduction of education to trade apprenticeships:

> It is not our intention to create apprentices, still less real workers, in our urban schools. The physical weakness of our students would alone prevent such a pretension. We should simply improve the dexterity of the children; ascertain their abilities and special aptitudes, their tastes, in order to direct them after leaving the urban school towards a professional school. Students in the middle grades and the upper grades, especially the latter, will therefore be taken to workshops and will learn the names of the tools of all the local trades, or most of them. They will know, by practice, what a trade requires, and that's all.[39]

Therefore, a pre-vocational program was to be provided, with real vocational training reserved for "professional schools" that Hardy established as separate, parallel institutions. As in the AOF, pre-vocational training was integrated into the language curricula as *leçons de choses*. The French language curriculum for non-elite urban primary schools, for example, was organized by subject around the various trades:

1st month: Wood. Different woods. Uses. Tools necessary to work with wood. Machine tools.
2nd month: Iron. Fitting [L'ajustage]. The forge. Tin-smithing [La ferblanterie]. Tools necessary to work with iron. Machine tools.
3rd month: Metals other than iron. Their industries.
4th month: Automobiles. Railroads. Transports in general. . . . etc.[40]

In the countryside, a similar curriculum included basic agricultural instruction and hands-on experience in the school garden. "The rural school," declared Hardy, "must not lose sight of its mission to keep in the countryside the people who are there, in better conditions, and not to create in children a desire to be functionaries. It is a regional institution that must serve the region."[41]

Such curricula reflected the limited goals of instruction for subaltern groups, regardless of their ethnicity or location. Knowledge was to be transmitted in restricted, finite packages. Language was not to become a tool of inquiry; French proficiency was to be restricted to the skills necessary for economic functions. In the urban schools, composition assignments were to focus on the production of commercial letters and business contracts. Geography was to concentrate upon map-reading skills. Mathematics emphasized basic geometry (volume, surface area, and scale). In the rural schools, the curriculum was even more restricted, with an emphasis on ungrammatical French, basic arithmetic, and agricultural techniques.[42] These schools were to create a compliant, economically productive, and unambitious labor force. Toward this end, the "Morality" curriculum told instructors in Muslim schools to "insist particularly on the nobility of manual trades, on the usefulness of the good worker. Develop a professional conscience, the taste for perfection, exactitude and regularity in work."[43] This version of Hardy's "moral conquest" seemed more determined by class than by ethnicity, contrary to his assertions about the importance of understanding the particular characteristics of ethnic groups and local contexts.

Arabic and Islamic Instruction

A cornerstone of Hardy's claim to provide instruction adapted to Moroccan needs was the inclusion of instruction in Arabic language arts and Islamic culture in the 1920 curricula. In the colonial school system these were treated as two distinct subjects. Arabic language instruction was provided by DIP teachers when personnel were available but was only offered in the urban primaries and in the schools for elites. In contrast, Islamic instruction focusing on the Quran was taught only by traditionally educated Moroccan teachers and was offered in many rural schools as well as in the urban areas. Arabic and Islamic instruction had great potential as a means for the French to shape Muslim students' understanding of their own culture and identity. However, although Hardy did expand Arabic language instruction in non-elite urban schools, these subjects played a much smaller role in colonial education for Muslims than the traditionalist rhetoric of Lyautey and Hardy might suggest.

The inclusion of Islamic education was a political necessity as well as an educational strategy. Such instruction conformed to Lyautey's conservative desire, shared by Hardy, to prevent cultural alienation and to maintain traditional values and institutions, but Arabic and religious instruction was also necessary in order to persuade Muslim families to send their sons to French schools. Yet Moroccan attitudes regarding religious education meant that Islamic instruction could not be integrated into the general life of the French schools, for religious instruction would not be accepted from a non-Muslim teacher. In 1921, Louis Brunot advised new teachers from France to speak of religious matters "with respect and as little as possible" for fear of offending student sensibilities.[44] Student attitudes forced the French-taught classes to be secular, creating a sharp divide between the "modern" and Islamic curricula. For religious education, the colonial schools solicited the cooperation of local, traditionally educated teachers, who offered instruction outside of regular school hours, either in the French schoolhouse or in a nearby traditional *msid* (Quranic school). This instruction was kept quite separate from the rest of the school's activities.

Traditional Moroccan Muslim instructors became essential to recruitment and to the goal of keeping students rooted in their own culture. However, the French were often distrustful of these local teachers. Outside of the French schools, the *fqih* (Quranic teacher) was seen as a competitor in the recruitment of students, and the "lethal propaganda" of the *fqih* was blamed for producing religious "fanatics" and for causing enrollment problems at the French-run schools.[45] A similar distrust was also directed at the traditional teachers who worked within the DIP schools (both elite and non-elite): they were suspected of sowing the seeds of rebellion by selectively choosing xenophobic passages from the Quran. Hardy insisted that there was no legitimate conflict between Islam and the goals of French rule. This, however, made the *fqih* all the more subject to suspicion. If resentment of the French occupation was expressed (or even sensed), then it was assumed that there had to be a malicious agent at work. These suspicions were exacerbated by the language barrier: school directors were often unable to understand the lessons themselves, and assumed the worst.[46]

In 1921 the French attempted to reform the instruction provided in colonial schools by traditional teachers, publishing guidelines for Quranic instruction. These guidelines were published in the educational bulletin, in French. Given the minimal supervision of such instruction and the probable resistance of the *fqih*, the effectiveness of these declared reforms is dubious. The only French methodological prescription with a clear impact was the prohibition of corporal punishment; the reported effect was that the *fqih* typically lost control of the class. Nevertheless, alleged improvements were used to justify the token amount of time allotted to Quranic instruction: supposedly, the traditional material could now be taught more efficiently, in less time. For the most part, Muslims were not convinced. It was plain that the French schools gave short shrift to Quranic instruction, while the rival private *msid* devoted the whole day to it.[47]

Arabic language arts instruction was easier for the French to control, for it could be provided by French teachers, or by French-educated Algerians or Tunisians. However, in the absence of a positive strategy for promoting French goals through Arabic instruction, the emphasis was again on restriction. In the *écoles de fils de notables*, the Arabic curriculum was to concentrate on grammar, and Hardy instructed teachers not to get into complex treatises by Muslim writers. For non-elite boys in the urban primary schools, Arabic was to be even more limited. A half hour per day, four days per week was considered sufficient.

These boys were to be literate enough in Arabic to read a letter, but that was all.⁴⁸

In the rural schools, Hardy excluded Arabic language instruction altogether. It is important to note that this was the case regardless of whether the inhabitants of the area spoke an Arabic dialect or a Berber dialect. Hardy was aware that the bureau of Indigenous Affairs hoped to promote divisions between Arabic- and Berber-speaking Moroccan Muslims, and stated that in "purely Berber" areas that did not already have a *fqih*, religious instruction was not to be introduced, in order to forestall the development of closer ties between Arab and Berber populations.⁴⁹ However, this ethnic division was otherwise absent in the 1920 curricula. Instead, Hardy emphasized rural-urban and class divisions, and he sometimes used the phrases *écoles rurales* and *écoles franco-berbères* interchangeably, as if all of Morocco's country people were Berbers. Hardy pointed out that classical written Arabic was an alien language to all rural Moroccans, even if some spoke an Arabic vernacular. Therefore, the preservation of traditional culture and social distinctions meant that Arabic literacy should not be introduced where it was not already common. Echoing metropolitan approaches to the maintenance of class segregation, Hardy declared that "the teaching of classical Arabic would be as out of place in a rural school as Latin in a hamlet in France."⁵⁰ As in West Africa, he upheld the introduction of French as a language of economic development and a means of communication with the colonizer. The minimum was to suffice; language instruction was provided on a need-to-know basis, and rural language instruction was to be restricted to "the rudiments of French."⁵¹ As with metropolitan working-class education and colonial education in West Africa, the goal of colonial education for Moroccan Muslims was economic development and social control, not cultural sophistication.

The Vanishing Point of Pedagogy: Muslim Girls
Hardy would devote little attention to the education of Morocco's Muslim girls. His 1920 curricular circular made no mention of the

schooling of Muslim girls. By 1921 he made it clear that he would follow the precedent set by Loth. Unlike boys' schooling, instruction for Muslim girls was to remain purely vocational, combining local crafts and textile production with domestic skills; academic instruction was minimized to the vanishing point. In 1923 Hardy explored the feasibility of opening an elite girls' school in Fez, but Fezi notables publicly opposed the idea (although some reportedly supported it in private). It was concluded that a girls' school in Fez was not worth the risk of angering public opinion in the protectorate's most conservative and most powerful Moroccan city.[52] Where girls' schools did operate, Hardy forbade the teaching of French, reportedly at the request of the sultan. French instruction might be given in rare circumstances where parents requested it, but even in such cases, Hardy urged teachers to attempt to dissuade parents who had "overly modern ideas." Lest there should exist a group of Muslim girls who were better educated than the illiterate masses of Muslim boys, Hardy ordered that classical Arabic be avoided as well, although Quranic instruction provided by a traditional teacher was permitted.[53] What mattered, above all, was that the French "do nothing to shock the traditions of their protégés."[54]

In Ponty's West Africa, Hardy had expressed a bit more enthusiasm for the education of girls. There he had praised schools for future mothers as a means to uplift the next generation of children, following a long tradition of rhetoric extending from Christine de Pizan to Mary Wollstonecraft to Qasim Amin. The 1914 West African curricular circular had displayed an unusually assimilationist orientation with regard to the education of girls, arguing that colonial schools were to "form good homemakers," but also to facilitate the spread of the French language throughout West African society by creating homes where French would become "in the precise sense, a mother tongue." This emphasis on French for West African girls contrasted sharply with Hardy's policy in Morocco.[55] However, Hardy had done little to expand education for girls in West Africa, citing the need to defer to the attitudes of African parents, especially Muslims, who were resistant to the idea of French education for their daughters; the number of West African girls in French schools seems to have declined during Hardy's administration.[56]

Upon arriving in Morocco, Hardy issued a directive to new teachers in which he stressed the importance of maintaining conservative traditions in Morocco: "Anti-clericalism is not an article to be exported. ... [W]e do not speak of the emancipation of the citizen, nor the liberation of the slave, nor of the liberty of the woman; these questions are not to be discussed in school."[57] The inclusion of the "woman question" in this general directive suggests that Hardy's passivity toward girls' education was not merely a practical concession to Muslim public opinion; it had become a fundamental part of his increasingly conservative approach to colonial education.

To Hardy, the maintenance of gender roles was as important as the maintenance of Islamic culture. Whereas he advocated an active role for the French schools in maintaining traditional culture in Muslim boys, protecting them against outside influences, when it came to Muslim girls he seemed to feel that the most dangerous influence came from the French: overzealous French *maîtresses* might infect their students with emancipatory ideas. Meanwhile, local hostility to changes in gender roles facilitated Hardy's agenda, making pedagogical action seem less necessary. In 1926, when Hardy left Morocco, there were still only 850 Muslim girls in French-run schools (though this was up from 450 in 1922).[58] Muslim families could be counted on to police their daughters (but not their sons) without help from the DIP. Later, Morocco's nationalists would take a more active approach to girls' education; they would see the controlled education of Muslim girls as vital to the maintenance and spread of Islamic and Arab culture.

The Other Others

Hardy also addressed the education of the twenty-four hundred Moroccan Jews enrolled in the DIP's *écoles franco-israélites*.[59] Unsurprisingly, his approach to Jewish education was based upon his belief in ethnic difference. Until 1920, pedagogy in the schools for Jews had followed the European programs, in part because, when the protectorate was established, AIU schooling had already created a class of Jews who spoke French and who were familiar with French culture. But Hardy did not want Moroccan Jews to become French, and he attempted to differentiate the *écoles franco-israélites* from the schools for Europeans. He declared that schools for Jews "address a student population noticeably different from that of French schools, and they must adapt as precisely as possible to the social milieu that they are committed to transform." However, Hardy seemed to conceive of the ethnic divide separating the European from the Moroccan Jew differently from that separating the European from the Moroccan Muslim. While Hardy defined Moroccan Muslim ethnic difference as psychological limitation, he saw the Moroccan Jew as suffering from "numerous physiological defects."[60] Therefore, like Loth, Hardy called upon the French to focus on the physical well-being of Jewish students. Whereas Loth had focused on the sanitation of buildings, Hardy stressed the need for physical education.

Hardy made it clear in 1920 that schools for Jews, like schools for non-elite Muslims, were to train workers, not an elite of educated intermediaries, and he aimed to lead the Jewish population away from commerce and toward farming and manual trades. He called for the development of vocational education for Jews and in the meantime instituted a "manual work" course. Just as Hardy had helped oppose the political aspirations of the urban *évolués* in West Africa, he promoted a Jewish curriculum that would avoid creating an indigenous urban elite in Morocco. However, he stated that French language education should be much more thorough than in the schools for Muslims. In addition, Hardy's desire to improve the physical condition of Jews and to lead the Jewish population toward farming suggests an attempt to lead them toward the muscular ideal of Lyautey's colonial man rather than merely to preserve their subordinate position in the society. But Jews were not to function as privileged intermediaries between the French and the Muslim masses; this role was reserved for the elite Muslims graduating from the *collèges musulmans*. In order to deflect Muslim complaints about the obviously superior quality of the schools for Jews, the DIP returned direct control of the Jewish schools to the AIU in 1924.[61] Thus Hardy succeeded in maintaining ethnic differentiation in the education of Jewish Moroccans, but relinquished direct control over pedagogy.

Conclusion

During his first years in Morocco, Hardy insisted that Lyautey's protectorate presented a variety of educational needs that were uniquely Moroccan and needed to be addressed accordingly. But it was hard not to fall back on familiar patterns of "different" pedagogy for a "different" population. In 1920 Hardy displayed little specialized knowledge about Morocco that might have addressed the question of just what needed to be different about these schools. As a result, the 1920 curriculum reflected metropolitan and West African strategies for using education to promote the economic development and social control of subaltern groups.

Because of Hardy's social conservatism and his beliefs about ethnic psychological characteristics, the pedagogical reformism that was developing in the metropole took on very different connotations in Morocco. The ideal of an active, practical education leading to the creation of a new man resonated with Lyautey's colonial philosophy and his disdain for metropolitan bureaucracy and intellectualism. But while Morocco became a laboratory for the new methods, the result was restrictive rather than liberating. In contrast to the new metropolitan reformism, which sought to increase access to first-rate education, Hardy's policies distanced protectorate education from the goal of developing the reasoning and critical thinking required for political agency in a republic. The AOF and metropolitan primary models were better suited than the *école unique* to keep busy a group whose economic activity was encouraged but whose political and social ambitions were feared. This was even true to some extent regarding the education of Europeans: Lyautey welcomed the economic activities of the settlers but hoped to avoid creating an Algerian-style *colon* republic. Consequently, the Residency did not want the settlers to be distracted from business by abstract political concerns. Colonial schooling aimed to create useful but compliant subjects who would not seek to alter the social hierarchy.

For Moroccan Muslims, the restrictive pedagogy of the colonial schools could be justified not only in Machiavellian terms or through the discourse of manly action, but also through discourse about the ethnic characteristics of Moroccans. For decades, colonial rulers and thinkers like Gallieni, Lyautey, and Delafosse had argued that colonial policy ought to be tailored to the particular needs of ethnic groups. Hardy soon became immersed in colonial ethnological discourse about Moroccan Muslims, and became one of its most prolific producers. Under his leadership, educational policy became intimately connected to the ethnology that he propagated through the publications and institutions of the educational system.

5. A Psychological Ethnology

> *Our goal is, in sum, to detach the Moroccan soul from the mass of picturesques, clichés, manias, phobias or philias that separate it from the [French] public; it is to convince writers of all sorts that their efforts should be oriented towards the only research that really counts in the troubled times we live in: the knowledge of men in front of you or next to you.* | Georges Hardy, *L'âme marocaine*, 1926

Since the beginning of the protectorate, ethnological knowledge had been considered essential to French rule in Morocco. If the French adequately understood the Moroccan context, they could conquer and rule the locals more efficiently. The early impetus for colonial ethnological projects in Morocco came from the leadership's recognition of French ignorance in the face of new and confusing challenges and a little-known society. This ethnological humility was short lived, however, because it was accompanied by the European conquerors' ever-present confidence in their ability to define, categorize, and comprehend the colonized society. That confidence was not always well founded, and the resulting miscomprehensions and errors exposed the weakness of imperial knowledge.

Georges Hardy recovered from the pessimism he had expressed after his expulsion from West Africa in 1919. In Morocco he transformed Lyautey's romantic desire to avoid the dull rigidity of metropolitan bureaucracy into an idealistic belief in the abilities of the colonial scholar to produce a transcendent new kind of knowledge. From the beginning it had been evident that the new colonial state needed agents and functionaries prepared to interact with the Moroccan population, and the educational service was to prepare them. But whereas Lyautey and Loth saw education largely as a tactic of colonial politics, Hardy came to see it as a comprehensive solution to problems of colonial rule, and indeed to the problems of his time.

Hardy became convinced that social and political strife could be prevented through the pedagogical dissemination of knowledge — especially ethnological knowledge, the knowledge of cultural and ethnic difference. He consistently asserted that only ignorance led to conflict. In maintaining this article of faith, Hardy ignored all manner of alternative explanations of persistent disharmony in West Africa, Morocco, and Europe: that inequities in power and wealth produce resentment, or that self-identified groups may have material or cultural objectives that conflict in an economy of scarce resources. He also ignored the possibility that discourses of knowledge and their centers of production are shifting and multiple — and therefore too slippery to be controlled by low-budget state institutions managed by bureaucrats, even those who, like Hardy, considered themselves to be examples of the new colonial man. Most importantly, he ignored the possibility that he might not possess the necessary knowledge about Morocco and its inhabitants.

The institutionalization of connections among scholarly research, teacher training, and pedagogical publication increased the expectation that scholarship would provide direct guidance to pedagogy, creating a demand for the kind of simple ethnography that could be transformed into policy. Hardy's attempt to harmonize Moroccan society through the use of education was in fact subverted by the relentless intrusion of chaotic reality. Nevertheless, Hardy was confident that he had knowledge about Moroccans that would ensure the success of the colonial project, and he worked to disseminate his vision of the "Moroccan soul" to Morocco's European and native populations.

An Ethnological Basis for Pedagogy?

The institutionalization of connections between ethnological research and pedagogy in Morocco had begun long before Hardy's arrival. In November 1912, the École supérieure de langue arabe et de dialectes berbères (ESLADB) was created in Rabat just days after Lyautey's appointment to the Residency. The ESLADB was to offer linguistic and ethnological training to French officers and colonial administrators, and was charged with developing a corps of professional translators.

The need for knowledge of Moroccan languages and culture was soon reinforced during the difficult "pacification" of the Middle Atlas. A committee on Berber studies was established in Meknes in 1913 to conduct research on the culture, society, mores, and politics of the Berber tribes. Soon, however, Rabat became the focal point for the colonial ethnological project. A central Berber Studies Committee was established in Rabat in 1915, and courses on Berber law and customs were introduced at the ESLADB under the direction of Mohamed Nehlil, a Kabyle Algerian.[1]

The Rabat Berber Studies Committee included some of the protectorate's top French officials, including the secretary-general to the Sharifian government, the head of the Cabinet politique, and Colonel Henri Simon, the director of the Indigenous Affairs service. Loth and Nehlil were also included, so that the knowledge produced could be disseminated through the educational system. The interconnections among administration, research, and pedagogy were also embodied in Biarnay, who was then head of the Service du contrôle des habous but was also a prominent researcher who would begin teaching Berber customs at the ESLADB in the fall of 1915.[2]

The production and dissemination of practical knowledge about Berbers was also to occur through the committee's journal, *Archives Berbères*. In the words of Colonel Simon, "Among the readers, some will find material for their own research, others, and principally among them the functionaries of the protectorate, will draw from it useful indications of the rules to observe in their relations with our indigenous protégés."[3] As Mohamed Zniber has noted, the committee and its *Archives* (unlike the later publication *Hespéris*) focused exclusively on Morocco's Berber populations.[4] This was a direct result of the difficulties involved in the wars of the Middle Atlas; the Middle Atlas Berbers presented stiffer and more persistent resistance to colonial attempts at conquest and rule, and thus prompted more study. The French believed that they understood Arabs well enough, based on a long tradition of scholarship. In contrast, the French authorities initially admitted that they had little understanding of Morocco's Berbers (notwithstanding the tendency to equate them with Algeria's Kabyles).

The study of Morocco's Arabic-speaking population was not neglected, however. World War I, like the wars of the Middle Atlas, increased the importance of the production and dissemination of ethnology within the educational system. Unlike the Middle Atlas campaign, the Great War put the entire protectorate at risk, not just the Berber-speaking mountains. French military resources were diverted to Europe, making well-designed policy and the understanding of Moroccan society more essential than ever. In order to produce and disseminate knowledge about both the arabophone and berberophone populations, the ESLADB was transformed into an academic institution concerned with all aspects of Moroccan culture. Ethnography was seen to be an "urgent" need, and Henri Basset, a young graduate of the École normale supérieure in Paris, set about assembling a library of French ethnographic writings about Moroccans. Documents available in *makhzan* or *habus* collections were also brought to the ESLADB. ESLADB professors were encouraged to conduct research and to publish their findings.

The ESLADB curriculum now included, in addition to language studies, courses in Moroccan law, customs, and history. The new courses were taught not by professional teachers but by experienced colonial administrators, an application of Lyautey's colonial philosophy of "the right man in the right place." This turned the ESLADB into a think tank for protectorate insiders. Because the chosen administrators held high-level posts, appointment at the ESLADB allowed them to train the functionaries whom they would eventually supervise, "keeping future heads of service in close contact with the methods according to which their future collaborators are being instructed."[5] This meant that the ESLADB, like the Berber Studies Committee, attempted to anchor policy making firmly in research and to bind instruction tightly to French policy goals. As colonial administrators set out to define and reinforce traditional Moroccan institutions, the knowledge they drew upon came from the research and instruction produced by these institutions. The link to pedagogy would be more ambiguous, however, because of the mediation of the educational leadership.

In 1920, after the arrival of Georges Hardy, the ESLADB and the Berber Studies Committee were absorbed into the Institut des hautes études marocaines (IHEM). Like its parent institutions, the IHEM was intended to provide guidance for policy. Degree programs in law and natural science were soon added to the courses on Moroccan ethnology and languages, but these concessions to the interests of the settlers were a minor distraction from the IHEM's intended role as a factory for knowledge about Morocco.

There were, however, ambiguities surrounding the research mission of the IHEM, reflecting tensions within the mission of the colonial state. The new institute inherited the goals and the members of the Berber Studies Committee, who upheld the conviction that research could and should "serve the cause of our influence in Morocco, in making us know better the populations that we are to govern and administer."[6] Lyautey's regular presence at IHEM meetings reinforced the notion that research ought to inform the policy of the Residency. The French leadership also made it quite clear that Morocco's development was to benefit France. Yet, in theory, the protectorate existed in order to develop Morocco, economically, institutionally, and technologically, for the benefit of the Moroccan state and its people. At the same time, the Lyautist approach insisted that traditional society, culture, and elites were to be preserved. The IHEM was to identify the characteristics of the traditional society so that these characteristics could be preserved in the new Morocco. Yet it was also stated, by Hardy and others, that the IHEM's work was important precisely because the old Morocco was vanishing: research was to preserve the old Morocco in the scholarly record, if not in the society itself.[7] The 1920 edict that created the IHEM declared that it would "have the pure goal of provoking and encouraging scientific research relative to Morocco, to coordinate such research, and to centralize the results."[8] Indeed, much of the research conducted had no apparent practical applications – such as the archaeological work devoted to Morocco's ancient Phoenicians and Romans.

Nevertheless, the IHEM was intended to embody Lyautey's colonial ideal of robust, flexible action, which was opposed to the decadent and stagnant institutions of the metropole. The IHEM was to be a new kind of academic institution. Hardy and Lyautey hoped that the new institute would be characterized by "a flexibility of function . . . the elimination of airtight boundaries, the assembling of very diverse forces"[9] and avoid the "self-referentialism [autogobisme]" which Lyautey believed characterized "certain academies, certain provincial societies, where they spend far too much time reveling in their own words."[10]

The key to the IHEM's hoped-for utility, vitality, and flexibility was to be its interdisciplinary collaboration and the inclusion of non-academic professionals: "doctors, officers, magistrates, administrators, colonists, engineers, etc."[11] Academic departmentalization was seen as an impediment to the exchange of knowledge, and Lyautey hoped that the IHEM's centralized institutional organization would be more productive. Fulfillment of this vision depended upon men as well as institutional structure, however, and many of the IHEM's members were career academics of metropolitan habits. Hardy hoped that the colonial context had produced or would produce a transformation in these men. In Hardy's words:

> God knows all the benefit each of us will receive from these varied elements; we have suffered, at certain moments of our careers and more or less consciously, from being locked within overly narrow social cadres, we have risked contracting the professional deformities so very dangerous to the freedom of spirit and the sincerity of research, and it will require for most of us a complete transformation of existence, a plunge into the swirling currents of colonial life in order to discover an intelligence which is not the monopoly of the corporation of which we have been members.[12]

Hardy's own work in Morocco would be shaped by this passionate belief in the colonies as a place where a new kind of knowledge could be achieved through a mystical transformation of the self. However, the requirement that research be not only useful but also "free" and "sincere" was a tall order. It reflected Lyautey's belief that success depended upon "the right man" more than the right policy: the success of the IHEM's mission depended upon the personal conversion of academics into "colonials." For most IHEM research, however, there is little evidence of such an existential conversion, although it remains unclear how "free" research might be distinguished from unfree, or "sincere" from insincere.

In any case, most of the articles published in the IHEM's scholarly journal, *Hespéris*, treated narrow topics that had no clear practical ramifications and did not seem to break from the metropolitan academic genre. Nevertheless, the portrayal of metropolitan academic discourse as self-indulgent abstraction allowed IHEM researchers like geographer Jean Célérier to console themselves that their detailed work, if not immediately subject to practical application, "added a note of realism" to a "general culture, essentially French, that risks losing itself in easy and sometimes dangerous abstractions."[13] Hardy also embraced the Lyautist approach, but he declared his intention to fulfill Lyautey's vision for the IHEM by fusing the philosophy of heroic action with a more calculated, intellectual approach, to demonstrate through the "belle passion intellectuelle" that "intellectual work and the colonial life are in no way contradictory."[14]

Hardy worked to increase the influence of the ethnological knowledge the IHEM produced. With the help of Henri Basset, who became the IHEM's director, Hardy sought to expand the institute's influence by using local committees to offer courses in various Moroccan cities, courses aimed at local French officials. The results were not encouraging, however, for such classes were rarely offered and were poorly attended. A wider dissemination of IHEM knowledge occurred through *Hespéris*, but this journal, published in Paris, was aimed mainly at a scholarly and metropolitan audience. In order to bring ethnological knowledge and the Lyautist approach to Morocco's inhabitants, Hardy looked to the schoolteachers as the shapers of the public mind. Teacher training at the IHEM provided a means to disseminate knowledge within the protectorate. In 1921 two new programs were added to the *collège musulman* in Rabat. The first was the *section normale indigène*, a teacher-preparation program for Muslim students; the second was the *section normale française*, which prepared young Frenchmen to teach in schools for Muslims. The Muslim students were given "a pedagogical education both theoretical and practical" in order to prepare them to teach French and Arabic in the Muslim schools as "indigenous adjunct teachers" (giving them second-class status at a lower pay rate). The French students had a more demanding curriculum, because they had the additional task of learning the ways of an alien culture. These French students were taught by the experts in Moroccan culture, the IHEM researchers. The French students spent the morning at the *collège* studying Arabic or Berber, as well as "the pedagogy specific to Muslim school," and in the afternoon walked over to the IHEM to study "general Moroccan culture."[15] These afternoon studies included Moroccan and Muslim history, ethnography, and agriculture. The knowledge produced in the IHEM was to flow downward into the schools for Muslims via the new teaching cadres. This gave Hardy a direct role in shaping the minds of Morocco's next generation of Muslim elites, because he taught first-year history in the IHEM program.

Despite the creation of teacher-training programs at the IHEM, however, the DIP would continue to recruit most of its teachers from the metropole. Hardy's attempt to connect pedagogy to ethnology would therefore depend upon his ability to influence in-service teachers. In West Africa, Hardy had worked to shape the *esprit moral* of the teaching corps, and he applied the same techniques in Morocco. He transformed the *Bulletin de l'Enseignement Public du Maroc*, previously used for official announcements and publication of curricular information, into a monthly forum for studies on Morocco. In Hardy's words, the mission of the *Bulletin* was "not to confine itself to narrowly pedagogical questions and to regard more broadly the land where we are called to labor; it is one of the essential points of its program to treat its readers as human beings, to convey to them the larger culture, to associate them as much as possible with the movement of research being conducted in all domains."[16]

As Hardy saw it, pedagogical research could not be divorced from ethnographic research; teachers needed to know the mentality of their students. However, the development of the *Bulletin* into an ethnographic review allowed for the development of an ethnological discourse distinct from that of the IHEM, a discourse that was dominated by the influence of Georges Hardy and his director of Muslim education, Louis Brunot.

Inventing the Moroccan

The structure and philosophy of the DIP demanded a connection between academic knowledge and educational policy, a goal that encouraged the construction of a simple credo about "the Moroccan child." The detailed studies of diverse minutiae published by IHEM researchers did not often translate clearly into policy. Nevertheless, the placement of the IHEM within the DIP and the IHEM's role in teacher preparation and elite secondary education reinforced the expectation that research and pedagogy ought to be linked, somehow. New teachers needed to be told what to expect and what to teach. Toward these ends, Hardy authored or coauthored works to bridge the gap between scholarship and pedagogy, works that were published by the *Bulletin*. The first major publication of this sort was his 1921 guide to Moroccan history, *Les grandes étapes de l'histoire du Maroc*, coauthored with Paul Aurès. In his last years in the DIP, Hardy translated his experience and studies into *L'enfant marocain: Essai d'ethnographie scolaire* (1925, coauthored with Louis Brunot) and, finally, *L'âme marocaine d'après la littérature française* (1926).

In these works, Hardy was not content with a dry, empirical cataloging of Moroccan social and cultural characteristics; instead, he sought to understand the "psychology" of the Moroccan, a "psychology" still synonymous with *âme* (soul) and *esprit* (spirit). His writings were permeated by a profound sense of the potential for intuitive understanding, an assurance that reflected Lyautey's faith in the agency of the colonial "man on the spot." For Hardy, first impressions were often the best, because they were based on an emotional perception of fundamental truths. He was critical of observers "who submit the acquisitions of the first days to the test of reality and are enriched by more nuanced ideas, but the acclimation to nuance kills in them the sense of color; the soul of strange men seem to escape them the closer they get, they lose their sense of psychological affirmation."[17]

An overly intellectualized approach, argued Hardy, distracted the observer from his initial recognition of the fundamentally unique characteristics of the Moroccan. Hardy argued that most French writers about Morocco had experienced the desired emotional "affirmation" upon first making contact with Moroccans but had turned their backs on it in favor of a more intellectual approach that corrupted their initial insight:

Most of the writers who have dealt with Morocco have felt, to an unusual degree, what Chevrillon called "the feeling of ethnic distances." They have confessed that they have been particularly alienated, disoriented by this country so long closed to European curiosity and whose inhabitants differ from us down to the smallest details of their external appearance. According to temperament, these voyagers have enjoyed this strangeness with delight or suffered from their isolation, but all have insistently analyzed their disarray, rejecting in the most fleeting impression the action of a human context that escapes the conventional forms of their thinking.... In their haste to understand the Moroccan soul and to arrange its elements into known categories, the European too often neglects the foundational characteristics of this soul and loses himself in abusive generalizations, in comparing superficialities, in false analogies, which weigh heavily on his judgment and complicate his relations with the indigenes.[18]

Hardy identified five false generalizations about Morocco, each based on the assertion that Morocco could be best understood in terms of its similarity to other places: Morocco as "medieval," that is, like the feudal Europe of the Middle Ages but unchanging, immobile; Morocco as "Islamic"; Morocco as "African"; Morocco as "Oriental"; and Morocco as "Mediterranean."[19] Hardy attacked such generalizations and set out to identify the unique characteristics of Moroccan psychology. He proclaimed that the DIP's mission was to achieve knowledge of the "real" Moroccan that had hitherto been obscured. Hardy aimed to achieve a scientific ethnographic understanding that transcended the usual colonial clichés; by 1926 he believed he had done so.

Hardy's critique of false analogies, "picturesques, clichés, manias, phobias or philias" prefigured Edward Saïd's, but unlike Saïd, Hardy wished to produce a knowledge of the colonized that was not "complicated" by nuance.[20] This made cliché inescapable. An examination of Hardy's work in Morocco suggests that he too was forced by the shock of disorientation to fall back on analogies and familiar patterns.

This is most evident in an early article he wrote for the *Revue de Paris*, "L'éducation française au Maroc," published in 1921.

The piece opens with a stereotyped "orientalist" description of an unidentified Moroccan *médina* (old city center), with the usual descriptions of narrow streets and secret passages, and in the omnipresent shadows, the teeming ("terriblement active") *mellah* (Jewish quarter). This ominous oriental scene is contrasted sharply with the brightness and open spaces of the European settlement. This scene is strongly reminiscent of the description of Fez in popular writer Pierre Loti's travel narrative *Au Maroc*, which had become a standard trope in writing about Morocco. Thus Hardy reproduced the ubiquitous clichés about oriental civilization: age and isolated self-absorption, the stagnation and decadence of Muslim elites trapped in a rigid and archaic state and decayed academic institutions. Jews were portrayed with a similar but more extreme image of moral and physical decay in the squalor of the *mellah*.

The article ascribed to the Moroccan Muslim a "double character" that also included "very real good qualities: intelligence and finesse, a sense of the beauty of shapes and nobility of feeling; a keenness for gain which is perhaps not very attractive at first but which combats in them the taste for indolence and fantasy."[21] This notion of a double character would remain a central feature in Hardy's descriptions of the Moroccan. His article also effaced differences among Morocco's Muslims – particularly Arab-Berber distinctions – another enduring feature in his writing.

In this 1921 article Hardy placed uncharacteristic emphasis on biological racial characteristics, referring to the "resistances that the blood of races can offer against the best attempts at education."[22] Elsewhere, however, he generally emphasized psychology rather than biology. His construction of Moroccan psychology was very much a collective endeavor, since he depended heavily on the work of DIP and IHEM writers. In many cases these were the men assigned to the ESLADB under Loth, men like Basset, who taught Moroccan geography at the IHEM and was an early scholar of Berber ethnography. Their works provided the details that Hardy used to flesh out his portrayal of "the Moroccan." But this particularistic research did not satisfy Hardy's drive for synthesis and intuitive psychological understanding. On the other hand, Hardy found a kindred spirit in Head of Muslim Education Louis Brunot. Brunot was a scholar of the Arabic language who produced detailed descriptive accounts of the characteristics of Moroccan Arabic dialects, accounts that were published in *Hespéris*. This academic precision did not translate into a similarly empirical approach to pedagogy, however. When he wrote about people rather than words, Brunot liked to make broad generalizations based on his observations of Muslim pupils, generalizations that ignored the regional variations he explored in his linguistic work, in addition to ignoring all individual variation. But Brunot was a "man on the spot," and his direct contact with such pupils gave his statements great weight. Hardy depended heavily on Brunot's 1923 *Bulletin* article, "Les caractères essentiels de la mentalité marocaine," for the essentials of Moroccan psychology.[23]

Hardy and Brunot recognized the problem of converting a wealth of particular ethnographic observations into formulas simple enough to guide pedagogy. In *L'enfant marocain*, a primer for new teachers, they apologized to ethnographers and veteran teachers for "the abuse of generalizations, the excessive rigor of affirmations, the lack of nuances."[24] Yet Hardy's recognition of this trap did not prevent him from falling into it. Despite the disclaimer, his basic conceptual approach prevented him from finding a middle path between the Scylla of monolithic dogma and the Charybdis of senseless trivia. Hardy and Brunot did present specific information that may well have been helpful background knowledge for new teachers – for example, *L'enfant marocain* offered descriptions of Moroccan child-rearing practices, games, family life, rites of passage, and educational and work experiences. But even such a condensed primer was too complex to answer the fundamental psychological question: What is the Moroccan child like? One approach to this question would be to dismiss it as misconstrued, but Hardy insistently believed that this question was answerable. His belief in difference never extended to a belief in local or individual diversity; he believed not only that a collective psychology was possible but that it was the key to adapted pedagogy. He aimed to communicate to new teachers "the sentiment of a difference, the desire to know more fully this difference, the wish to adapt their daily actions to it."[25] Brunot shared Hardy's preference for an intuitive experience of the Other:

> The language that we use, adapted to our habits of thought, is extremely ill-suited to express a foreign mentality, and our reasoning is inapt to explain ways of judging and beliefs which are not our own. Only a sympathetic sensitivity toward the indigenes can vibrate in harmony with the Moroccan soul and feel what it is; in effect, you sense the soul of a people more than you understand it; cold analysis, however subtle, leads to monstrous absurdities or to colossal psychological errors.[26]

Hardy and Brunot recognized that experience would lead properly inquisitive teachers to a more subtle understanding of this difference, but they never questioned that there was *one* difference, that a collective Moroccan psychology existed and was knowable. In December 1920 Hardy had told the IHEM that the study of Moroccan psychology should avoid general analysis of the "Moroccan soul" and should focus on specific manifestations thereof, such as politeness, irony, anger, and play.[27] However, the Lyautist principle that knowledge ought to be quickly applied to action pushed Hardy to embrace Brunot's more holistic and romantic approach to Moroccan psychology. Hardy found the detailed work of scholars like Henri Basset useful for later chapters but less helpful for introducing the essentials of "the" Moroccan psychology. Brunot's experience in the classroom and his preference for intuitive generalizations made him an attractive collaborator for Hardy, but given the wealth of knowledge available to

Hardy through the IHEM, his collaboration with Brunot reflected a search for simple affirmations among the ethnographic complexity of the IHEM scholarship.

In his 1920 curriculum, Hardy had depicted Moroccans as having the same characteristics he had ascribed to West Africans while he was posted in the AOF: "laziness, vanity, irregularity, indolence, egotism, lying, [and] hypocrisy," along with a talent for memorization.[28] With Brunot's help, however, Hardy soon set out to produce a more differentiated view. Brunot introduced his 1923 article with the caveat: "One hardly ever speaks of the indigene's mentality except to proclaim it inferior to the European mentality, to indicate its faults, considered wholly from our point of view, to justify our economic, political, or simply scholastic failures; one only thinks of this mentality to declare it inscrutable or to complain about it."[29] Brunot and Hardy both expressed the notion that the Moroccan was not inferior but simply different, but there is much to suggest that they failed to transcend the ethnocentric griping that Brunot described.

Hardy and Brunot boiled down "the Moroccan" to a finite set of psychological affirmations. This required some intellectual dexterity, given the obvious diversity of the Moroccan population. But they were not the first colonial writers to confront this hurdle, and like many before them, they resorted to the idea of "contradiction." This was a powerful concept because it allowed the authors to maintain their belief in a unitary object of analysis despite conflicting evidence. Contradiction became a characteristic of the Moroccan soul rather than a sign of analytic failure. The essential characteristic of the Moroccan psyche was dualism, accompanied by a lack of balance or moderation, leading to excess: "for us, instincts, the same instincts as the Moroccan's, act simultaneously and tend towards a harmony guided by reason; instincts, for the indigene, seize in turn the entire consciousness and execute in alteration a brilliant and rapid solo . . . in sum, what mostly differentiates this mentality from our own is above all a question of equilibrium and regularity."[30]

Accordingly, Hardy and Brunot's Moroccan soul could be both selfishly individualistic and "muttonishly" gregarious. Individualism manifested personally as inconstancy, vanity, and selfishness, and politically as anarchy. Hardy and Brunot claimed that "the words solidarity and cooperation can be translated into Moroccan, Arab or Berber, because all the words translate, but the concepts that these words evoke in our minds are radically inaccessible to a Moroccan brain."[31] Yet at the same time, the Moroccan (child or adult) was incapable of individual action and wholly dependent upon the group for direction. This resulted in a tradition of political tyranny and social conformity. These psychological traits implicitly justified centralized French rule as well as pedagogical autocracy. Both power and knowledge had to be dictated from the center, since the Moroccan was too individualistic and too conformist for self-rule or independent learning.

Intellectually, the Hardy-Brunot Moroccan was mnemonically gifted but creatively deficient and poor at abstract reasoning (still bearing an uncanny resemblance to Hardy's view of West Africans). Affectively, the Moroccan was detached and resigned, when not consumed by fleeting passions or sensuality. The positive side of this serenity was a gift for contemplative patience. The downside was passivity and resistance to change. On the other hand, the Moroccan responded actively when there were obvious concrete benefits to be had. This portrayal of Moroccans also legitimated French rule and the DIP's curricula for Muslims. Moroccan economic development and political reform were only possible if organized by the French; Moroccans would respond to concrete incentives but lacked the abstract reasoning for successful leadership. Teaching abstract concepts was a waste of time; only simple, concrete instruction would bear fruit. By asserting the "concreteness" of the Moroccan intellect, Hardy also excluded Moroccans from contributing to the analysis of their own psychology; Moroccans were to be involved in the French ethnological project only as informants. Hardy quoted Henri Terasse:

The Moroccan can hardly conceive that there could exist, along with knowledge of the outer world, a knowledge of himself. Very rarely does he project into himself the bright light of reflection: his interior life is composed of simple tendencies and violent desires which he submits to without analyzing. Opposed to these compulsions are moral or social prohibitions that don't need to be understood to be effective. In this rudimentary spiritual life, all which concerns the practical life arrives without difficulty into clear awareness, but all that would furnish material for a disinterested inquiry remains in unsuspected crevices of the soul.[32]

There is an obvious continuity between Hardy's emphasis on practical instruction for Moroccan Muslims and his goal of turning West Africans into "useful men." Moreover, his belief that psychological understanding came through personal contact meant that he required little empirical evidence for these generalizations. His personal impressions and Brunot's anecdotal evidence were sufficient to reinforce prevailing clichés about colonized peoples.

Brunot drew his supporting examples from a variety of contexts, which Hardy quoted at length. Brunot was impressed by Muslim memory. Muslim *qadis* and *ulema* (jurists and scholars) were "living juridical encyclopedias" who relied solely on memory. A Moroccan domestic servant could cook European meals from memory without ever tasting them. But comprehension and reason were lacking. The servant could arrange European furniture according to memorized instructions, but would arrange it irrationally if given free reign; schoolchildren could recite passages without being able to explain them. Educated Moroccans were good at arithmetic but poor at algebra; Moroccan histories were full of dates but lacked analysis. Moroccans who could pursue higher education preferred medicine and law rather than mathematics or abstract science, and found critical history useless.[33]

The shortcomings of this anecdotal approach are obvious, and it would be tedious to present case-by-case counterarguments here.

Brunot did, however, consider the argument that the Moroccan inclination toward memorization was a product of instruction and educational culture rather than an innate psychological trait. Some French observers had argued that the memorization of the Quran in the traditional primary school (*msid*) trained young Moroccans to memorize. This was a critical question for the DIP. If traditional schooling had created the perceived psychological tendency, then French schooling could remedy it. If, however, mnemonic strength and abstract weakness were fundamental traits, then Hardy's approach dictated that schooling ought to adapt to these traits. Brunot dismissed the notion that the *msid* had created this tendency, noting that only a small proportion of Moroccan children received such an education. He asserted that traditional Moroccan educational methods were the result of Moroccan psychology rather than the cause of it.

In 1925, Hardy and Brunot briefly considered an alternative factor: second-language acquisition. The Moroccans they encountered did not speak French as a native language, and even Brunot, the Arabic professor, did not speak the Moroccan Arabic vernacular (much less Berber) with a native's proficiency. The same could be said of virtually all of the DIP's French staff. Limited language proficiency often manifests in a lack of complexity, with the result that cross-linguistic contact (colonial or otherwise) creates the risk of mutual underestimation. Hardy and Brunot came close to recognizing this in 1925:

> When he expresses himself in French ... the Moroccan child uses words he could only acquire at school, and these are sharp-edged words, the content of which are bigger than his little ideas: it is very excusable not to possess the art of our nuances, and it is always through familiarity that one recognizes the flexibility and the richness of our language, from the difficulty of grasping it at first. Moreover, memory, which language teaching must make heavy use of, furnishes the child with stereotyped formulas and phrases and invites him to make use of them automatically.[34]

Thus Hardy and Brunot recognized that the process of language acquisition and language teaching restricted the Moroccan child's ability to express subtlety. Yet their interpretation of this fact encouraged the colonizers to dismiss any discontent expressed in "sharp-edged" French ("des mots à arêtes vives"). No matter how grand (or political) the language, there was nothing behind it but "little ideas." Evidence for the conceptual limitations of Moroccans came from comparing the French expression of Moroccan children to French expression by French children, without an examination of Moroccan native-language expression. Hardy and Brunot failed to consider the existence of a complex Moroccan intellect hidden behind the epistemic curtain of mutually limited language proficiency.

The epistemological arrogance of the colonizer (the failure to admit the limits of one's own comprehension) undermined the principle that alien psyches and civilizations should be respected as different but not inferior. Hardy and Brunot claimed to recognize the intellectual equality of the native, but they could only describe it in negative terms. Difference, for them, was always subtractive. The Hardy-Brunot Moroccan "is normally intelligent, but not like us, and always his intelligence isn't directed at the same objects as ours. . . . [M]ost of the time, when the indigene doesn't understand us, it is because we speak to him about things that have never interested him, and, if we find him stupid, rest assured that he finds us stupid also, to have spoken to him about things that are useless in his opinion."[35]

In this analysis of difference, the Moroccan is missing something – he or she is uninterested in substantial French knowledge. On the other hand, the Moroccan has no substantial knowledge that the Frenchman lacks. Hardy and Brunot's confidence in the colonizer's ability to know the native prevented them from considering whether apparent Moroccan irrationality was the result of a logic the French could not see (e.g., that Brunot's maid arranged his furniture rationally but according to principles of which he was ignorant). This subtractive recognition of difference did little to encourage further inquiry; it became a self-perpetuating paradigm.

Pedagogy and Ethnology

During Hardy's tenure as director of Public Instruction (1920–26) and Brunot's as head of Muslim Education (1920–39), the ethno-psychology of Hardy's "Moroccan soul" inhibited the adaptation of pedagogy to a changing situation. The DIP's ethnology was in turn reinforced by curriculum and method in the schools. Under Hardy the DIP became a highly centralized organization with standardized curricula and an official viewpoint. The curricula of Muslim schools – especially non-elite schools – served to reinforce the Hardy-Brunot description of Moroccan intellectual limitations. Instruction was to be simple and practical, avoiding complexity and abstraction. In non-elite schools, French instruction was limited to a concrete, object-based vocabulary (*leçons des choses*). In the rural schools, even verb inflections were considered unnecessarily complex. History and geography were also restricted in scope and depth.

These curricular guidelines not only restricted the linguistic and intellectual tools available to the student but also created an environment where children were not encouraged to discuss complex or abstract topics. If French was presented as a language of simple practicality, it is hardly surprising that children's behavior failed to disconfirm the DIP view of Moroccan psychology. Insofar as children responded to the DIP curriculum, it was taken as confirmation of their simple, pragmatic intellects. Hardy, for example, related an anecdote in which a rural schoolmaster had ordered the planting of a garden and asked the children to perform chores. "When it concerns personal interest," Hardy stated, "expression is sharpened by desire, and the most clumsy among them states clearly what he wants to say: for example, the day when work began on the school garden in Sefrou, each student asked the teacher the same question, in a perfectly precise form: 'Sir, are the vegetables for us? Will those who work well in the garden get more vegetables than the others?'"[36]

The rural language curriculum had prepared children for just such practical situations, and when the pupils expressed themselves clearly, this demonstrated the "concreteness" of their intellects. Hardy complained that when the children were asked to speak on other topics, their speech became wordy and imprecise. Rather than conclude from this weakness that a more challenging language curriculum was necessary, Hardy believed this confirmed that Moroccans were ill-suited for complex topics. The curriculum gave Moroccan students little opportunity to prove otherwise.

Metropolitan psychologists had also introduced an empiricist approach to children's behavior which in the colonial context helped maintain beliefs about the psychological limitations of non-Europeans. The "law of economy" (a version of Occam's razor) stated that "in no case may we interpret an action as the outcome of the exercise of a higher psychical faculty, if it can be interpreted as the outcome of the exercise of one which stands lower in the psychological scale."[37] Combined with the Delafosse-Hardy principle that universal human traits ought not to be assumed, this created a presumption that the Moroccan Muslim or West African did not possess higher-order thinking skills until it was proven otherwise. Moreover, even when colonized individuals, whether Moroccan schoolchildren or Senegal's ambitious *évolués*, expressed an understanding of abstractions and political ideals, the behavioralist approach made it easy to dismiss their speech as mere "verbalism," the parroting of French ideas without comprehension. Starting from a presumption of ethnic inferiority, a difficult burden of proof was placed on non-European colonial subjects. Claparède had warned that "it is not always the process which we conceive to be simplest which is simplest in reality. If it is legitimate to account for the mental life of the child on the most economical principle, one must nevertheless make sure that the simplicity involved in the explanation squares well with the facts."[38] However, the ethnological approach to pedagogy led the educational leadership to dismiss facts that did not correspond to their notion of the authentic Moroccan. In 1923 Brunot wrote: "It is preferable . . . to look for the traits common to all these [Moroccan] types, considering only the large mass of people; the modern or modernized elite which tends, at least in appearance, to approach us, is less interesting in this regard than rural people or old women living in a world radically different from our own."[39]

This approach to ethnology underlay the DIP's restrictive approach to education for Muslims. A Moroccan Muslim who discoursed articulately and rationally in French was, for ethnological purposes, not a real Moroccan; therefore, discourse about the "Moroccan soul" did not need to take these examples into account. Hardy recognized the danger of this circular reasoning in 1926: "Yet, here as elsewhere, ethnography cannot explain everything; sometimes it even happens that it constructs a kind of tautology, because it presents the ethnic temperament as given once and for all."[40] Nevertheless, Hardy and Brunot seem to have been unable to avoid this tautological thinking. The desire to identify and maintain pure, aboriginal ethnic characteristics reflected Hardy's distrust of westernized urban elites and helped maintain pedagogical and ethnological discourses about the limited intellectual capacity of Moroccans. Hardy acknowledged that the global economy and the spread of education and culture (whether French or Arabic) were in the process of changing the identity, capabilities, and goals of Moroccans, but he never accepted this transformation. Moroccans who became discontented with the status quo or with the restricted education provided by the DIP were seen as inauthentic. Their intellectual achievements, aspirations, and complaints were considered illegitimate – to be ignored, if not suppressed.

Of course, the most effective strategy of resistance against pedagogical regimes has often been non-attendance, and this was certainly true in Morocco. Hardy's desire that DIP schools should play a major role in the colonial relationship was frustrated by limited Muslim interest in French schooling. But rather than see limited demand as a sign that French education had to be adjusted, Muslim attitudes toward French schooling were viewed as a barometer of political sentiment or of moral progress. When Moroccan schoolchildren dropped out of French schools, this was seen as a sign of defects in the Moroccan character rather than in the French curriculum. "When children arrive at school, they want to know everything, learn everything; the programs, for them, are not heavy enough, the days are too short and the vacations too long; this beautiful fire lasts a month or two, then the student disappears."[41] It never occurred to Hardy or Brunot that these students might have intellectual curiosity or social ambition that was not satisfied by the restrictive French curriculum ("1st month: wood. . . . 2nd month: iron. . . . 3rd month: metals other than iron," etc.).[42] Instead, the dropout rate implied Moroccan shortsightedness and inconstancy. Enrollment problems in schools for Muslim boys reinforced the DIP's ethnology and the administration's faith in the restricted curriculum. This "colonial knowledge" was no doubt reassuring to the colonizers, but it was not conducive to solving the underlying causes of Muslim resistance to colonial schooling.

The Berber Question
The French administration of Morocco's Berber-speaking populations was another issue in colonial administration that ethnological discourse tended to occlude rather than illuminate. It was also an area where the discourse of the DIP diverged from the prevailing discourses of the colonial state.

By the time Hardy arrived in 1919 to become the new director of Public Instruction, ethnic differentiation between Berbers and Arabs had become a fundamental principle of protectorate ethnography and political strategy. Yet Hardy asserted that, psychologically, all Moroccans were the same. Like the nationalist ideology that would eventually supplant it, Hardy's psycho-ethnography argued for the existence of a unitary, common Moroccan identity. His assertion of this unitary identity was at odds with the dichotomous ethnography that supported the Berber policy, but it drew on another strand of French discourse about Morocco, which asserted that all Moroccans were Berbers, even if some of them were superficially arabized. Hardy's view produced discord between the ethnology promoted within the educational system and that of the Residency, the military authorities, and many of the experts in the IHEM.

Although Hardy accepted the idea of creating *écoles franco-berbères*, he consistently avoided portraying Berber-Arab differences as a matter of ethnicity, culture, or even language. His 1920 directive that there was to be no Arabic literacy instruction in any rural schools made the Berber-Arab distinction unimportant. In his ethnological writings Hardy avoided using the term "Arab," preferring to refer to "arabized Berbers" and "Berbers remaining Berbers."[43] Yet he produced an ethnology that was more nuanced than the "all Moroccans are Berbers" thesis.[44] In the *Revue de Paris* he described Moroccans as "arabo-berbères," each possessed of a "double origin" and a "double character." This contradicted the idea of the pure Berber whose culture the French would protect from the alien forces of Islam and Arabic. Hardy argued that Islam acted as a powerful unifying factor in Moroccan society: "they are all Muslims, to different degrees it is true, but only the title of Muslim matters, because religious pride compensates for what might be lacking in faith."[45]

Hardy's 1921 pedagogical history of Morocco, *Les grandes étapes de l'histoire du Maroc*, placed great emphasis on Morocco's natural unity and made a muddle of the supposed dichotomy of Arabs and Berbers. Hardy and his coauthor, Paul Aurès, wrote that the Moroccan people had been geographically defined by the natural boundaries of the Atlantic, the Mediterranean, and the Sahara; isolation behind these boundaries had led to the development of a Moroccan race, the Berbers. Hardy's emphasis on the unique and unitary character of the Moroccan people seems to have been shaped by his desire to suppress pan-Arabism and pan-Islamism among arabophones. Not only did he prohibit Arabic instruction in arabophone rural areas, but he sought to separate urban Moroccan arabophones from Arab culture outside of Morocco by ending the recruitment of teachers from Algeria and Tunisia and by proposing that student readings be purged of Arabic literature from the Middle East.[46] Similarly, *Grandes étapes* attempted to discourage young Moroccan Muslims from identifying with Arabs abroad by emphasizing the distinct, unitary, and Berber character of Morocco.

According to Hardy and Aurès's account, the Berbers were initially too fiercely independent to organize themselves into a state, but they were "a very resistant, courageous, hard-working and ambitious race" that had never truly submitted to foreign invaders.[47] One such group of invaders was the Arabs, whose corrupting influence had failed to dilute the Berbers' good qualities. This reflected the prevailing French discourse. But in *Grandes étapes* the Arab-Berber distinction did not clearly correspond to the *makhzan-siba* distinction, and the term "Arab" disappeared after the rise of the Almoravides, replaced by the term "Moroccan."

Rather than define the Berbers as dissident rural tribesmen, resistant to a decadent, theocratic, and alien Arab tyranny, *Grandes étapes* legitimated the *makhzan* as a semi-Berber institution. It also related Moroccan unity to Islam and to the religious status of the sultan, and declared the sultan's sovereignty over all Muslim Moroccans: "It is thus, as in the past, the Sultan alone who, for the indigenes, is the sovereign judge, and the rules that apply are those of traditional law originating in the Quran."[48] This was problematic in the light of the Berber policy, to say the least; the nationalists would make the very same claim in their protests against the 1930 Berber *dahir*. Hardy and Aurès, in their history written for schoolteachers, made no suggestion that teachers ought to promote a Moroccan identity or a concept of *makhzan* authority that did not include the Berbers.

Hardy's challenge to prevailing doctrines soon drew a response. Six months after the publication of *Grandes étapes* as an edition of the *Bulletin de l'Enseignement Public du Maroc*, the *Bulletin* published another special edition: an article by Maurice Le Glay titled "L'école française et la question berbère." Le Glay gently rebutted Hardy's portrayal of Moroccan unity and argued for the necessity of making policy distinctions between Arabs and Berbers in order to distance the Middle Atlas Berbers from *makhzan* authority. Le Glay conceded that all Moroccans were "vaguely Muslim" and of predominantly Berber racial origin, but he argued that these facts were largely irrelevant to policy. Geographical differences had created social and cultural differences. The fact was, argued Le Glay, that Morocco's towns and plains contained groups that were "arabized in language and religion," possessed a highly developed Islamic civilization, and were loyal to the sultan, while the Middle Atlas tribes remained Berber in language, custom, and law. Le Glay reiterated the Berber policy, warning against repeating the error of allowing the arabization of the Kabyles in Algeria. He also called for the creation of schools to promote the evolution of Middle Atlas Berbers separately from the Arabs. The most important aspect of these schools would be the exclusive use of the French language.[49]

As indicated by the publication of Le Glay's essay in Hardy's educational bulletin, Hardy had no intention of standing in the way of the implementation of the Berber policy. In the summer of 1923, Hardy charged Paul Marty, director of the Collège Moulay Idriss, with the development of a plan for Berber schools. Marty was uniquely qualified to turn the Berber-Arab dichotomy into educational policy. In West Africa he had helped to solidify the French concept of a division between *Islam noir* and the more orthodox *Islam maure*, a concept that had inspired a policy of preventing the arabization of *Islam noir* and which paralleled the Berber-Arab discourse in North Africa.[50] In West Africa, Hardy had echoed Marty, declaring that was no need for the French to try to co-opt Islam, because African Islam posed no threat; African Muslims learned Arabic only for its "magical value" and did not understand the meaning of the verses they recited.[51] Marty described non-Arab Muslims as if they were not really Muslims at all, writing that "the black mentality is completely incapable of bearing the metaphysical concepts of the Oriental semites and the ecstatic digressions of the Sufis. . . . As Islam distances itself from the cradle

... as races and conditions change, it becomes increasingly deformed. Islamic confessions, be they Malaysian or Chinese, Berber or Negro, are no more than vulgar counterfeits of the religion and state of the sublime Quran."[52] Although in West Africa Marty had presented this argument to downplay the alleged danger posed by Islamization, in Morocco Marty portrayed the spread of "Arab" orthodoxy as a grave threat to an essentially non-Muslim Berber culture. Hardy, however, would not adopt this view of Morocco.

In 1923 the ideas of Le Glay and Marty were incarnated in five Berber schools in the Middle Atlas. The following year, a teacher-training section was created at the IHEM to prepare European teachers for these schools. However, the Berber primary schools required little curricular modification. Instruction was officially in French at all the French-run rural schools; consequently, the Berber primaries were not much different from the other rural primaries, except that the occasional oral use of Arabic was to be avoided in the Berber areas. There was, however, a significant difference in policy concerning elites. Berbers could not be sent to the Fez and Rabat *collèges*, nor could Moroccan graduates of the Fez and Rabat normal sections be used to teach in the Berber primary schools, lest the Berber students become arabized. Yet the French needed to train Moroccan teachers for the Berber primary schools, and needed to produce French-speaking administrative employees for use in the Middle Atlas. Consequently, an *école primaire supérieure* was opened in Azrou in 1927. The French-only curriculum of this school, later known as the Collège Berbère, contrasted sharply with the bilingual program at the *collèges musulmans* for arabophones in Fez and Rabat.[53]

However, the creation of the Berber schools (which were placed under the authority of the Indigenous Affairs service) had little effect on DIP psychology and pedagogical practice in the arabophone areas. Marty took an assimilationist approach to the schooling of Berbers, calling for a renaissance of the "strong, ordered, and clear disciplines of Latin civilization" among the people of Tertullian and

St. Augustine.[54] Yet his emphasis on ethnic differences and his respect for the Arab-Islamic tradition led him to support a parallel Islamic renaissance at the Fez *collège*. Hardy, in contrast, supported the creation of the Berber schools but continued to deny that there was a fundamental ethnic division between Moroccan Arabs and Berbers. Instead, he merely conceded the political expediency of a policy of "divide and conquer," declaring, "we must treat them separately and maintain the divide that separates them from the city dwellers, in order to allow us, when the opportunity arises, to find, here or there, the counterweight necessary to maintain order and authority."[55] Patricia Lorcin has argued that French ethnological discourses about Arabs and Berbers were not the product of "divide and conquer" tactics in Algeria and Morocco; such tactics were derived from the ethnological discourses.[56] Hardy, it seems, had accepted the derivative tactics without accepting the underlying ethnological beliefs.

In the works Hardy published through the press of the *Bulletin* after 1921 he modified his theoretical position only slightly. In *L'âme marocaine* (1926) he paid more attention to rural-urban differences and made use of work by Le Glay and by IHEM scholars Biarnay, Laoust, and Henri Bruno. There were no more statements about the sultan's sovereignty over all Moroccans. Hardy also took pains in *L'âme marocaine* to point out that Moroccans' common characteristics did not imply national unity in the French sense of a *patrie*. Nevertheless, he declared that "in this country there has lived and still lives a 'people.'"[57] Hardy continued to assert a common "arabo-berber" mentality that was more Berber than Arab, and he stressed the importance of a common religion that was everywhere fundamentally Berber. The comparison to Algeria was invalid, according to Hardy, because in Morocco everyone was much more Berber. Ironically, *L'enfant marocain* (1925) offered a description of the Moroccan child that was based primarily on the arabophone urban bourgeois. But this did not matter, because Hardy and Brunot transformed the Berber-Arab ethnic dichotomy into an internal psychological dualism: Berber individualism and Arab collectivism; industrious Berber pragmatism versus Arab indolence; Berber honesty versus Arab deceitfulness—all became oppositions within "the Moroccan soul" and "the Moroccan child."

Hardy and Brunot continued to reject the notion that psycho-ethnography should distinguish among Muslim Moroccan social and ethnic groups. Brunot wrote: "We know different types of Moroccans: the Chleuh [Berber], the Arab, the rural, the urbanite, the black, the islamified Jew, the merchant, the artisan, the *fqih*, the marabout, etc. . . . [M]ust one describe the mentality of each? This would expose one to fastidious repetitions which would only serve to expose the nuances, omitting the fundamental characteristics."[58] Hardy and Brunot continued to assert their ability to induce (or intuit) a psychological commonality which they assumed to be more fundamental than the obvious surface diversity. This allowed them to reconcile their own simple generalizations with the prevailing ethnology and with a wealth of specific research produced by the IHEM writers. The diversity of specifics, the "nuances," could be conveyed without calling into question the generalizations. This provided simple formulas that could be invoked to guide pedagogy.

Hardy and Le Glay's disagreement over the Berber question did nothing to improve the pedagogy in DIP schools or to promote harmonious colonial politics. Instead, their efforts perpetuated policies that embodied the defects of both positions. Hardy's belief that arabization had been an ephemeral phenomenon throughout Morocco legitimated the minimal provision of Arabic-language instruction in the arabophone cities and the outright omission of Arabic instruction in the countryside before 1926. On the other hand, Hardy correctly maintained, in opposition to Le Glay and Marty, that Islamic identity was a strong unifying force even in the Berber-speaking Middle Atlas and that Berber customary law was largely derived from Islamic law. In this, however, Le Glay prevailed, and Quranic instruction was prohibited in the Berber schools, despite complaints from Berber families and dissent from at least one outspoken French schoolteacher.⁵⁹ The neglect of Arabic education and the attempt to suppress both Arabic and Islam among the Berbers impeded student recruitment and the spread of literacy in the mountains.⁶⁰ Moreover, these policies would soon provoke accusations of assimilationism from the political dissidents who emerged in Morocco's cities.

My Brother the Wolf

Meanwhile, international hostilities that had led to World War I had persisted and intensified, even as new threats to world security (i.e., to the European-dominated global system) had arisen in the forms of Bolshevism, pan-Islamism, and anticolonial nationalism. Despite these impending crises, the ethnological discourse of the *Bulletin de l'Enseignement Public du Maroc* reflected Hardy's idealistic belief that an educational system could produce and manage knowledge in order to create a harmonious society, not just in Morocco but around the world. Hardy saw colonial schools as a laboratory for a new approach to peace through ethnological understanding.

Hardy's ideas about education, ethnology, and psychology were expressed most fully in 1925 in a manifesto titled *Mon frère le loup: Plaidoyer pour une science vivante* (My Brother the Wolf: Call for a Living Science), published as an issue of the *Bulletin*. *Mon frère le loup* was clearly rooted in the colonial discourse of both Delafosse and Lyautey, and can be read as a reaction against the West African movement for legal and educational equality. Hardy's book also reflected diverse trends in 1920s metropolitan thought: disenchantment with Enlightenment intellectualism, loss of faith in universal humanity, and the desire, embodied in the new League of Nations, to reject old patterns of thought in an effort to find a new basis for peace. Hardy was convinced that in such times of crisis and danger, academic scholarship should no longer seek to be objective and disinterested; the idea of "pure" science was "a monstrous callousness, an egotism to be combated." He declared that the human sciences had lost sight of their original role and had become irrelevant and "anemic." History, for example, had lost sight of its "traditional role as the tutor of princes and of people."[61]

By denouncing the objectivity of academia as "anemic," Hardy echoed Lyautey's muscular anti-intellectualism. Hardy wanted the protectorate's educators and scholars to share in "the exaltation the whole being, which seizes the soldier or colonist at the sight of the 'great silent land' that he must conquer or claim."[62] He echoed Lyautey's hope that the invigorating experience of "the colonial" might rescue Europe from its decadence. But the idea that Europe's salvation lay in the colonial experience went beyond the emphasis on manly action as the cure for feminine decadence. The salvation of Europe, like the creation of colonial harmony, required not only the recognition of difference but also the careful cultivation and application of knowledge about differences. Hardy began to portray his ethnology as a more scientific endeavor, perhaps reflecting the increasingly empirical orientation of ethnology as it became established as a social science. He quoted the metropolitan director of Public Instruction, Anatole De Monzie: "Peace is no longer a desire of the heart, ill-defined by the intellect: it is a great technical idea that ought to be seen as such, which requires the knowledge and the work of the elite more than the troubled sentiments of the street."[63] Nevertheless, Hardy still demanded that such technical knowledge be combined with emotional "exaltation."

The title of *Mon frère le loup* referred to St. Francis of Assisi, who counted the wolves as his brothers. Hardy asked why it was that St. Francis could live in harmony even with the beasts of the forest but that the human nations of the world were so hostile to one another – even closely related European nations. Hardy's answer, and his prescription for peace, insisted upon the importance of knowledge and the recognition of difference.

The looming conflicts between nations and peoples, argued Hardy, were the result of a lack of knowledge and mutual understanding, and even a disinclination to understanding. A League of Nations and international courts of justice were well and good, but such institutions alone could not preserve peace. What was needed was the dissemination of knowledge, a "re-education of minds."[64] Old, false doctrines had to be renounced, and a new "living science" of humanity had to replace them. The old doctrines to be replaced were universalism, evolutionism, and historical materialism; the new "living science" was colonial ethnography.

To Hardy, the grave error of universalism was that it presupposed a universal humanity which did not exist; it ignored human reality in the pursuit of an abstraction, a fantasy. The universalist tradition insisted that all men were in essence the same. Hardy argued that this rendered impossible real understanding between peoples because it illegitimated differences in ways of thinking. Universalism was particularly pernicious because it permeated popular notions as well as academic discourse, and this led to a dangerous intolerance: "In sum, this trend of thought, scientific or popular, has reinforced among social groupings and peoples the illusion that they speak the same language, that no profound difference separates them, and that as a result those intentions opposed to their own are essentially bad intentions. Intellectuals' manifestos and dinner-table conversations are rooted in the same principles and lead to the same perils."[65] As Hardy saw it, the universalist cannot understand why others disagree with him, and finds them simply wicked; the result is often war. In the colonies, everything became clearer. People were not all the same, and the key to peaceful coexistence was the recognition of difference.

Hardy formulated his argument in terms that the twenty-first-century reader will recognize as racist but which Hardy saw as reflective of a respect for other races not found in universalist ethnocentrism. St. Francis, argued Hardy, did not insist that all the animals of the forest live the same or think the same. The genius (or metaphorical value) of St. Francis was that he spoke to each animal in its own language, recognizing the particular traits given it by the Creator. Instead of insisting on a false universality, humans ought to show a similar respect for human difference. Hardy had learned this in his long years in the colonies, as he explained in an anecdote:

> My boy Mahmadou, clever Senegalese, only wants to do whatever comes into his head; he is kind, nevertheless, and devout; he correctly performs his small services; but once free from his professional obligations, he claims to be the master of his moral attitude. I tried hard to tell him: Mahmadou, this is good, that is bad; he resists all my sermons and concludes, smiling with all his teeth: "the reason of a white is not the reason of a black." Mahmadou denies the existence of universal Man.
>
> Back then, Mahmadou's formula irritated me. Today, after long years spent among blacks and among whites not of my blood, I have frankly come around to it, and I assert it without shame.[66]

Drawing upon his West African experiences, Hardy went even further in his assertion of human difference:

> The Black of the Congolese forest is without a doubt my brother, and I spare no trouble, sentimentally, to treat him as such; but I cannot help but think that he is my brother in the sense understood by St. Francis of Assisi: my brothers the birds, my sister the ewe, my brother the wolf. I know for certain that his representation of the world in no way resembles mine, and that his mind functions according to special laws. I can only get along with him if I research and fully admit these differences.[67]

These excerpts betray the patronizing arrogance of the European colonizer and the gross inequities of power in the colonies. By putting the European in the position of St. Francis and the colonized in the position of the animals, Hardy endorsed the notion of a racial hierarchy. However, while acknowledging the repugnance of Hardy's metaphorical equation of the Congolese to animals, it is also important to recognize that the heart of his argument in *Mon frère le loup* was the extension of this metaphor to the Europeans. To Hardy, human differences became obvious in the colonies, but he argued that real differences in "human" nature also existed among Europe's nations and among Europe's social classes. Idealist notions of universal humanity had led to mutual miscomprehension in Europe, because differences in opinion, interests, and behavior could only be conceived of as aberrations. Hardy argued that the recognition of legitimate differences among European groups was the only road to international and social peace in Europe.

European colonialism might seem a strange model for world peace, for colonial history was hardly devoid of conflict, hatred, and bloodshed. Hardy argued that the reasons for conflict in the colonies had been the same as in the metropole: the failure to appreciate difference. In the early stages of colonization, colonial policy had been based on a "grave error of psychology," the belief that the colonized populations could be transformed and assimilated to European ways of thinking and living. This led to trouble, he argued wryly, because "there is just as large an abyss between the European and the Bambara or the Annamite as between the Frenchman and the Englishman."[68] But before long, some colonizers recognized the importance of these differences and adopted policies that "scrupulously respected the heritage of beliefs, institutions, and customs" instead of trying to transform the colonized into Europeans. The result, Hardy claimed, was "profound peace."[69]

Hardy's hope for European and imperial peace was based on the presumption that his work in Morocco had been a success. Hardy believed that respect for difference and knowledge of "the Moroccan" had helped him create an educational system that led to social harmony. In truth, Hardy's faith in his ability to understand the Moroccan had prevented him from grasping the complexity and diversity of Moroccan capabilities, ambitions, and self-conceptions. This inadequacy was exacerbated by the pressure to transform knowledge rapidly into educational policy and curricula. The IHEM was meant to be a source for complex and accurate ethnographic information about

Moroccans. But Hardy and Brunot showed great flexibility in their ability to incorporate IHEM "nuance" about Moroccan diversity, traditions, and customs while maintaining their psychological generalizations. Despite Hardy's late endorsement of a more "technical" approach to ethnology, his work in Morocco privileged the intuitive experience of the Other as a source of knowledge, and the search for cultural authenticity disqualified all contradictory evidence.

The ethnological discourse that permeated the colonial educational system in Morocco provided the educational leadership with comforting guidance for policy making and pedagogy. These apparently useful certainties did not always contribute to the success of French efforts to control the Moroccan Muslim population, however. Moroccan Muslims responded to French educational agendas through diverse strategies, and the ability of the French to respond to these strategies was often hampered by the habits and limits of the prevailing ethnological and educational discourses. For Hardy, the colonial schools aimed not at repression but at responding to "men and things as they are," that is, as he imagined them through the lens of colonial ethnology and psychology.[70] Before long, however, "men and things" would turn out quite differently. The era of French rule would be short lived, and the educational system would be at the center of Moroccan efforts to first subvert and then unseat their European overlords.

6. "A Worker Proletariat with a Dangerous Mentality"

> *The indigene doesn't imagine that a child would take courses at a school in order to become a worker. Far from it: the artisan only sends his son to school to avoid the hardship of the father's trade.* | Direction générale de l'instruction publique, *Historique*, 1930

Throughout the colonial period in Morocco, the leadership of the Direction générale de l'instruction publique struggled to increase enrollment in the colonial schools for Muslim workers and farmers. Considering the fact that by the end of their reign the French in Morocco were still schooling little more than a tenth of the protectorate's Muslim children, this endeavor cannot be considered a success. Nevertheless, the administration did work to expand Muslim schooling. The administration was motivated both by a desire to promote the "modernization" of the economy and by fears of the disruptive effects of modernization. The colonial state wanted schools to recruit more students in order to produce a cheap and compliant skilled labor force that would meet the needs of the colonial state and settler businesses, but they also feared the social consequences of economic change. Such fears intensified after Moroccan workers joined striking Europeans in 1918 and 1919.[1] Roger Gaudefroy-Demombynes echoed the anxieties of his DIP informants in his 1928 doctoral thesis, warning of the "great danger" inherent in the economic transformation of Morocco, leading to "the formation of a worker proletariat with a dangerous mentality.... These are ... workers who will quickly adopt the worst mentality and habits of European workers. The passage 'from souk to factory,' aside from the possibilities of unemployment, will make the advantages and charm of a coherent domestic economy disappear, giving birth to the horrid factory with its banality and misery. To replace this insouciance, this gaiety, he [the worker] will drink in honor of modern progress and the benefits of European civilization, and will be quickly conquered by communism."[2]

Although Gaudefroy-Demombynes was fatalistic about this process, Morocco's French educators hoped that colonial schools could counteract the dangers of uncontrolled modernization through cultural suasion, if only Moroccans could be persuaded to send their children to French-run schools. As a result of French recruitment efforts, enrollment in non-elite schools for Muslims climbed slowly but steadily throughout the 1920s. Official figures (no doubt inflated) for the primary and professional schools for Muslims rose from thirty-two hundred in 1919–20 to more than fifty-seven hundred in 1925–26.[3] The French educational leadership recognized, however, that this remained a minuscule fraction of the Moroccan Muslim population. Dissatisfaction with the limited extent of colonial schooling for the Moroccan masses became a common theme in the discourse of the educational administration.

The primary impediment to the education of Muslims was not, initially, a lack of money. True, the protectorate's budget in 1920 allotted only 14,784,000 francs for education, up from a paltry 998,000 in 1913–14. The education budget grew steadily in the 1920s, surpassing 26,500,000 francs in 1926, but this was offset by inflation. In 1926 education still accounted for only 4.56 percent of the protectorate's budget, and the majority of funds for education went to the education of Europeans.[4] Nevertheless, during Georges Hardy's directorship (1920–26) the shortage was not of seats, schools, or staff; the shortage was of Muslim students to attend the schools.

The Moroccan upper classes, hoping to benefit from economic modernization, generally encouraged French efforts to educate non-elite Moroccans. As Hamid Irbouh has stated, "the Moroccan *Makhzan* and aristocracy supported the French educational project because . . . it correlated with their own social aspirations."[5] Irbouh notes that this upper-class support was reflected not only in the pronouncements of *makhzan* ministers but also in the local advisory committees and the Arabic-language Moroccan press during the 1920s. Nevertheless, the DIP had difficulty orienting the Muslim masses toward the agendas of colonial education. Through the mid-1920s the colonial schools, shaped by the colonial theories of the French administrators, had limited appeal to most Moroccan Muslims. Consequently, the primary and vocational schools for Moroccan Muslims were plagued by low enrollment, high dropout rates, and truancy, while the French educational leadership struggled to increase and maintain Muslim enrollment.

Colonial pedagogy was intended to convince the European and Moroccan populations that the colonial relationship would bring material benefits to metropole, settler, and native. There were, however, genuine conflicts between the goals of the educational administration, the European businesses, and the Moroccan workers – conflicts that inhibited the adaptation of colonial schooling to Moroccan needs and thus inhibited recruitment. Because of French ambivalence toward the modernizing effects of colonial rule, economic utility was not always the main goal of colonial education, and this made it less attractive to working-class Moroccans. Meanwhile, the DIP was constantly defending its policies against critics within the settler and business communities, who would have preferred purely manual education for Muslims, or no education at all.

Flexibility was a central principle in the Gallieni-Lyautey colonial theory, and "adaptation" became the mantra of the DIP. In theory, the cultures, desires, and interests of the collaborators were to be accommodated in diverse ways, to be determined "on the spot" by vigorously flexible colonial men. In practice, however, DIP responses to the problems of colonial education were often determined by an internal logic based on ethnological discourse and doctrine rather than by Gallienist pragmatism. The political and intellectual culture of the colonial educational system blinded the colonizers to the economic and cultural agendas of Moroccan Muslims, resulting in a failure to accommodate the colonial schools to the needs of their Moroccan clientele.

The pseudo-psychological discourse fostered by Georges Hardy and Louis Brunot tended to obscure the causes of the problems at hand, leading the DIP to squander its resources on attempts to preserve or re-create authentic Moroccans, while excusing policy failures as results of Moroccan psychological limitations. Difficulties of collaboration were often explained with reference to the Moroccan psyche rather than to structural elements or policy choices, producing lowered expectations and a continued emphasis on the restriction and control of curriculum. Hardy's DIP failed to convince many Muslims of the value of colonial education, and at the same time it frustrated those Muslims who did hope to use the colonial schools as the key to a better future in protectorate Morocco. Hardy's approach to colonial pedagogy continued to have a stifling effect on educational policy after his departure in 1926, not least because of Brunot's continued presence as head of Muslim Education. By the time the Great Depression struck Morocco, the DIP had done little to strengthen the position of the average Moroccan, and little to convince Moroccan Muslims of the benefits of French rule.

Primary and Vocational Education

Since the beginning of the protectorate there had been tensions between the goals of the French educational administration and those of the European business community. The educational leadership, influenced by years of academic training and the metropolitan and imperial models of the past, tended to prefer a well-rounded curriculum. In addition, Lyautey's fear of repeating the mistakes of Algeria by creating an "atomized" population reinforced the administration's preference for general education for working-class Muslims, so that the Muslim poor could be shaped politically and culturally as they made the transition to the modern economy. General education (French, arithmetic, morality, etc.) was to convince Morocco's Muslims that their cultural and political interests lay in the preservation of tradition, while providing skills that would make them prosperous in agriculture and traditional trades, keeping them on the land and in the professions of their fathers.

Representatives of the European business community called for more "narrowly professional" education, however.[6] Since 1916 the Association du commerce, industrie, et agriculture (ACIA) had been advocating purely vocational apprenticeship programs to meet the immediate needs of European enterprises. Some colonists argued that general education merely distracted from the learning of a trade; employers complained that Muslims who graduated from colonial schools would not be content to work for Europeans but would have vain hopes of becoming shop owners or businessmen. Manual apprenticeship, it was argued, "reduces to a minimum the spiritual troubles [and] allows the management of the stages of moral and intellectual re-education and especially assures the easy placement of its products [i.e., the graduates], avoiding the continuous creation of jacks of all trades, masters of none."[7]

A compromise resulted: the colonial educational service, in addition to providing "general" education in urban and rural primary schools, created separate "professional" schools to provide vocational instruction preparing students for employment in European industries. Later, "traditional" crafts courses were also introduced in the professional schools. In 1917 the ACIA began offering night courses that offered practical classes open to Europeans and Muslims alike, as well as basic French language instruction; in the same year, the DIP opened the École industrielle et commerciale de Casablanca. Elsewhere, the

DIP simply designated certain existing urban schools as professional schools. There were sixteen such schools by January 1926.

Hardy, although supportive of the professional schools, promoted general education throughout his career. He believed that such an education was necessary for the *conquête morale*; he had never trusted that "moral and intellectual re-education" could occur through purely technical training. His 1920 programs, inspired by the West African model, gave the urban and rural primary schools a vocational flavor within the context of a general education. French language instruction was peppered with vocationally oriented vocabulary and themes. There was also, in addition to academic subjects like history and geography, a modicum of handicrafts or agricultural instruction. In 1925 the DIP declared that "a workshop is not required, not even a small portable vice. For tools, scissors, knives, hammers, pliers, tongs. For initial materials, paper, cardboard, small boards, nails, wire, glue. With these ad hoc materials, students make diverse objects: (boxes, little benches, etc.) and learn above all how to use their hands: sharpen a pencil, make a whistle, drive a nail, sharpen a knife, etc. . . . The more advanced children learn to solder iron, install an electric buzzer, re-upholster a chair."[8]

This "pre-apprenticeship" training was not meant to fully prepare students for the practice of a trade, however. The primary schools remained focused on providing a carefully restricted general education, while genuine vocational training was reserved for the professional schools. However, the mission of the professional schools was plagued by problems of student recruitment and job placement, and the training at these schools often fell short of expectations.

Hardy had initially hoped the students would attend the professional schools after completing primary schooling. In practice, however, demand for schooling was so weak that the professional schools were forced to accept students with no prior French education, and few students who had completed the primary school program went on to the professional schools. Consequently, in the 1920s the professional schools became a parallel educational track rather than a form of post-primary schooling. Meanwhile, low enrollment led the primary schools to permit older students to attend, so both sorts of schools served a largely adolescent clientele. Hardy also promoted the inclusion of some general education in the professional schools, with the result that these sometimes became little different from the primary schools. This emphasis on general education continued to prevail in the DIP after Hardy's departure. From 1920 to 1930 vocational training for Muslims was progressively diluted.

The technical education for Muslims in the professional schools was to involve a period of classroom instruction, both theoretical and practical, followed by apprenticeship. This technical training was to have sharply distinguished the professional schools from the urban primary schools: professional schooling was to produce fully trained craftsmen. It soon became evident, however, that professional schools were unable to do this; instead, they produced *demi-ouvriers* (pseudo-workers) without a specialty.

The most critical problem in the professional education system was the reluctance of employers to cooperate with DIP efforts to place students as apprentices. European shop owners generally refused to take on Muslim apprentices from the DIP schools (the Legrand company in Safi was an exception). In 1920 Hardy had attempted to organize *chambres de métier* (crafts chambers) to facilitate collaboration between European business and the DIP, but this had failed because of employer apathy. European workers also opposed Muslim apprenticeship, presumably fearing that the student-apprentices would depress wages.[9]

Because apprenticeships outside the school were difficult to arrange, in 1924 the professional schools fell back on a policy of in-school *preapprentissage*. This formal in-school instruction also proved problematic, however. Experienced vocational instructors were virtually unavailable, so French or Moroccan craftsmen were hired as *auxiliaires*. School directors were trained for general school administration, without any preparation in vocational education. Most students entering the professional schools had not attended DIP primary schools, and consequently few students arrived able to understand French, the main language of instruction. Nor did students arrive with hands-on skills, for few were the sons of craftsmen themselves. Paul Marty argued that this allowed students to learn manual skills and the French language at the same time, but he admitted that to be successful the schools needed students who already spoke French.[10] Not until the 1930s would unemployment drive primary school graduates to enter the professional schools.

Through the mid-1920s, finding and keeping any sort of student in the professional schools was a challenge: recruitment was difficult and attendance irregular. This was not always a form of resistance; most Moroccans from the laboring classes had little choice but to accommodate the French presence and seek work where they could, but the growth of the "modern" economic sector pulled potential students away from the colonial schools. The *certificat d'études professionnelles* and *certificat d'apprentissage* had little value, and few students spent the three years necessary to obtain a degree. Most students departed when an employment opportunity arose; a bird in the hand was worth two in the bush, since there was no guarantee of a higher-quality job upon graduation. Poor families needed money, and until the late 1920s a labor shortage on large commercial farms and in the construction and shipping industries meant that work was available in the countryside and in the city, a powerful magnet drawing students away from the schools.[11]

The DIP tried to retain students by providing stipends and by allowing students to form cooperatives for the sale of crafts, but such income was still too meager to compete with salaries available outside of the school. Students reportedly felt they were being exploited as cheap labor, apparently considering the equally meager instruction to be a mere facade. The most important issue was job placement, however; without good jobs for graduates, professional schooling could not succeed. In 1921 the failed *chambres de métier* were replaced by *offices des métiers* (offices of crafts), but without the collaboration of the business community, these became committees of educators who could only try to assess local business needs and tailor instruction accordingly. In practice, job placement became the task of the school directors, with poor results.[12]

Traditional Crafts
Although the professional schools were intended to provide a skilled workforce for European businesses in Morocco, the protectorate leadership did not wish to allow European industry to eradicate traditional crafts or displace traditional craftsmen. The danger posed by European competition was painfully evident, especially in the Moroccan shoemaking and tanning industries. Since the 1910s, European footwear had competed successfully with the leather *babouches* that were handmade by some of Morocco's most prestigious craftsmen. The result was the proletarianization of numerous apprentice shoemakers and tanners, who then sought work as unskilled urban laborers. The Moroccan textile industry was also threatened by Japanese, French, and German imports.[13]

As Irbouh has explained, the initial French response to the predicament of traditional crafts had been to impose reforms on the Moroccan guilds, in hopes of opening threatened industries to French control. In 1917 a *dahir* had diminished the powers of the *amin* (guild leader) and the *muhtasib* (city market inspector), reducing them to the status of dependent intermediaries through whom the French could gain influence over the tight-knit communities of artisans. In 1920, Hardy, freshly arrived, had proposed further reforms giving craftsmen the status of independent business owners who had the power to elect the guild *amin*, thus breaking the power of the guild leadership and opening Moroccan crafts to French influence. His proposal met opposition from Indigenous Affairs director Charles Huot and Grand Vizier El Mokri; both objected that this would increase the independence of craftsmen and would lead to trade unionism. Mokri proposed instead that the *amin* be appointed by the *makhzan*, a reform that would increase the authority of the central state. The French Conseilleur du gouvernement chérifien, de Nazière, was persuaded by the arguments of Mokri and Huot and decided that the guild hierarchy would come under the control of the *makhzan*.[14]

As was so often the case, however, French administrators simply sidestepped the *makhzan* hierarchy, and the colonial educational service set out to control Moroccan crafts through the Service des arts indigènes, established in 1920 under the umbrella of Hardy's Direction de l'instruction publique. The mission of the Service des arts was shaped by French nostalgia for Moroccan tradition and ambivalence toward the modernization of the Moroccan working class. Consequently, the new Service des arts struggled against market forces and against the influence of European culture. It worked to maintain old-fashioned crafts threatened by competition from "modern" products, while discouraging the adaptation of Moroccan crafts to European styles and methods. This involved a mission "de propagande et de contrôle" targeting both the craftsman and the consumer.[15]

Prosper Ricard, charged with the task of reforming Moroccan crafts, advocated efforts to preserve Moroccan tradition against modernizing and globalizing "influences that offend taste." He mentioned the "avid interest of the European public" as a reason to try to keep traditional crafts alive, but this European interest was a double-edged sword. On the one hand, European buyers were a potential market for traditional crafts; on the other hand, their influence tended to promote the assimilation of Moroccan crafts to European tastes. Another potential threat was European influence on the taste of the Moroccan consumer. Ricard saw the "bad taste" of both European and Moroccan buyers as a threat to the authenticity of indigenous crafts.[16] The French administration was fearful of cultural hybridization and appalled by improvisations of artisans who combined local and European styles, such as the use of oriental geometric design on tabletops supported by Louis-Philippe legs. In response, the administration set out to define and reinforce "authentic" Moroccan culture, to "favor the development of an artistic industry according to a logic befitting the Arab soul."[17]

A museum and an officially sanctioned workshop were established in Rabat to show European and Moroccan consumers what truly traditional crafts looked like. The Service des arts also provided an official stamp of authenticity to approved products. It was recognized, however, that these efforts would be insufficient. Consequently, the Service des arts sought to gain influence over Moroccan craftsmen by subsidizing apprenticeships within the Moroccan workshops. For the administration, apprenticeship had three advantages over formal school instruction. First, it would not disrupt the traditional social organization of artisans; second, it would avoid the confusion of traditional and modern crafts that would occur if traditional crafts were taught within the DIP professional schools; and third, it would be cheaper than building new schools.[18]

This approach was soon frustrated by the resistance of the Moroccan craftsmen: they were unwilling to obey the directives of their French supervisors. This is unsurprising considering that the Service des arts directives were intended to lead the craftsmen away from the changing demands of the market. In addition, these craftsmen were often reluctant to train apprentices who would be future competitors, despite financial incentives provided by the DIP.[19] Rather than confront the flaws in its own policies, the DIP blamed this resistance on the culture of the craftsmen and declared that the decay of indigenous craft production was too advanced for a solution to be found within the traditional shops. Seeking greater control over the training of craftsmen, Inspector of Professional Education Gabriel Rousseau declared in 1922 that "it is only within the professional schools where apprenticeship is organized in a rational and progressive way toward the goal of regenerating trades currently in a state of decadence, that we can succeed in producing satisfactory results."[20]

The DIP therefore began to develop courses for traditional crafts within existing professional schools or within urban schools converted to professional schools. In such schools, a Moroccan instructor was responsible for hands-on training; instruction in "theory" was to be provided by a French instructor. Eventually, students were to be placed as apprentices to Moroccan craftsmen; the authenticity of the crafts produced by apprentices was to be policed by the Service des arts.

All of this proved difficult. Under-resourced and separated by distance, the schools reportedly received minimal guidance from the Service des arts. The Moroccan master craftsmen had no formal education (beyond perhaps the *msid*) and found the school routine quite alien. The school directors and "theory" teachers often lacked the manual skills necessary to be of any relevance to the craftsman. And then there was the persistent abyss of language: the French supervisor and the Moroccan instructor could sometimes barely communicate.[21]

A larger issue was raised by Gaudefroy-Demombynes. Unlike his DIP informants, Gaudefroy-Demombynes had little faith in the power of education to prevent Morocco's decline into the horrors of industrial capitalism, and he argued that the traditional crafts programs in Morocco were futile because they served no market demand. Moroccan demand for traditional crafts was diminishing: *habus*-funded commissions for traditional decorative work were drying up, and the Moroccan elite was turning to European-style consumer goods. The French effort to prop up traditional crafts in the 1920s was futile. Traditional shoemaking and ceramics continued to dwindle. In the 1930s, Japanese imports – most notably cheap plastic footwear – joined European goods on the Moroccan market.[22] Gaudefroy-Demombynes asked: "Why be surprised under these conditions that all the indigenous crafts are in decadence, and that some are even disappearing? The establishment of the Protectorate profoundly changed the environment in which Moroccan crafts evolved. It will be truly difficult for the Service of Indigenous Crafts to artificially preserve a Moroccan character. The arrival of the Europeans, one must recognize, entailed the more or less rapid death of the old domestic economy."[23]

This analysis aptly described the futility of the DIP's project of cultural control. Even the DIP professional schools were subject to the tyranny of the market, for meager budgets made them dependent on the sale of goods. Consequently, the schools had to cater to consumer demand, introducing economically viable crafts in many regions rather than preserving the characteristics of locally indigenous work. Meanwhile, the doomed efforts of the Service des arts meant that funds were diverted away from modern vocational training into programs that promoted the preservation of traditional crafts. Yet another layer of differentiation was added to the colonial educational system, further diffusing resources and limiting economies of scale. The Service des arts absorbed almost six million francs from the DIP budget in the 1920s, above and beyond the cost of instruction in the schools.[24]

Reform and Negotiation

In the mid-1920s the DIP attempted to address the problems of professional school recruitment and job placement. In 1925 a new inspector's office for professional education was created, and Hardy called a conference to discuss reforms. The resulting proposals were quite modest. The importance of suppressing artistic innovations designed to interest European consumers was reiterated, despite the fact that sales of crafts had become a vital source of supplementary income for students in the professional schools. Recognizing the poverty of the students, conference participants proposed an increase in stipends. This recommendation was put into practice, and stipends were soon doubled, but the amount remained lower than wages in the private sector, and therefore inadequate. Conference participants also called for improvements in pedagogy and the training of teachers, and their recommendations led to the opening of a section to train European craftsmen-instructors at the École industrielle et commerciale de Casablanca, although a proposed parallel program for Moroccans was not realized. Some proposals called for more coercive measures: one suggested extending the practice, initiated in Oujda, of obliging students to sign a three-year contract, subject to the forfeiture of a deposit.²⁵ Another area of attention was the desire to orient training to the needs of the local job market. Much was also said about improving job placement, but for the most part this lay outside DIP control. The DIP alone could not make professional education viable. Conference participants proposed to solve this by attempting to place only the best apprentices.²⁶

Ironically, the clearest outcome of the 1925 conference was an increased emphasis on general, nonvocational training in both the urban primary and professional school programs, reducing the differentiation between the two types of schools. Professional schools increasingly focused on French and arithmetic instead of technical skills, in hopes that European employers would be more willing to take on apprentices who could speak French and figure. By the end of 1926, five of the sixteen "professional" schools were redesignated as general "primary" schools.

This trend toward general education continued after Hardy's departure. In 1930 the DIP declared that "the causes of the inferiority of the Moroccan worker lay in the ignorance of the French language, which prevents him from understanding what is expected from him, [and] in the ignorance of drawing, arithmetic, and the metric system. ... [T]he same conclusions impose themselves when one examines indigenous crafts. These techniques are in decadence because the indispensable knowledge of drafting and geometry are completely lacking among apprentices."²⁷ The educational leadership hoped that improving the general education of vocational school graduates would make Muslim apprentices more attractive to European employers, as well as improve the quality of their work.

There was another reason for the rejection of "narrowly professional" programs, however. The shift toward more general education was also the product of tacit compromise and negotiation with the schools' Muslim clientele, in an attempt to improve recruitment. The DIP had long struggled with the gap between the Lyautey-Hardy ideology and Moroccan attitudes toward French education. The stated goal of non-elite education was to impart skills that would allow craftsmen and farmers to continue to practice their trades, but to do so with improved results. This would keep people rooted in their family occupation and avoid the social dislocation that might lead to atomization and Bolshevism. Non-elite schooling was not to promote upward mobility, aside from a tiny number of talented students who were allowed to transfer from urban schools to *écoles des fils de notables*.

This served the interests of the colonial state and of the Moroccan elite, but it ran counter to the goals and strategies of the non-elite Moroccan families whose sons the DIP sought to recruit for the urban and rural schools. The DIP soon recognized that these Moroccan families were interested in French schooling primarily as an opportunity for upward mobility. Artisans and farmers who had learned their trade from their parents or in a guild workshop saw no reason to send their sons to French schools except in hopes of escaping manual work in favor a more prestigious and lucrative profession. A survey published in the *Bulletin de l'Enseignement Public du Maroc* in 1924 confirmed that many students entered the urban and rural schools hoping to become functionaries, merchants, or schoolteachers rather than artisans or farmers.[28] However, the curricula in these schools were ill-suited to such aspirations. This limited the possibilities for social mobility, as was intended, but it also impaired recruitment.

In the cities, artisans disdained the urban French schools, which offered low-quality vocational training and substandard wages; instead, the schools attracted youth from the poorest classes of workers, attracted by the meager stipends en route to jobs as semiskilled laborers. This was a major problem for the DIP, because the failure to recruit the sons of artisans exacerbated the system's structural problems. Artisans' sons would have arrived with better manual skills, raising the general level of instruction. Although a higher quality of student would not have eliminated European resistance to hiring Muslims, it might have helped. More significantly, students from artisan families would have been able to make use of family contacts to obtain apprenticeships and employment in Moroccan shops; instead, the schools attracted precisely those students who lacked such contacts.

Similarly, the rural schools failed to attract the peasants whom the DIP wanted to keep on the land. Instead, they attracted both an overly elite clientele (the sons of rural merchants and civil servants) and a growing class of uprooted rural proletarians. To some extent these problems were the inevitable result of demographics and geography: the rural population was dispersed and in many places semi-nomadic, but the schools could only attract students who lived within walking distance. These schools had typically been established in administrative centers, near the offices of Affaires indigènes or Contrôle civil. These administrative centers had been established as points for collaboration with local merchants and elites.[29] Nevertheless, the school programs emphasized hands-on agricultural training. This acted as a brake on recruitment. Teachers complained that students resisted hands-on agricultural work. The requirement that students work in the school garden was reportedly seen as "dishonorable," a demeaning corvée that treated students as day laborers – a sign of downward mobility even for the peasants.[30]

At first the DIP had been unresponsive to these problems. In 1920, Head of Muslim Education Louis Brunot initially responded to these reports by browbeating the teachers, accusing them of laziness and "a regrettable incomprehension of the role of the schoolteacher in the countryside."[31] Brunot denied teachers' requests for funds to provide clothing or stipends to attract students. The role of the schoolteacher, he reminded them, was not to influence students through bribery but to exert moral influence over their aspirations, directing them toward the life of the farmer, dissuading them from more lofty goals. However, Brunot allowed that funds raised through the sale of produce from the school garden might be used to operate a school cantina. He also suggested that the teachers were expecting too much manual labor from young children; the heavy work should be done by a concierge-gardener, or perhaps by prisoner labor. Moreover, the sons of the rural elite were not to do any manual labor at all, although they were still to be taught agriculture in order to orient them toward rural life.

In 1924, Lyautey and Hardy hoped to address the distinct needs of rural elites by creating regional agronomy schools for the sons of large rural landowners. The first such school was established in Fez, but the rural aristocrats, if they opted for French schooling, preferred to send their sons to Rabat, the center of power. The Fez agronomy school was closed in less than a year. Rural French schools were mainly of interest to the landless poor, who were attracted by the possibility of finding work on a *colon* farm. Consequently, the rural schools that succeeded in recruiting students were those located near European settlements. The poorest students were also attracted by the free lunch provided.[32]

The DIP was thus presented with a sort of paradox. Non-elite schooling was intended to keep Muslim artisans and farmers rooted in their professions, to avoid displacement, and to protect the status of the traditional elite. Yet the more vocational the orientation of the colonial schools, the greater the tendency to attract uprooted proletarians rather than the desired Muslim craftsmen and farmers. Yet insofar as these families had not yet been displaced (by European competition, by shrinking markets, or by drought), they saw little reason to send their sons to French schools, except in hopes of achieving upward mobility in the form of an administrative or commercial position. The greater the technical orientation of the schools, the less appeal they had.

In this context, the dilution of professional training and increase in general education beginning in 1925 appears to have been a double game, both accommodating and thwarting artisans' and farmers' disinclination to vocational training. General education was to lure students into the schools with the hope of upward mobility. However, the overarching goal of non-elite education remained the orientation of students toward manual vocations, and the curricula of both the primary and the professional schools continued to reflect this. However, the gap between the aspirations of Muslim families and the goals of the DIP shifted the function of the professional school away from imparting technical skills and toward exerting psychological or social influence on the students, making the professional school resemble the primary school. The Congrès de l'enseignement professionnel indigène declared that "pre-apprenticeship is not just manual, it is also intellectual; by the choice of exercises in math and drawing, by *leçons de choses*, even the readings themselves, one ceaselessly pushes the spirit of the child toward the professions and trades of the city."[33] Similar prescriptions for rural schools were issued, indicating that rather than teach new agricultural techniques, rural schools should give students "the taste, the sense, and the intuition" for farming as well as respect for hard work and property.[34] These attempts at social control justified the existence of such schools, since it was evident that the actual vocational training offered in the school was insubstantial.

The use of general education in the professional school was reaffirmed under Hardy's successor, Jean Gotteland. Recognizing that artisans saw little use for French schooling if it was not to lead out of the manual trades toward a more elite career, the DIP's 1930 *Historique* declared that "to combat this fundamental prejudice . . . we have been led to give apprentices general instruction, adapted nevertheless to professional goals, and we will establish the principle that the apprenticeship school's only reason for being is to teach the child something besides what he would learn more or less rapidly in the workshop of an artisan or an industrialist."[35]

The deprioritization of technical skills did little to address the resistance of European and Moroccan employers, who were reluctant to provide the necessary post-school apprenticeships. The effort to recruit (or convince) students to be skilled manual workers was doomed if the schools offered neither quality skills training nor access to apprenticeships. No matter how much French educators might discourage Muslim students from seeing French schools as a route to administrative posts, the fact remained that the schools generated minimally educated generalists with mediocre manual skills.

The 1930 *Historique* recognized that the schools would have little success in recruiting students in the long run if market forces did not cooperate. It expressed the hope that high salaries for graduates of the professional schools would eventually convince Moroccan Muslims that the schools provided an opportunity for success in the manual professions rather than an escape from them. The global economy would not cooperate, however, as wages fell in the 1930s. In the end, non-elite education for Muslims was itself a jack-of-all-trades, doing everything poorly but nothing well.

The Impact of Theory

The obstacles to the success of DIP education for non-elite Muslims were legion. As Richard Rothstein has pointed out, it would be foolish to assume that "schools are independent actors whose ability to generate student outcomes and, through them, to affect other social and economic institutions is limited only by schools' own effort and skill."[36] Without a shortage of highly skilled craftsmen, there was little the DIP could do to get European or Moroccan employers to offer apprenticeships to students or graduates. Nor could the DIP alone alleviate the poverty that led Moroccan Muslim students to leave or eschew French schooling in favor of unskilled or semiskilled work. Nor could the DIP abolish the population dispersion and transhumance that kept rural students away from the schools.

However, the DIP success in schooling was also impaired by the DIP ideology, derived from Lyautey's principles and developed and promoted by Hardy and Brunot. This ideology created contradictory goals for schools and then blamed their failures on Moroccan psychology. First and most concretely, contradictory elements in the DIP's mission led to the diffusion of scarce resources, already highly diffused by the redundancies of separate systems for Europeans, Muslims, and Jews. The cultural conservatism which demanded that the DIP work to preserve traditional social structures was at odds with the DIP's mission to promote the economic exploitation of Morocco. It was a tall order to expect that French schooling should prevent proletarianization and preserve traditional social structures while at the same time strengthening the economic position of Moroccans *and* meeting the needs of European companies, which wanted laborers, not apprentices. The DIP's efforts were fragmented by its attempt to simultaneously offer general education, preserve traditional crafts, and provide modern technical training, while making grudging concessions to Muslim social ambitions. The resulting compromise, offering low-quality general education and low-quality vocational training, did little to achieve any of the DIP's goals.

Meanwhile, however, the influence of an official psychological ethnology took pressure off the schools themselves. Hardy and Brunot's ethno-psychology reinforced a tendency to blame failures on static psychological characteristics of the student population rather than to address structural problems inside or outside the schools. This tendency is evident not only in the writings of Hardy and Brunot, who blamed high dropout rates on Moroccan impulsiveness and inconstancy, but also in the statements of other writers who discussed the problems of educating non-elite Muslims.[37] When discussing the difficulties associated with the vocational education of Moroccan students, DIP writers invoked the notion that these students were different, not as individuals but as an ethnic group with traits distinguishable from those of European students, traits that were psychological in origin rather than the result of social or economic conditions. For example, Camille Mattieu began his 1929 report in the *Bulletin de l'Enseignement* on "Le dessin, le travail manuel et les écoles indigènes" with a "psychological study." In this analysis, Mattieu asserted that "the indigene who frequents our schools has certain traits in common with the children in European schools: he is a child and must be treated as one; but he also possesses qualities, and, it must be said, faults, which are inherent in his nature." Although Mattieu admitted that there were exceptions, he claimed that the Moroccan student was "indolent by nature," motivated only "by the will of the teacher or the attraction of compensation." This was exacerbated by "defective" visual memory, which Mattieu contrasted to the strong auditory memory noted by Hardy and Brunot, and "a severely limited attention span."[38] The result was shoddy work; the remedy, according to Mattieu, was not to lobby for more apprenticeships and better employment opportunities for graduates in order to attract better-prepared students and motivate them to work harder. Rather, it was that instruction should proceed at a very slow pace, focusing on the simplest tasks, demanding absolute precision in technical exercises involving only pencils and scissors. This "professional" education was to address tasks of practical relevance to "pre-apprenticeship" only at the final stages.

The psychological characteristics of "the Moroccan" were invoked even by writers who were generally critical of Hardy-era DIP policy. Gaudefroy-Demombynes recognized that poverty and economic pressure were the main obstacles to recruitment and regular attendance in the professional schools, but he simultaneously blamed Moroccan character flaws: "It must also be said that the Moroccans are very imprudent: they prefer immediate profit to future advantages which are in Allah's hands.... Moroccans are very impulsive, very extreme, very inconstant, very fanciful; they are easily inspired, but their ardor disappears at the first obstacle or difficulty."[39] Thus the colonial vision of the Moroccan was invoked to explain the Muslim laborer's willingness to abandon the French school in favor of employment, and even to switch trades when necessary. Even Brunot's successor as head of Muslim Education, Lucien Paye, looking back from the more egalitarian perspective of the Popular Front and the Fourth Republic, would find it necessary to acknowledge the accepted wisdom that the Muslim "doesn't like to plow" and "dislikes working the land" before going on to analyze the problems of DIP vocational education.[40]

The psychological portrait of the Moroccan took much of the pressure off the colonial school system: the goal of the primary and professional schools became the transformation of this Moroccan mentality rather than the provision of valuable skills or quality job placement. Poor enrollment and retention of students only meant that continued focus on this psychological transformation (and thus on low-level general education) was necessary. Under Gotteland, the DIP officially gave up the notion that education was the key to economic modernization, declaring that "professional education should prudently follow, and not precede, industrial evolution."[41] All that remained was the goal of creating political compliance, the *conquête morale*.

The Tide Turns

In the second half of the 1920s, the political and economic situation in French Morocco changed dramatically. In 1925 an anticolonial uprising in the Rif Mountains, led by Muhammad bin Abd al-Karim, spread south into the French zone and pushed Lyautey's troops back to within twenty-five miles of Fez. This seemed to signal the failure of Lyautey's politics of collaboration. Abd al-Karim was defeated, but only after Paris transferred military authority over French forces to Philippe Pétain, prompting Lyautey's resignation from his position as resident-general. Lyautey was replaced by Théodore Steeg, a Radical Party politician and former governor of Algeria. Hardy, dispirited by the departure of his mentor, began to search for a post in France. In 1926 he departed to head the École coloniale in Paris, leaving Brunot in charge of Muslim education under the direction of Hardy's successor, Jean Gotteland.

That year also saw the end of widespread Moroccan resistance to French schooling, as recruitment became less difficult and enrollment began to rise. The educational leadership associated this with the victory over the Rif rebellion, believing that the defeat of Abd al-Karim had made it clear to Moroccans that their future lay in collaboration with the French, ending the uncertainty caused by World War I and then the Rif War. The political impact of Abd al-Karim's defeat may indeed have contributed to the new influx of students, but according to Daniel Rivet, the Rif rebellion had few sympathizers in the cities of French Morocco.[42] There were certainly other factors. The social dislocation that Hardy had hoped to prevent had in fact occurred. Transhumance had diminished, collective-use land had been appropriated by the *makhzan* and sold to settlers, and water had been diverted to meet settler needs. The protectorate state subjected Moroccan farmers to the *tartib* (agricultural tax), and by 1926 many farmers had fallen into debt and lost their land. Many resorted to working on large settler estates or migrated to the cities in search of work on urban construction projects or as domestic workers in European homes; others emigrated to work in France. As urban shantytowns grew and more and more Moroccans were forced into wage labor within the new colonial economy, French education became more popular. The landless, tradeless wage laborers who had initially been attracted to European schooling were now a significant portion of the population. DIP schooling offered a nontraditional strategy to cope with the new realities of protectorate life, a strategy that became increasing popular as traditional strategies became unviable.[43]

When Muslim demand for French schooling increased, the DIP no longer had to struggle to fill the schools. In October 1926 the educational service was forced for the first time to refuse admission to students because of a lack of places in the classes for Muslims. Soon, Muslim demand for schooling had outstripped the resources of both the *collèges* and the non-elite urban schools, although enrollment remained weak in the rural schools into the 1940s. The DIP responded in two ways: it expanded schooling in order to accommodate new students, and it created policies to exclude some children. For the first time, finances, rather than the supply of staff or students, became the primary impediment to educational expansion. Gotteland began to lobby for additional funds, and the proportion of the colonial budget allocated to education would go up to 7.41 percent by 1930. In 1931 he pointed out that this percentage was still inadequate for a modern country or even a modern colony: it compared unfavorably to Prussia (16.5 percent), the Philippines (11 percent), and Geneva (25 percent). Moreover, most funds for education went to schools for Europeans: the education of Muslims received less than 22 percent of the total educational budget through the mid-1920s, rising to 22.9 percent under Gotteland in 1932–33.[44]

Nevertheless, the DIP was opening new classes at a rate of thirty per year by employing monitors and other auxiliary staff, allowing enrollment increases of more than 1,000 students annually. Total Muslim enrollment, which had risen slowly from 4,272 to 6,228 under Hardy, jumped to 11,813 by 1931. Most of these were in primary schools, although enrollment in professional schools rose to about 1,200 by 1935. The DIP could not meet demand and had to reject large numbers of applicants to its non-elite schools: up to 1,200 applicants may have been rejected in 1933.[45]

Rather than reject students indiscriminately, Brunot embarked on what Wayne Schaefer has called "a policy of weeding and exclusion."[46] For the first time, student age was to be "normalized": a standard age was established for each class (at a slightly older level than in France), and students who were too old were turned away — regardless of how long they had already been in the colonial school system. In no case were students to be allowed to remain in the primary school past age fifteen. In addition, students would be prohibited from repeating a year more than once, and those with poor attendance would be expelled. Brunot made a virtue out of this necessity by claiming, in contradiction of earlier statements and policies, that only students of the proper age were psychologically suited for the schools. As a result, he was unapologetic about the exclusion policy: "we cannot turn away students of school age . . . for the benefit of adolescents whose parents should have sent them to school sooner than they did."[47] Brunot also advised teachers not to tell students or their families that the exclusions were due to a budget crisis. He may have intended to avoid undermining French prestige, but in retrospect this was a mistake, creating the impression that the colonial state was deliberately withholding instruction from the Muslim population.

The increased demand for colonial education was also felt in the girls' schools, and by 1929 there were almost two thousand Muslim girls enrolled; some parents even consented to let their daughters join boys' classes.[48] As Muslim opposition to girls' schooling dissipated, so did the influence of Hardy's warnings against academic instruction for girls. There was still no common curriculum for the girls' schools, but now the schools were shaped less by the desires of Muslim parents than by the interests and abilities of the French women who directed and taught in the schools. Often French language instruction was introduced, but not Arabic. The result was that, quite contrary to Hardy's vision, the schools for girls had a greater French orientation than did the schools for boys. Moroccan Muslim women continued to teach manual skills in these schools, and sometimes the Quran, but female teachers of Arabic language and literature were rare.[49] This prompted complaints from Muslim parents, but still the demand for schooling exceeded supply. As one Marrakesh parent, Abdallah Ben Brahim, argued, this steady demand was the result of desperation and poverty, not satisfaction with the content of instruction:

> If the Direction de l'enseignement has observed in the last two years a certain affluence in the schools for Muslim girls, this is not because the current programs of feminine education are satisfactory. It is rather because of the economic crisis and poverty, nothing more. All the families that suffer from poverty, for whom the crisis imposes restrictions, send their daughters to the schools to try to live off their funds! . . . [E]liminate the school cantinas for just three days and the number of girls will diminish and return to what it was before this fragile "progress" which the girls' schools have witnessed these past two years.[50]

As Ben Brahim pointed out, the increased demand for Muslim schooling did not correct the problems that had limited demand until 1926. This was as true of boys' schools as it was for girls' schools.

After 1926, the DIP's shortcomings in popular education can easily be blamed on budgetary and economic constraints. However, the policies of the Lyautey-Hardy period were also responsible for the DIP's new predicament. First, the limited appeal of Hardy's schools to Moroccan Muslims meant that infrastructural growth had been slowed from 1920 to 1926, leading to a crisis of capacity when demand did increase sharply. The low enrollment prior to October 1926 was a direct result of the educational leadership's official hostility to social mobility, its ambivalence about economic modernization, and its insistence on cultural control. If Hardy's schools had offered routes to administrative posts, Muslim students would have been eager to take advantage of the opportunity, and the school system would have grown more quickly between 1920 and 1926. Instead, low Muslim enrollment was blamed on collective psychological flaws and excused by the doctrines of cultural preservation and gradual evolution. Because of Hardy's ideology, the DIP did less than it might have to strengthen the position of Moroccan Muslim workers within the new colonial society and economy.

Continuing economic growth in the protectorate might have allowed the DIP to receive the funds necessary to catch up with Muslim demand. Such economic expansion might also have created a shortage of skilled labor which might have led European employers to cooperate with the DIP, creating the apprenticeships and job opportunities necessary for meaningful vocational training. Instead, the Great Depression struck Morocco in the early 1930s, accompanied by drought. The protectorate's economic policies aimed to protect the settlers; as a result, Moroccans suffered the most. As unemployment rose, French education attracted Muslims seeking a way out of their growing poverty. The DIP had finally convinced Moroccan Muslims that French education was a route to success, but the DIP could not fulfill this promise: it could neither build enough schools to serve all the applicants nor provide an education that would lead to quality employment, much less upward mobility. Consequently, the *conquête morale* would prove to be a pyrrhic victory. The frustrations bred by lack of access to educational and economic opportunity would soon bridge the gap between the Moroccan masses and the intellectual elites who began to speak in the name of all Moroccan Muslims.

7. Elite Demands

Neglect no occasion to feed them the milk of knowledge, so that they obtain the desired results as rapidly as possible. | Mohammed ben Abd el-Ouahad, 1920

The receptive soul of the indigene is prepared to receive the instruction that we want to give him, if one takes care to serve his instincts and his tendencies instead of substituting impulses which are alien to him. | Louis Brunot, 1928

In 1920, the sultan's *naïb* (representative) for education, Mohammed Ben Abd el-Ouahad, accompanied by Head of Muslim Education Louis Brunot, addressed students and faculty at the École de fils de notables de Casablanca. "Knowledge is in fact the only way to well-being and glory," Abd el-Ouahad declared to the students. "It is an essential factor in prosperity and peace. It is materially necessary for all nations wishing to leave darkness and escape the yoke of laziness to reach the summit of glory and happiness." He then exhorted the teachers to "improve their morality, develop their intellectual faculties, inculcate in them generous ideas, neglect no occasion to feed them the milk of knowledge [science], so that they obtain the desired results as rapidly as possible. At the same time, persuade them to remain faithful to the traditions of their ancestors, to observe their customs and to conform to the principles of living [savoir-vivre] that the pure doctrine of Islam has not neglected to proclaim."[1]

Abd el-Ouahad's speech was no doubt shaped by a desire to please his French hosts, who reproduced (and perhaps redacted) it in the *Bulletin de l'Enseignement Public du Maroc*. There were, nevertheless, subtle notes of discord. Abd el-Ouahad's equal weighting of the importance of modern science and Islamic moral instruction was not matched in the curriculum of the French schools, and his expectation of academic results "as rapidly as possible" stood in stark contrast to Hardy's emphasis on restricted pedagogy and Brunot's belief in slow, gradual change.

Yet the Direction de l'instruction publique's claim that it would provide a modernizing technical education and a firm grounding in Muslim culture had much appeal for those who, like Abd el-Ouahad, advocated the reform and renewal of the Moroccan state, the *makhzan*. Nor was Abd el-Ouahad the only member of the old elite who was willing to actively collaborate with French educational efforts in hopes of advancing *makhzan* agendas. Grand Vizier El Mokri's 1918 request that the *collège musulman* diploma be made equivalent to the French baccalaureate had been rebuffed, but in 1920 Mokri presented a request better suited to the French policy of association: he asked that a program be created at the *collèges* to train a future generation of *qaïds* (rural governors) and a corps of secretaries for the *qaïds* and for urban pashas.[2]

By requesting that the *collèges* turn the sons of the rural elite into civil servants of the *makhzan*, Mokri put the Treaty of Fez to the test. Would the French use education to promote the modernization of Morocco and prepare it for independence by creating a true professional class and by allowing the central government to replace the rural aristocracy with a modern civil service? Unlike Lyautey's original vision for the *collèges*, Mokri's proposal would not have given the French control over the education of high-level officials in the central *makhzan*; instead, it would have diminished French control at the local level by requiring French officers to work through Muslim intermediaries trained and chosen in Rabat and Fez. Such an arrangement would have enhanced the importance of the DIP, but Indigenous Affairs preferred to rule the countryside with the help of pliable local agents dependent upon the support of the local Indigenous Affairs officer. Although Hardy embraced Mokri's proposition immediately, the military and political authorities did not trust the DIP to vet aspirants to positions of rural authority. General Maurial and Raoul Marc, counselor to the Sharifian government, decided that "it is preferable to give the sons of rural notables a good education without directing them toward the career of *qaïd*, which would certainly create administrative if not political difficulties. It is for the Service des renseignements [Intelligence Service] to survey the young people coming out of the *collèges* and returning to their regions, and to discern among them, should the case arise, those who could become real chiefs. The real school for *qaïds* is not the *collège*, but the Bureau des renseignements."[3]

In effect, the Intelligence Service (i.e., Indigenous Affairs) was unwilling to cede political power to a reformed Moroccan state with a centralized civil service. Meanwhile the *makhzan* remained reluctant to cede control over its own reproduction by opening a path for French-educated Muslims that would allow access to high-level positions in the *makhzan*. The defense of entrenched interests by both the *makhzan* and Indigenous Affairs diminished the influence of the educational service and left little room for the new class of students graduating from the *collèges*. Qadis were still trained by the Qarawiyyin; the *qaïds* still arose through traditional local networks of politics and kinship, or were selected by Indigenous Affairs.

The conflicts between the goals of the French and the agendas of the Moroccan Muslim elite influenced the entire relationship between colonizer and colonized in Morocco. However, because of the ethnological assumptions of Hardy and Brunot, the DIP in the 1920s refused to recognize its relationship with its elite Muslim clientele as a site of real political conflict and negotiation. The DIP leadership persistently interpreted Franco-Muslim relations as a psychological and pedagogical problem. Rather than seeking to make compromises between French interests and Muslim interests, the administration continued to hope that schools could educate elite Muslims into accepting French agendas without protest.

During Hardy's term as director of Public Instruction, one result of the DIP's refusal to adjust its policies and curricula was that its elite system for Muslims, like the non-elite primary and technical schools, struggled to recruit students. Just as the technical schools had little to offer the sons of artisans in the way of career advantages, the colonizer's elite schools offered true notables no access to power.

Hardy opposed the assimilation of Muslims into the colonial administration, and he reversed the decision made under Loth that would have allowed access to French higher education and to the legal and medical professions. Hardy warned against giving students too much knowledge or too much of a taste for analysis: "French literature, mathematics, physical and natural sciences; all these, which already so unbalance European heads, should be measured out parsimoniously to Muslim heads, and above all should be distanced from all rationalism: it is not the school that teaches reason . . . it is life — and I would like our French instruction in the collèges musulmans to be limited to wholly practical elementary knowledge, in constant relations with the concrete."[4]

Yet even as he sought to restrict the education of collège students, Hardy recognized that finding appropriate career opportunities for collège graduates was one of the most pressing problems for the DIP's educational mission, because frustration among underemployed collège graduates might lead to political dissent. Hardy maintained the hope that collège graduates might gain access to the Islamic magistrature, a career path that had been blocked by Mokri's objection to religious instruction in the collèges and the refusal to allow collège students to take courses at the Qarawiyyin. Hardy said that Mokri had been correct in his judgment that collège students were too young and ill-prepared for the Qarawiyyin, but Hardy blamed the inexperience of his predecessors for Mokri's insistence that all religious instruction be excluded from the programs. Hardy argued that a "misunderstanding" had led the *makhzan* to suspect that the French goal had been to use the *collèges* to rival or supplant the Qarawiyyin in training future *ulema* and *qadis*. He instead presented the *collèges* as prep schools for the venerable mosque-university: "if the grand vizier had known that the *collèges musulmans* were modestly proposed to prepare students to study the religious sciences later on, and at least, to teach them what no good Muslim should be ignorant of regarding his religion and his social status, he would have approved the programs that were presented to him, which included elements of the religious sciences."[5] Hardy therefore set out to restore Islamic instruction to the programs. A compromise was eventually reached that allowed Fez *collège* students to resume lessons at the Qarawiyyin.

It was clear, however, that opening a path leading from the *collèges* to the Islamic magistrature would involve, at best, a small number of students. For the rest it was evident that the *collège* diploma lacked value on the job market. In order to improve the utility of a *collège* education, the DIP resolved that additional post-secondary training was needed. Hardy initially envisioned that such *enseignement supérieur musulman* might include French-run professional schools where elite Muslims might study subjects such as agronomy or electrical engineering. This was never realized, however; elite families had little interest in a second-rate technical education for their sons, and the few students who completed the *collège* programs were inclined toward academic or administrative careers. In recognition of this fact, four advanced *collège* students were given internships within the French administration in 1922, with the idea of preparing them for later appointments within the *makhzan*. Within the year, however, this program was terminated in favor of creating a post-secondary program for Muslims within the Institut des hautes études marocaines. The goal of this new program at the IHEM was to "form a nursery of functionaries and magistrates, capable of understanding perfectly our intentions, acclimating, within the indigenous administration, our habits, methods and regularity, but at the same time clothed in the eyes of their coreligionists with traditional prestige, not suspected of excessive modernism, and suited to truly serve as the liaison between all classes of indigenes and ourselves."[6] Thus the new program was to take over the original role of the *collèges*: the preparation of future *makhzan* officials who would be willing to collaborate with the French. This did little to alleviate the job-placement problem in the *collèges*, however; the French administration recognized that they would still be able to place very few students in such positions, and therefore the IHEM program for Muslims accepted only a handful of students per year. For the vast majority of *collège* students, a DIP education did not lead to the sort of prestigious positions that the allegedly "elite" students expected in exchange for their hard work and for their goodwill.

Consequently, the *collèges* were no longer expected to produce a future ruling class, the leaders of the new, reformed *makhzan*, as had been originally intended. It had proved easier and quicker to deprive the *makhzan* of real authority than to persuade the old guard to allow the integration of a new French-educated administration into the *makhzan*. Nevertheless, it was still hoped that *collège* graduates would serve as intermediaries between French and Moroccan society, whether in commerce or in administration. It was therefore necessary that the students gain a thorough understanding of French culture and society, without losing touch with their Muslim roots. The tension between Hardy's restrictive pedagogical philosophy and Lyautey's desire that the schools create true elite collaborators, not subaltern clerks, was reflected in Hardy's statements about the mission of the *collèges*. Hardy's writings on the *collèges* oscillated among a variety of formulas, ranging from the more restrictive "humanités musulmanes et instruction française pratique" or "une culture islamique et une instruction française" to the more expansive idea of providing "une double enseignement — traditionnel et moderne" or "une double culture musulmane et française."⁷ This inconsistency was not trivial: a "double culture" implied that Arabic and Islamic instruction would accompany a rigorous French-style secondary education, while "French practical instruction" recalled the more restrictive model of the *écoles primaires supérieures*.

Teacher, Teacher

The nature of French-language instruction in the *collèges* also depended upon the individual *collège* directors and teachers. There was considerable pressure on school personnel to conform to the anti-assimilationist Lyautist philosophy. The first *collège* directors, especially Brunot, had embraced Hardy's approach. However, when Brunot was made head of Muslim Education in 1920, his replacement as director at the Fez *collège* was of a more republican, assimilationist bent. The new director, Immarigeon, advocated increased Moroccan access to the French *lycée* and managed to alienate elements of Fezi society, whom he described as "disguised nationalists" who promoted "fanaticism."⁸ Lyautey fired Immarigeon in the summer of 1922, citing the director's failure to embrace the conservative and traditionalist mission of the *collèges*. Immarigeon would later become provost of the Lycée Gouraud in Rabat, but he was unsuitable for Lyautey's *collèges musulmans*.

Immarigeon's replacement at the Fez *collège* was Paul Marty. Marty had been the head of Muslim Affairs in the AOF under Ponty and was an influential ethnographer of West African Muslims. In Morocco he exhibited some ambivalence regarding the tension between the assimilationist tradition in French education and Hardy's doctrine of ethnic preservation and pedagogical differentiation. Marty played a major role in developing the French-only schools for Berbers, and before 1922 he had been an advocate of making the *collège* diploma equivalent to the French baccalaureate. Arriving in Fez to replace a man sacked for assimilationism, however, Marty recanted his earlier views about the baccalaureate. In Fez he stressed the need to keep students rooted in their own culture and to discourage them from seeking entrance to French higher education, which might germinate dissidents like the Oxford-educated Indians and Egyptians who had dared to criticize British imperialism. In Marty's words, the *collèges* needed to avoid "the creation of a class of lawyers without causes, of jurists and men of law, unutilized and unusable, of unemployed journalists, recruits for the army of jealousy and disorder."[9]

Marty declared that assimilation was therefore to be rigorously avoided. Nevertheless, he allowed the French teachers at the Fez *collège* to continue to teach French literature and philosophy, including such authors as Voltaire and Montesquieu. This was not an absolute contradiction: Marty's approach fit the idea of providing a "une double culture." Marty stressed that this French instruction was to be accompanied by an equal emphasis on Arabic literature and, in the broader context, by a renaissance of Islamic culture in Fez, an "intellectual renovation" centered around Arabic-language academic conferences held at the *collèges*.[10] Nevertheless, the *collèges* became embroiled in controversy when the anti-assimilationist writer Louis Vignon visited the Fez *collège* and observed an instructor, Charles Sallefranques, giving a lesson on plays by Marivaux. Vignon published an article in the August 1923 issue of *Correspondant*, attacking Sallefranques as an assimilationist. Vignon privately appealed to Lyautey to end the teaching of French literature to Moroccans, who, according to Vignon, were congenitally ill-suited for such topics, "so great is their intellectual retardation, their habitual lack of reflection, their incapacity for abstraction."[11]

It is unclear how Lyautey responded to this controversy, but French literature was not removed from the curriculum; Hardy and Brunot simply continued to counsel the teachers to avoid unnecessary abstraction and complexity. Sallefranques defended himself: he denounced the "utopian educators" of the assimilationist tradition but pointed out that his students were often as old as twenty, could speak French, and had access to French bookstores and periodicals. His job, therefore, was not to avoid Enlightenment writers, especially the most "dangerous" ones like Voltaire, Rousseau, and Diderot, but rather to guide students in reading them. Like Hardy and Brunot, he emphasized the moral guidance of the teacher through the medium of general education. Sallefranques, whom the nationalist press would later denounce as a "reactionary," added that none other than Philippe Pétain had observed him teaching Beaumarchais, and had approved.[12] Marty also defended the literature curriculum, expressing confidence in the ability of the teacher to exert moral and intellectual influence over the students, leading them to reject radicalism: "The task of the professor has been to restrain a bit their corrosive enthusiasm, and, without veiling what remains of the great critical effort of the eighteenth century, to insist on its fairly narrow limits." According to Marty, these studies served to "open them to the salutary influences of our civilization, of which one moreover spares them the purely negative aspects."[13] This approach stretched the limits of Hardy's instructions to measure out French literature parsimoniously, but it was framed within the anti-assimilationist goals of the *collèges*. Although the French-based pedagogy in the *collèges* engaged the ideas of the European Enlightenment, instructors were pressured to foster skepticism toward these ideas. Faced with mature and intellectually curious students, the French educators conceded that the danger of French ideas could not be avoided by restricting the reading list; instructors had to confront French ideas head-on, in order to minimize and control their impact. In this, of course, the *collège* instructors were not entirely successful, and the intellectual renaissance of the Muslim elite did not take the form that Marty had envisioned.

Voting with Their Feet

In 1920, Ben Abd el-Ouahad had exhorted the boys at the Casablanca *école de fils de notables* to believe that "children today, you will be important men tomorrow."[14] But this did not happen. Of course, those who were truly sons of notables could live off family landholdings and business interests, or perhaps become *qaïds* like their fathers. While such careers might have been enhanced by knowledge of French, they did not require a degree, and most *collège* students departed before receiving the diploma. A *section normale* was also created at the IHEM so that *collège* graduates could go on to teach in the DIP primary schools for Muslims as second-class *adjoints* (assistants). This, however, was not an attractive option for members of the Moroccan elite. Rather than complete a long program of study with limited utility, some *collège* students dropped out and settled for clerical positions within the French administration; others accepted low-level positions within European companies. In 1924, end-of-year exams were introduced in the *collèges*, making it more difficult for students to reach the certificate and diploma exams and ensuring a high rate of dropout and failure. By October 1926 only seventy-two students had received the certificate for the first cycle (*certificat d'études secondaire musulmanes*: CESM), and only seventeen had achieved the terminal diploma (*diplôme d'études secondaire musulmanes*: DESM).[15]

The total enrollment of the French-run *écoles de fils de notables* and the *collèges musulmans* stagnated and even declined, from 565 in 1920–21 to 505 in 1924–25.[16] Meanwhile, the French need to maintain political compliance took priority over educational agendas. Indigenous Affairs provided the schools with a list of eligible notables, thereby restricting recruitment efforts in order to exclude the politically disgruntled or uncooperative. As in non-elite education for Muslims, weak student demand meant that there was little pressure for the quantitative expansion of DIP elite schooling during this period.

As head of Muslim Education, Brunot echoed Loth's 1917 warning against scholastic conscription. When carried out by the French, this was seen as foreign innovation and a kind of corvée, and it was especially ineffective for the recruitment of notables: when Muslim agents were given the responsibility for conscription, the better families used their influence to avoid being included, and so the schools ended up with the riffraff: "a few poor devils who flee the school after a few days."[17] When eager French schoolteachers canvassed local families and hung around outside the local Quranic schools to solicit students, the results were also poor. Brunot believed this was because Muslim families ignorantly thought that the French teachers had a personal financial stake in the schools; as a result, these pedagogical panhandlers had little appeal to respectable families.

According to Brunot, these enrollment problems were easy to resolve: the Frenchman simply had to "put himself in the shoes [lit., skin] of the indigene, capture his thoughts, the reasons for his attitude."[18] Once the Moroccan was understood, the solution to the problem would be obvious. This followed Hardy's principle that only ignorance led to conflict. As usual, however, Brunot then asserted that the real locus of ignorance lay in the mind of the Muslims, not the DIP policy makers: he argued that the Moroccan elite knew nothing about what went on in the French schools and therefore kept their children away.

The solution Brunot proposed was typical Lyautist "oil stain" theory. Brunot hoped that the local Muslim "patronage committees," which had failed to generate much in the way of financial contributions, would at least lead to better recruitment simply by associating French schools with the dignity and status of Muslim notables. He also hoped that this would also result from academic conferences, such as those held at the *collège* in Fez, and by inviting important Moroccans like Ben Abd el-Ouahad to visit and give speeches. The focus was on creating an aura of *makhzan* legitimacy and prestige around the French schools. Once the Muslim leadership recognized that French schooling was useful, this appreciation would spread to a broader segment of the population. This was a very gradualist approach: Brunot argued that, given time, French schooling would appear to be a part of elite Moroccan society. There was no question of whether the education offered was indeed "useful" to the goals of the Moroccan elite (who a priori could have no legitimate interest that differed from that of the French). All that was needed was time and a French offer of "sympathy, cordiality, and moral dignity."[19] This meant that the DIP accepted the small scale and low enrollment of the elite system and waited patiently for Muslim attitudes to change.

Not all Moroccan families who avoided the *collèges* rejected the modernizing promise of French education: some preferred to seek access to the schools for Europeans. Many families were suspicious of the segregated schools for Muslims and the differentiated curriculum, fearing that the schools for Muslims would not prepare students to compete effectively with Europeans and Moroccan Jews in the new economy. This was a fairly accurate assessment of the situation. If the refusal of baccalaureate equivalency for the *collège* diploma was not enough, the superior facilities for Europeans made it quite obvious which schools were first-class. Lyautey and Hardy, despite their anti-assimilationist convictions, cautioned that the European secondary schools should not be wholly forbidden to Moroccan Muslims, for fear of provoking political opposition, and for fear that overly westernized Moroccans might contaminate the Muslim character of the *collèges*. However, many obstacles kept Muslim students out of the European system. They could be admitted to schools for Europeans only with the approval of the colonial authorities (Indigenous Affairs or the DIP). However, most Muslims were kept out of the *lycées* simply because they could not meet the age and academic requirements for entrance. The restriction of the French curricula in the DIP schools for young Muslims made it difficult for students to transfer into the European system: few Moroccan Muslims could pass the entrance exams before they had surpassed the maximum age limits. The inadequacy of primary education for Muslims, combined with linguistic and cultural barriers and the inflexibility of the age requirement in the European schools, created an effective barrier to educational integration at the secondary level.[20]

Nevertheless, some did manage to enter the system for Europeans. The most influential Moroccan notables could persuade the authorities to bend the rules to allow their sons into the French primary schools, and from 1920 to 1923 there were more than two hundred Muslim students per year in primary and professional schools for Europeans. The *écoles de fils de notables* enrolled fewer than six hundred students per year in this period, which meant that more than a quarter of all French-educated "elite" Muslim schoolchildren were educated in the schools for Europeans. Once the segregation barrier was breached at the primary level, exceptionally dedicated students immersed in these francophone environments could study their way into the secondary schools. By 1926–27 there were more than fifty Muslims in secondary, upper primary, and technical schools for Europeans (although about a third of these were Algerians, mostly in Oujda). These numbers represented a significant proportion of all Muslim students in DIP post-primary education, since the *collèges musulmans* enrolled fewer than 150 students during this period.[21]

Other elite families avoided the French system altogether. The Qarawiyyin university in Fez and the Ben Youssef *médersa* in Marrakesh provided a traditional education to about seven hundred students. A few wealthy families continued to send sons to study in Cairo or Nablus, arousing French fears that Morocco might be contaminated by the nationalism that was stirring abroad. A more accessible option for families who could pay the modest tuition were the private Salafi *msids rénovés* (new *msids*, also known as "free schools" because they were free from French control). Salafiyya was a religious reform movement founded by the Egyptian Muhammed Abduh, a student of Jamal al-Din al-Afghani. Abduh and the Salafis sought to create a renaissance of Islamic culture and society, bringing an end to the corruption and decadence of Muslim societies, which was seen as the root cause of Western domination. This was to be accomplished through a renewed commitment to orthodox Islamic practices and Islamic law and through educational reform. Although Salafiyya would later become increasingly militant and rigid, in the late nineteenth and early twentieth centuries it was a forward-looking intellectual movement. Salafi education embraced Western methods and subjects, including mathematics, science, and foreign languages, while remaining rooted in Arabic and Islamic law. Salafi free schools began to open in Morocco by 1921, and by 1924 more than twenty-five such schools had opened, serving between fifteen hundred and two thousand students. These schools offered a modern education rooted in the Arabic language and Islam but including arithmetic, history, geography, and sometimes French. They constituted an important source of competition for the French-run institutions, and soon the free schools became centers of political dissent. However, the free schools initially enjoyed the blessing of the DIP, and even some practical support. By 1925 the DIP had come to see these schools as a threat, but Marty still praised them as a complement to the French system; as he saw it, they served the French goals of modernizing Moroccan society within the context of Muslim culture.[22]

Competition from the free schools made it even more difficult to persuade the Moroccan ruling class to send their children to the French-run *collèges*. Consequently, the *collèges* ended up educating Moroccans from a variety of social groups. The wealthy urban bourgeoisie outnumbered the children of *qaïds* and high *makhzan* officials (although these groups were not entirely separate), and the proportion of students from humbler backgrounds gradually increased, although they remained a minority.[23] The result was the creation of a new intellectual class, distinct from the political class and the religious intelligentsia. This tiny new class of French-educated Muslims embraced the French schools as a tool of modernization but challenged the schools' limitations by demanding integration into the French metropolitan educational system, with unimpeded access to French higher education. Such demands were contrary to the politics and pedagogy of the protectorate in the 1920s, however, and were refused by the DIP and by the Residency.

Seeing Muslim dissatisfaction as a symptom of Muslim ignorance, the DIP did little in the 1920s to make elite educational programs more palatable or more useful to the Moroccan political class, or even to the bourgeoisie. Hardy's ethno-psychological approach to colonial education was ill-suited to the negotiation of compromise between the colonial state and the Muslim elite, because Hardy was dedicated to the suppression of new (supposedly inauthentic or premature) Muslim ambitions, rather than to their accommodation. Because of slow recruitment before 1925, there had been little incentive to expand infrastructure and staff, leaving the DIP ill-prepared for the increased demand for French education in the late 1920s and 1930s. As was the case with the non-elite primary and vocational schools, demand for French-sponsored schooling increased among the Muslim elite beginning in 1926. The defeat of the Rif rebellion made it clear that the French regime controlled the future of Morocco; meanwhile, economic hardships and French opposition slowed the growth of the free school movement, weakening the DIP's main competitors. Enrollment in the French-run *écoles de fils de notables* and the *collèges* rose from 620 in 1925–26 to 1,072 two years later, and surpassed 1,600 in 1930–31.[24] As in non-elite DIP education, the dynamic had reversed: now the DIP was preoccupied with repelling students rather than recruiting them. This did not mean that the Muslim population passively accepted what the DIP offered them, however. Muslim dissatisfaction with the nature of elite DIP education remained, and pressure for change now came from within the schools, and from the new class of pseudo-elite, French-educated Muslims the schools had created.

Associations des Anciens Élèves

In 1920 a group of forty Muslim notables and former *collège* students in Fez became alarmed at the anti-assimilationist trend in French educational discourse when a speaker at the annual meeting of the Casablanca Chamber of Commerce and Agriculture suggested that indigenous students should be restricted to purely primary education. Addressing its concerns to the French leadership and to Grand Vizier El Mokri, the Moroccan group demanded that the French follow "principles of equity" in two senses: they asked that Arabic instruction be given treatment equal to French, and they asked that the schools provide programs for Muslims that matched the programs in schools for Europeans, granting access to French schools of medicine, law, and engineering.[25]

The French administration was able to reassure the petitioners that the views of the offending speaker did not reflect those of Hardy or of the DIP, as would be demonstrated when the *collèges*' secondary classes reopened for the fall 1920 term. However, the group's petition had gone beyond the specific question of vocational versus general education, and the group declared its intention to form an "Association indigène relative à l'enseignement des langues arabes et française" in hopes of influencing the French administration. This became the Association des anciens élèves du Collège Moulay Idriss in Fez, an organization soon imitated in Rabat. Former students from the *écoles de fils de notables* also began to form associations.

These "Associations of Former Students" were not, strictly speaking, alumni associations, for they included students who had studied at the *collèges* but had not completed the diploma, and they initially included interested Muslims who had never studied at the *collèges*. Despite the boldness of the requested reforms, the educational leadership did not object to these organizations, for they represented an important point of contact and collaboration with the Muslim elite. Hardy saw these groups as a potential ally in efforts to spread French influence and recruit students, and as a means to extend DIP surveillance into post-scholastic life. "Well counseled and discreetly directed," he wrote, "the Association of Former Students and of friends of the *collège musulman* can be an interesting organ of liaison between the government and the indigenous population."[26] Hardy also saw these organizations as a necessary social complement to the educational institutions the French had created in Morocco. Regarding the association in Casablanca, Hardy wrote:

> The former students do not have, unlike Europeans of their age, the resource of meeting each other in a café, for football, meeting at home and seeking to complete, through reading, the instruc-

tion that they find insufficient. The question, then, is to know if this organization of former students which exists virtually may, as they request, come under the tutelage of Mr. Dumas, director of the school [the *école de fils de notables* in Casablanca], or if we should let it evolve alone, by chance, under various influences, without the counterweight of a sympathetic surveillance.[27]

Marty echoed Hardy's sentiments when he wrote about the Anciens élèves organization at the Fez *collège*, declaring that "the goal of these young men is far from bad: they want, first of all, to maintain the connection, a bit sentimental, to their youth, but they also want to help each other materially and morally, and to perfect their intellectual training through post-scholastic studies." Marty recognized that these organizations could be dangerous if they "angrily transformed themselves and turned to political adventures."[28] However, he argued, in typical DIP fashion, that such dangers could be avoided by a mixture of goodwill and supervision. These organizations were to receive encouragement, but were required to meet at the schools themselves, in the presence of the school director. Eventually, outsiders were excluded from even honorary membership, as were students who had been expelled for any reason or who had attended the school for less than a year. Like Hardy, Marty assumed that there was no legitimate cause for conflicts between the students and the DIP. Dissidence, therefore, could only arise from malevolent forces outside of the school.

Under French supervision, the Anciens élèves organizations continued to work quietly for reform of the educational system. Some DIP teachers and metropolitan academics were sympathetic, recognizing that Moroccan students were intellectually as capable as French ones. Even among top protectorate administrators there was considerable debate over whether the DESM ought to be made equivalent to the baccalaureate after all, in order to improve recruitment and to appease the Anciens élèves. Hardy himself apparently came close to conceding baccalaureate equivalency in 1922, but with Lyautey's support he ultimately remained true to his principles, although he exhibited some flexibility regarding whether the DESM might be declared equivalent within Morocco, without providing access to opportunities in France. Hardy and his colleagues articulated three main objections to baccalaureate equivalency, however. First, it was argued that the *collège* diploma could not be made equivalent, because the *collège* education was simply not on par with that of the *lycée*. Second, the French leadership noted the varied nature of Moroccan demands: it would be difficult to reconcile baccalaureate equivalency, which would presumably mean increasing the orientation of the *collège* programs toward French, with the new demand for improved and expanded Arabic and religious instruction in the *collèges*. Finally, the leadership feared that political dissidence would result from Muslims pursuing careers in law.[29] The baccalaureate was denied.

In March 1926 the Fez Anciens élèves organization again presented a set of demands similar to those articulated in 1920. They asked that the diploma be made equivalent to the baccalaureate, or at least to the *brevet supérieur*, to allow students to transfer into the French system more easily and gain access to higher education in metropolitan France. Seeking better employment opportunities, they also demanded access to better positions and better salaries within the protectorate administration, and criticized the administration's hiring of Algerians, Tunisians, and Syrians rather than the local *collège* graduates. The Anciens élèves' request for the equivalency of the *collège* diploma to a French degree would have effectively turned the *collèges* into *lycées*, ending the curricular differentiation that was the cornerstone of the Lyautey-Hardy approach. Predictably, despite a few sympathizers among the French, this request was again refused in 1926.[30]

The matter was far from settled, however. The discontent produced by the refusal of the baccalaureate was only exacerbated in 1927, when a baccalaureate program was instituted at the Collège Sadiqi in Tunis. Morocco's Anciens élèves were acutely aware of this new inequity. That same year, the handful of Moroccan Muslims who had squeezed through the cracks in DIP segregation and were studying in France joined Tunisian students to form L'association des étudiants musulmans nord-africains en France (AEMNAF; Association of Muslim North African Students in France). The availability of the baccalaureate in Tunis made its denial at the Moroccan *collèges* even more aggravating. For the next three years, Morocco's Anciens élèves lobbied the protectorate leadership with letters and petitions; meanwhile, the AEMNAF launched a campaign in the French press. They not only demanded that a baccalaureate program be created in the *collèges* but also pushed to make colonial education accessible to more Moroccans. In 1926 they asked for — and received — the abolition of fees for the *écoles de fils de notables* and called for the construction of more primary schools in Fez.[31]

Brunot's Response

After Hardy departed to become director of the École coloniale in 1926, Brunot held the middle ground, attempting to preserve Hardy's approach to Muslim education under a new educational director, Jean Gotteland. Brunot showed little sympathy for the aspirations of the Anciens élèves. However, the changes that had taken place in Morocco had put him in a difficult position. Under the Residency of Lyautey's successor, Théodore Steeg, the settler population increased in number and influence, forcing Brunot to defend his educational policies on two fronts. On the one hand were the ambitious Anciens élèves; on the other hand were French critics who saw the new class of French-educated Moroccans as a threat, and opposed all but the most rudimentary instruction for Muslims. As Hardy had done throughout his career, Brunot continued to assert that a general education was appropriate for Muslim students, but only in a segregated, restricted form. He also held fast to Hardy's belief that the school system was capable of convincing Moroccan Muslims to remain content with such restrictions. These beliefs meant that there was little need to make concessions to the Anciens élèves — concessions that would have outraged the opponents of Muslim education.

Hardy's goal had been to create students with Moroccan mentality and European skills. In theory, the language curriculum was to have enforced this separation. However, the acquired bilingualism of the pupils did not conform to Hardy's neat categories. The DIP's approach to education was predicated on the assumption that the French instructors understood (or could understand) their Muslim students but that Muslim students could only understand the French insofar as such knowledge was parceled out in careful lessons. This may have been true of schoolboys in the classroom during the years when Moroccans were still strangers to French culture, but by the mid-1920s the balance of epistemic power had shifted. In the Anciens élèves the DIP faced a group of young adults who had learned to speak French, in most cases far better than their French teachers spoke Arabic. These young bilinguals were in a privileged position to understand both cultures. Educators like Immarigeon and school directors like Marty may have come close to realizing this, but Brunot and the colonial leadership continued to insist that Moroccan biculturalism was an arrogant delusion. As Hardy and Brunot saw it, Moroccan Muslims, despite their apparent "grandiloquence," could learn to parrot their textbooks, but they did not learn to think as Frenchmen.[32] Even the relatively assimilationist Roger Gaudefroy-Demombynes accepted the view of his DIP informants that these educated young Moroccans were not bilinguals with bicultural understanding, but rather semi-linguals suffering from "confusion dans l'esprit."[33]

As a result of this attitude, Brunot approached the rumblings of discontent among French-educated Muslims in the late 1920s as a pedagogical problem to be overcome by instruction rather than as a political disagreement to be negotiated. He remained committed to Hardy's faith in the power of the schools to create the mutual understanding that would lead to harmonious colonial relationships. If harmony was not prevalent, and if the structure and curricula of the schools were adequately "adapted" to the characteristics of Moroccan Muslims (as Brunot believed they were), then the problem and the solution lay with the teachers.

The DIP leadership had always been very concerned that the teachers might subvert the conservative mission of the DIP by promoting the assimilation of Muslim students to French culture. Brunot sought to remedy the gap between DIP theory and classroom practice by focusing on the "moral spirit" of the teachers. For the most part, he continued to reiterate the pedagogical theory of the Hardy era. In 1934 Brunot produced a fat new handbook consisting of old DIP publications repackaged for new teachers: *Premiers conseils: Collection d'instructions et de manuels pédagogiques pour les maîtres des écoles musulmanes*. Among other bits of Hardy's doctrine was his 1920 directive that teachers forget any notion of promoting secularism or political or social reform: "Anti-clericalism is not an article to be exported. . . . [W]e do not speak of the emancipation of the citizen, nor the liberation of the slave, nor of the liberty of the woman; these questions are not to be discussed in school."[34]

Brunot continued to promote the idea that an emotional communion with the "Moroccan soul" could make teachers, and through them the students, see the wisdom of the official DIP approach. In 1928 the *Bulletin de l'Enseignement Public du Maroc* upheld the belief that the schoolteacher, face-to-face with the indigenous population, had the ability "to look deeply within the indigenous soul."[35] This did not mean that the teachers ought to listen to the grievances of the Muslim students, however. The teacher's task was to gently lead the student to accept the DIP's curricula and policies rather than to challenge them. According to Brunot, "the receptive soul of the indigene is prepared to receive the instruction that we want to give him, if one takes care to serve his instincts and his tendencies instead of substituting impulses which are alien to him."[36] This implied that the teachers need not listen to the "alien" ambitions voiced by their students or by the Anciens élèves; the DIP understood the "instincts and tendencies" of these educated Muslims better than they understood themselves.

In order to convince metropolitan-trained teachers to reject their republican universalist habits, Brunot invoked metropolitan writers who emphasized the importance of adapting instruction to the developmental needs of the child. He cited Jean-Jacques Rousseau and repeated the arguments of Edouard Claparède and Henri Roorda that the pedagogy of the Third Republic was too difficult and tedious for children, with too much rote memorization. Brunot then linked Hardy's ethnology to metropolitan psychological theory by means of analogy: native is to European as child is to adult. To Brunot, the injunction to avoid treating a child like an adult was identical to the principle that one ought not to treat a Moroccan like a Frenchman, lest one create "an alien personality in which the instincts of the race mix bizarrely with the acquired principles of Western morality."[37] He cited Claparède and Roorda to try to convince the teachers not to teach too much material, and to eschew the temptation to attempt to match the educational standards of the metropole: if these writers claimed that education for children ought to be simpler and more concrete than instruction for adults, then did not Moroccans need even simpler and more concrete instruction than did European children? Taking the prescriptions of these metropolitan writers to an extreme, Brunot asserted that the purpose of education was not the transmission of knowledge but the cultivation of personality and emotion. Teachers were to focus on the affective development of the child's personality. Presumably, the resulting emotional health would prevent the sort of disaffection expressed by the Anciens élèves.

In Brunot's thought, political dissidence was misinterpreted as mental instability, and emotional health was believed to be inversely proportional to intellectual rigor. To Brunot, the damage done by education came from teaching too much information and from teaching concepts that Moroccans were not capable of understanding.[38] Like Hardy, he cloaked the anti-intellectualism of his restrictive pedagogy in a seemingly progressive language of needs-based adaptation: "And, when we know the intellectual mechanism of our indigenous student, we should, on the one hand, as Claparède recommends, adapt our instruction to the student, and on the other hand, orient and develop his intelligence, progressively, to lead it to be not too different from that of the European."[39]

This would appear to be an assimilationist statement, except that Brunot had already clearly defined his view of the limited "intellectual mechanism" of the Moroccan mind. The key word was "progressively," that is, gradually, without sudden changes. Indeed, Brunot attempted to dissuade teachers from teaching new ideas to their pupils, even as they taught them a new language: "lead them to form easily, in this language that is alien to them, ideas that are always personal" – personal, not abstract, not foreign, and above all not political.[40] In other words, ideas in keeping with the DIP understanding of what ideas could be "personal" to the authentic Moroccan.

In addition to citing Rousseau and Claparède, Brunot reinforced his argument by referring to more recent "back to basics" discourse in metropolitan pedagogical theory. The *Bulletin de l'Enseignement* excerpted an article from the *Journal des Instituteurs et des Institutrices* which claimed that metropolitan students arrived at university with inflated egos but poor basic skills because "one doesn't demand of them the necessary effort to learn the most humble things."[41] Brunot explicitly drew support from metropolitan writers who blamed overly intellectualized education for the bureaucratic *functionarisme* of democratic states. Brunot quoted a recent issue of *École et la Vie*: "scholastic education has killed democracy: instead of making citizens capable of judgment and sacrifice, it has created individuals who, upon leaving the primary school, know nothing of practical life, have no judgment, but unfortunately think they have learned all knowledge and are capable of judging everything."[42] This scornful view of the French primary school graduate also summed up Brunot's view of those Muslim students who expressed discontent, ambition, or worse, political resentment.

Brunot argued that the danger of egotism, arrogance, and misjudgment was particularly grave among Moroccan students, because of their ethnic tendency to excessive individualism and anarchy. Education ought therefore to emphasize the ability to distinguish between "healthy suggestions" and "bad impulses."[43] Students had to be taught to distrust language and ideas; they needed to become anti-intellectuals. "Above all, let us put them on guard against the deceptive power of words," declared Brunot.[44] Students had to become critical of words and ideas if they were to resist the insidious discourses that, by 1928, were evident among elements of the Moroccan Muslim community. Brunot maintained the hope that pedagogical restriction would lead to political contentment; he shared Hardy's "out-of-balance conviction" that curriculum could shape politics and culture, and bring an end to Muslim students' vain desire for increased integration and opportunity within the French system.[45]

Finally, the Bac

In the 1930s, despite Brunot's reluctance, the DIP gradually changed its approach to Muslim education. As anticolonial movements grew in North Africa and the Middle East during the interwar period, it became increasingly important for the DIP to maintain the support of French-educated Muslim elites. This meant that the discontents of the Anciens élèves could no longer be brushed aside or dismissed as inauthentic. Notwithstanding Brunot's exhortations to teachers, the colonial regime could not wait for pedagogues to indoctrinate a new generation of more amiable collaborators; the current generation had to be placated.

The first concession to the Anciens élèves' demands for increased educational integration and opportunity came on 16 May 1930, when it was declared that the baccalaureate would be offered at the *collèges musulmans*. The French baccalaureate immediately became the preferred goal of the *collège* students, who henceforth saw the old "adapted" DESM as inferior, since it provided no access to metropolitan higher education. However, the baccalaureate was instituted in such a way that it became extremely difficult to obtain in the *collèges*.

In 1929 the Anciens élèves and the AEMNAF had asked that the DESM be made equivalent to the baccalaureate. This proposal would have allowed a small but significant number of Moroccans access to metropolitan education via the current *collège* programs (with some improvements). Instead, the DIP required students to take the regular French baccalaureate exam, but the *collège* programs were not transformed to match the *lycée* curriculum. Instead, the DIP maintained the doctrine of providing students with a "double culture" of French and Arabic. This made the route to the baccalaureate exceedingly difficult, because students had to complete the requirements for the baccalaureate while still fulfilling the *collège* requirements in Arabic, Islamic religion, and Muslim law, although Arabic instruction was reduced to five hours per week. The resulting program involved significantly more class time than that followed in the *lycées*: thirty-five hours per week in the *collèges*, on average, compared to twenty-five in the *lycées*. As if the modern baccalaureate were not difficult enough, students at the Collège Moulay Idriss in Fez were encouraged to take the more difficult classical baccalaureate, which required Latin. As a result, the baccalaureate was achieved only by the most determined and talented minority; the rest were forced to settle for the old "adapted" *collège* degrees. In 1933 only four *collège* students succeeded in obtaining the baccalaureate.[46] Perhaps as a result, Muslim families in Fez and Rabat put increasing pressure on the authorities to admit their children to the French *lycées*.[47]

In its immediate practical effect, the introduction of the baccalaureate at the *collèges* was only a tiny step toward increasing access by Moroccan Muslims to opportunities for success within a French-dominated society. Baccalaureate or not, careers in the French administration remained closed to Moroccan Muslims. As head of Muslim Education, Brunot continued to believe that the key to educational success was the recognition and preservation of ethnic difference. He urged teachers to read the ethnography in the *Bulletin de l'Enseignement*, along with the work of racial theorists such as

Gobineau, in hopes of minimizing the assimilatory effects of French schooling. Well into the 1930s, Brunot and the *collège* directors continued to resist the pressure to create genuine parity of educational opportunity for Moroccan Muslims.[48] By this time, however, it was becoming evident that the assimilation so feared by Brunot was not in fact the greatest threat to French power in Morocco.

8. Nests of Nationalism

They think of us as their dogs. | Abdelqader Tazi, 1923

In this country there has lived and still lives a "people." | Georges Hardy, 1925

In September 1923 a young man named Abdelqader Tazi was elected president of the Fez *collège*'s organization of former students. The son of the sultan's delegate (*naïb*) in Tangiers, Tazi was a twenty-nine-year-old former *collège* student who was continuing his education in Fez by studying at the Qarawiyyin. There was initially no sign that Tazi would become a problem for the authorities. Paul Marty, the school director charged with supervising the Anciens élèves, found the organization's elections somewhat ridiculous but harmless: an "amusing spectacle." Marty praised the members for their enthusiasm and described Tazi, the winner, as "a boy not well read in French, but learned in Arabic; intelligent, reserved, a bit self-effacing perhaps."[1] As such, Tazi was the ideal *collège* student, according to what Fanny Colonna has called "the principle of proper distance": well grounded in traditional Moroccan society, and intelligent, but not so at home in French as to pose a threat to the "social distance" that colonial relations demanded.[2]

By mid-October, however, Tazi was identified as a threat to the colonial state, a man "naturally predisposed to rebellion against all authority," a rebel even within his own family.³ General Decherf, commander for the region of Fez, informed Lyautey that Tazi was attempting to use his status as president of the Anciens élèves and the son of a high *makhzan* official to transform the student organization from an organ of pro-French collaboration into a center of anti-French discontent. Tazi was not yet a nationalist in 1923, and no Moroccan nationalist movement would emerge in that year, but he had alarmed Decherf by sending him a rambling letter which began as a passionate but respectful petition for the redress of grievances and then rose to a defiant crescendo.

Tazi's letter to Decherf illuminates the ambiguities of anticolonial sentiments among young, French-educated upper-class Muslim men in the 1920s. Tazi's complaints diverged sharply from the prevalent demands of elite Moroccan Muslims for educational parity and career opportunities, and reflected the ways in which those demands had failed to address the concerns of young Muslims like Tazi. Tazi's trembling outrage was occasioned by "the contempt, the humiliation, the oppression, and the vexations" to which the Muslims of Fez were subjected on a regular basis by the European population:

> For a long time, we have been patient.
>
> For a long time, we have waited for these people who humiliate us to spontaneously cease to do so.
>
> We have experienced from them only redoubled arrogance and obstinacy.
>
> Most of the French who inhabit the city cannot pass through the streets without unjustly striking or publicly insulting, and for the smallest reason, the Muslims whom they encounter, whoever they might be, in the presence of indigenes and foreigners of all origins.
>
> They think of us as their dogs and strike us with their feet; they always throw at us these words "bicot" and "dirty Jew,"

these words that can only be pronounced by the vilest creatures of God.⁴

Tazi claimed that the offenses against the Muslim population were too numerous to recount: "I would like to give you examples, but I am overwhelmed and my pen shakes, so many examples arrive in my mind." He therefore limited himself to two concrete cases. The first concerned a dispute over water rights. French settlers' disruption of traditional and local arrangements for the division of water for irrigation and personal use was a cause of significant hardship for the Moroccan population, especially the poor. Tazi described how a certain Mr. Barraux, director of the Compagnie Marocaine, refused to let representatives of the Muslim community in his quarter enter his land in order to redirect the flow of water and divide it among the local residents. On one occasion Barraux reportedly responded to a visit from the *muezzin* of the local mosque by striking and kicking the man severely. Tazi called Barraux a "ferocious lion" and portrayed the event not just as an assault, or even as a case of economic injustice, but as a religious affront, since Muslims deprived of water could not properly perform their ritual ablutions.

Nevertheless, Tazi's description of the Barraux water incident was rather matter-of-fact compared to his descriptions of the verbal insults that he and his friends had personally endured. Of these, he related one in particular:

> On October 4, young Haj Larbi ben Abdeljalil, son of the pasha's *khalifat*, who is part of the elite of our cultivated youth, was passing down the rue du Douh, in the company of the contrôleur de l'enregistrement (Mr. Andrieux), his wife, and the director.
> Animals that were passing through obliged Haj Larbi to step back. Without realizing it, he pushed lightly a foreigner who found herself behind him, a Dutchwoman, Madame Mesker, who was with her husband. She set about insulting him and calling him "dirty Jewish pig."

This very gentle young man wanted to respond to the insults, as anyone else would have done, but the Muslim education he had received prevented him from taking to task a foreigner of lower status and of the poorest education.

The hostile encounter between Larbi ben Abdeljalil and Madame Mesker was not an isolated incident, and General Decherf acknowledged that some settlers did indeed treat Muslims with disdain. However, Decherf emphasized that this was a two-way street and claimed that more often it was foreigners who were abused, as everyone from old people and women to French notables was subjected to "the arrogance and the bad attitude of the young people for whom Si Abdelkader Tazi has made himself the spokesman."[5]

This apparently mutual hostility reflected not only the tension between Moroccan Muslims and foreign settlers but also tensions between different elements of colonialist culture in Lyautey's protectorate. Tazi sought to defend a class hierarchy that was rooted in Moroccan Muslim society and which was supported by Lyautey's discourse. Lyautey had always opposed the elevation of low-class *colons* above the native elite, just as he had discouraged the French from seeking to alter gender roles within Muslim society. Tazi, the son of a high *makhzan* official, expressed shock that even a high-class Frenchman like Barraux, director of the Compagnie Marocaine, had conducted himself so poorly: "If an action so ugly has been committed by this important person, who considers himself among the elite of his compatriots, what can one expect from the French of low class?" However, the insults to Larbi ben Abdeljalil were particularly objectionable because they came from a person of lower social class, in the presence of three of Abdeljalil's high-status French acquaintances. There also seems to have been a gendered element: the insult was more grievous because it came from *une étrangère*, and in the presence of the wife of the *contrôleur*.

In 1916, Lyautey had promised the Moroccan elite that he would preserve their status "so that rank and hierarchy are preserved and respected, so that people and things stay in their ancient places, so that those who are the current leaders command, so that others obey."[6] However, this emphasis on preserving the class hierarchy in Morocco conflicted with the ubiquitous belief in racial hierarchy, a belief buttressed by European discourses of anti-Semitism (extended to Arab Muslims) as well as broader discourses of racism and orientalism. As David Prochaska has noted, "the maximum points of friction occur where ethnic and racial divisions are exacerbated by socioeconomic ones; in other words, for those at the top of indigenous society and those at the bottom of settler society."[7] Moreover, Lyautey's personal emphasis on the preservation of class status within Moroccan society was undermined by the official emphasis on ethnological discourse, which produced a tendency to identify generalized characteristics of ethnic groups across class lines. Such discourse was infused with the belief in European cultural and psychological superiority (despite the occasional statement to the contrary). The result was friction between the class status of the Moroccan notable and the ethnic status of the European.

Tazi's letter also reflected the tension between his resentment of French domination and his apparent acceptance of elements of the colonialist ideology. Tazi echoed French discourse about French civilization and the *mission civilisatrice*, and asked only that the French hold to the high standard of conduct that was expected of them ("From what quarter, my General, comes this tyranny? Is this evidence of correctness and humanity?"). He also understood and accepted the role of intermediary that the French had designated for the students of the *collèges* and the Anciens élèves. He spoke of "the essential task to which we have set ourselves, and which should extend to dissipating the misunderstandings existing between the French and our fathers." Rather than reject this role, Tazi complained that European hostility was undermining the ability of the French-educated Moroccan elite to promote the cause of the French:

What line of conduct should we follow vis-à-vis our fathers who weep in secret, at home, due to behavior they encounter every day in their relations with certain Frenchmen?

My General, you have often told us that you desire to see us heart and soul with you. How can you ask this from those who are the butt of such humiliations?

Rather than reject the colonialist discourse of the protectorate, Tazi merely complained that the European population was violating Lyautey's principles. However, the letter took on a more defiant tone, and a more nationalist and Islamist argument, as he worked himself into an apparent rage:

To these French (those who humiliate us), we say this as a warning.

Be assured that we alone are the people of this country—and that is the reality—and that you are only with us as guests charged with a civilizing mission.

The error that is at the root of your base and miserable actions comes from your thoughts to the contrary.

Do not forget, where just, that we are Muslims, that this forms a community very attached to its religion, to its country, to its home, and that if they had attained the degree of civilization of other peoples, you would find them among the toughest and most refractory.

The Muslims do not accept injustice; they refuse to perish until the last, by the power of their unity. This is written in their history and constitutes a known aspect of their character.

Three forces are combined in us.

Arab nobility.

The Islamic spirit.

The sentiment that we are in our own country.

I address this complaint in my name and in the name of humanity.[8]

In his conclusion, Tazi returned, more or less, to the position of a respectful petitioner. However, although he finished by celebrating France and French justice and expressed confidence that Decherf would make things right, this confidence was combined with a veiled threat against the general's eternal soul:

> I had first hoped to address Marshal Lyautey, but it is enough to write you.
>
> I hope that you will do what is necessary and that you will make visible the true French justice that we know.
>
> Know that you will be responsible for what happens to us on this earth the day that you answer before the Unique, the All-Powerful, for great and small sins. You know only to respond.
>
> I beg you to believe, my General, in all my respect.
>
> I am ready, when you desire it, to render myself before you to give you all useful information or clarification.
>
> In conclusion, I say, "Vive la France and Vive Sa Justice."

This was not a revolutionary manifesto. Tazi addressed his grievances to the region's French military commander, and he made no attempt to rally the masses. His discourse suggests that French-educated Muslims attempted to derive political leverage from their designated role as intermediaries between the French and the traditional society of their elders. This was a strategy that aimed to make the most of the opportunities available to upper-class Moroccan Muslims within the context of a colonial field shaped by Lyautey's associationalism. In 1923 Tazi held to this strategy of accommodation, but he obviously found it extremely unsatisfactory. Collaboration with the French leadership did not shield the Moroccan elite from the racism of the colonists in the street; nor did it shield their poorer Muslim brethren from the economic disruptions caused by colonialism.

Whether or not Tazi's letter was composed, as he claimed, in a fit of psychological distress, it expressed a defiance and a sense of national identity based on Arabness, Islam, and territorial nativism. In the long term, this discourse of defiance would lead Moroccan nationalists to a more commanding position than collaboration could offer them. In the short term, however, Tazi's uncertain combination of accommodation and rebelliousness led to a loss of status. His tentative defiance was sufficient to alarm General Decherf, who initiated an investigation. As French authorities made their displeasure clear, Abdelqader Tazi was denounced by many of his peers, including the Anciens élèves' vice-president and former president, and by his own brother, Mohammed Tazi. Mohammed Tazi, however, shifted the blame from Abdelqader to a circle of malcontents who had allegedly corrupted his brother; this circle included the future nationalist leader Mohammed al-Kholti. On 15 October 1923, Abdelqader Tazi was discreetly exiled from Fez and sent to Rabat, and Decherf recommended a tightening of French control over the Anciens élèves.

The expulsion of Abdelqader Tazi did not silence the Anciens élèves. But the demands of the Anciens élèves in the late 1920s did not yet publicly address the concerns raised by Tazi in 1923; nor did they echo his rhetoric. Instead, these organizations continued to pursue the goals of increased educational parity and more freedom to integrate into French society. This strategy accommodated French rule while resisting the Lyautist vision for colonial society. Not all graduates of the colonial schools found this strategy satisfactory, however.

A New Opposition

In 1925, two years after Tazi was expelled from Fez, a "secret society" was formed there by a group of *collège* students seeking a forum for political discussion and intellectual inquiry free from the surveillance of the DIP. Its members included Tazi's friend Mohammed al-Kholti and Mohammed al-Fasi, who would later become independent Morocco's first minister of education. This group soon fused with a clandestine group of Qarawiyyin students led by Alal al-Fasi. The following year in Rabat, Tazi joined a group of French-educated Moroccans to form a secret society together with several young men who had received a traditional Islamic education. A third group was formed in Tetuan, in the Spanish zone.[9]

These three secret societies produced the leadership for the nationalist movement. In 1930, in order to organize protest against the French Berber policy, approximately two dozen dissidents grouped themselves into a new organization called the Zawiya, which directed a network called the Taifa in cities throughout Morocco. These dissidents began to mobilize the Anciens élèves organizations and launched a press campaign in Morocco, in France, and in the Arab world. Zawiya funded the publication of a Moroccan nationalist journal in Paris, *Maghreb*, which appeared in 1932. The following year, Zawiya also sponsored the first nationalist newspaper in Morocco, *Action du Peuple*. Both of these papers were published in French; in the case of the latter (briefly renamed *Volonté du Peuple* from December 1933 to March 1934) this was because the French refused permission for an Arabic-language newspaper.

By early 1934, Louis Brunot and the DIP's director, Jean Gotteland, had become alarmed that nationalists had taken over the various Anciens élèves organizations throughout Morocco. The Anciens élèves were now seeking to band together in a national federation, were sending financial support to Moroccan nationalists in Paris, and were reading *Maghreb* and the works of the Lebanese pan-Islamist Shakib Arslan. Meanwhile, Zawiya had founded a Comité d'action marocaine (Kutlat al-Amal al Watani, lit., "national action bloc") to develop a formal proposal that would be presented to the French authorities.[10]

These Moroccan dissidents of the early 1930s did not call for the French to withdraw from Morocco, but they did demand that the French honor the terms of the Treaty of Fez. This accommodation of French power made them no less nationalist, however; their vision for Morocco reflected the European notion of a modern nation-state: a national people, united within a bounded territory, under a sovereign governing authority. According to the Moroccan nationalist reading, the Treaty of Fez committed the French to assist in the reestablishment of such a state. As the nationalists explained in *Tempête sur le*

Maroc, a pseudonymous tract published in Paris in 1931, the French protectorate was a tool "to reestablish the spiritual and temporal authority of the sultan throughout all the territory of the Sharifian empire."[11] *Maghreb* reminded the French authorities that "Morocco is, in effect, according to all the international treaties currently in force, a free country."[12]

Yet the reality of French power meant that the nationalists were forced to adopt a "gradualist course."[13] Consequently, the proposal presented by the Comité d'action marocaine in December 1934 to Foreign Minister Pierre Laval, Resident-General Henri Ponsot, and Sultan Sidi Mohammed was not a declaration of independence but a *Plan de réformes marocaines*. This *Plan* stated that, "in making public today our program, our wishes and our aspirations, we would like to believe that we are contributing to the preparation of this good and useful policy which alone is capable of leading the Moroccan people in the evolution which it hopes to realize with the constant help of the French Nation."[14] Nevertheless, despite this accommodation of the protectorate, the *Plan*'s authors portrayed Morocco as a nation and "people" and demanded that Morocco be treated according to its rightful status as treaty partner rather than as a colony. A decade later, the nationalists would become bolder and demand immediate independence: *istiqlal*.

Genealogies of Moroccan Nationalism

Discussions of the origins of Moroccan nationalism often focus on the influence of Salafi Islamic reformism and pan-Arab nationalism. Others argue for the roots of nationalism in the reform efforts of the *makhzan* in the late nineteenth and early twentieth centuries.[15] However, it has also been recognized that the Moroccan nationalist political discourse was infused with European ideas and bore the stamp of Muslim dissidents who had been educated in French-run schools.

Benedict Anderson has suggested that, however complex the origins of anticolonial nationalism might be, "the immediate genealogy should be traced to the imaginings of the colonial state."¹⁶ Stated thus, Anderson's hypothesis is too unequivocal, but there can be no doubt that the terrain from which nationalism grew was shaped profoundly by the colonial state and that "much of what appears to be resistance by local groups to the colonial state is, in fact, inseparable from that state and unattainable without using its resources."¹⁷ To note the role of the colonizers in shaping anticolonial resistance is not to deny agency to the colonized but merely to recognize that the imperial influence permeated every part of the colonial terrain. As Georges Balandier has observed, it is a characteristic of colonial situations that "colonial society, the seat of domination, is not separable from the colonized society, the object of domination."¹⁸ Notwithstanding the distortions and confusions that characterized the colonizers' and colonized's perceptions of each other, colonial situations consisted of inextricable interactions between these groups, and the cultures of the colonizers and the colonized must be seen as the product of this interaction.

Homi Bhabha has argued that resistance occurs precisely because the colonizers are unable to maintain their separation from the colonized, and vice versa: "If the effect of colonial power is seen to be the *production* of hybridization rather than the noisy command of colonialist authority or the silent repression of native traditions, then an important change of perspective occurs. It reveals the ambivalence at the source of traditional uncertainty, that turns the discursive conditions of dominance into the grounds of intervention."¹⁹ As the colonized were transformed by the colonial situation, the agendas of the colonizers were simultaneously and ubiquitously transformed by the resistance of the colonized. The Lyautist approach to colonialism emerged from this mutual transformation, reformulating the imperial agenda in response to the blurring of lines separating the French from their French-speaking colonial subjects in Algeria, Senegal, and Indochina.

Some twentieth-century anti-imperialists (Franz Fanon, e.g.) believed that the colonized could escape this process of hybridization, uprooting themselves from the colonial terrain. In this view, "the hegemonic discourse is ultimately abandoned as scorched earth when a different discourse, forged in the process of disobedience and combat, occupying new, never-colonized and 'utopian' territory, and prefiguring other relationships, values and aspirations, is enunciated."[20] Yet this reflects the prescriptive discourse of anticolonial rhetoric rather than an empirical description of events. As Bhabha has written, "The place of difference and otherness, or the space of the adversarial . . . is never entirely on the outside or implacably oppositional. It is a pressure, and a presence, that acts constantly, if unevenly, along the entire boundary of authorization."[21] The relationship between domination and resistance was always intimate, both when resistance took the form of the inarticulate avoidance and noncompliance of the subaltern and also when the dominance of the colonizers was challenged by the eloquence of men like Blaise Diagne, Grand Vizier El Mokri, or Morocco's budding nationalists.

Morocco's colonial schools were intended to control and regulate this intimacy, preventing contaminating exchanges of cultural and political ideas, but this was futile. Perhaps the greatest error in the Hardy-Brunot approach to education was the belief that French schools were capable of controlling the culture and ambitions of young Moroccans by parceling out only the knowledge "adapted" to the students' alleged psychology and the needs of the colonial state. French educational policy in Morocco was explicitly opposed to the transmission of Western liberal ideas, in hopes of forestalling the formation of a class of dissident "*évolués*" like the groups that had appeared in Senegal and Algeria; curricula for Moroccan Muslims were designed to prevent the transmission of republican ideas about self-government or the Rights of Man. Yet the colonial leadership did not have a monopoly on the intellectual formation of the students. Even if the teachers could be persuaded to comply with the official policies (a question that caused Hardy and Brunot considerable anxiety), the careful restriction of schoolhouse discourse could not control the ideas that students, former students, and non-students encountered outside the classroom. The discursive influences on the early Moroccan nationalists were therefore legion.

By the early 1920s, the DIP's urban students and former students were increasingly in contact with French society and with ideas and events throughout North Africa and the Middle East. The colonial administration was well aware of this, but it believed that French supervision could prevent undesired effects. From 1922 to 1925, Lyautey and the DIP had even organized annual trips to France, lasting five to eight weeks, in which a small number of students and young notables were taken to Marseille (with a visit to the Colonial Exposition in 1922), Bordeaux, and Paris. The days these students spent in the capital included visits to the Sorbonne and to the presses of *Matin*, *Petit Journal*, and *l'Intransigeant*. Lyautey's decision to bring these students to France reflected his confidence that cultural hybridity could be prevented by colonial paternalism. The chaperones, including Paul Marty and Charles Sallefranques, were confident that they had control over the student's impressions, exerting "intellectual hygiene" in Paris just as they did in Fez. However, the trip to Paris offered opportunities and freedoms otherwise closed off to *collège* students—including the opportunity to do the foxtrot in a Parisian nightclub.[22]

Meanwhile, back in Morocco, students and former students of the schools for Muslims were exposed to a wide range of influences from the metropole and from across North Africa and the Middle East. According to General Decherf and Mohammed Tazi, Abdelqader Tazi had been politicized by the influence of Mohammed al-Kholti and several other students who had returned from Egypt with foreign ideas. Since the beginning of the protectorate, the French authorities had expressed trepidation about upper-class Moroccan families sending their sons east to Egypt, Syria, or Palestine for higher education, for fear that pan-Islamic and pan-Arab influences might find their way into Morocco. However, Moroccans did not have to travel abroad in order to encounter these ideas. In the 1920s, urban Moroccans were reading and discussing newspapers from France, the Middle East, and Tunisia. Theater provided another medium of political discourse and intellectual exchange. Inspired by a touring theater troupe made up of Egyptians, Tunisians, and Moroccans in 1923, Anciens élèves groups in several Moroccan cities began giving performances of plays in Arabic. These plays ranged from *Romeo and Juliet* to *Salah al-Din al-Ayyubi and the Conquest of Andalusia*.[23] Urban Moroccan Muslims, whether French-educated or not, were living in a cultural environment increasingly infused with discourses and images from Europe and from the Middle East. Despite the best efforts of Hardy and Brunot, young Moroccans were acutely aware of not only French republicanism but also religious, nationalist, and anticolonial movements in Turkey, Syria, Palestine, and throughout the Maghreb.

Despite French fears that the imprudent declarations of Woodrow Wilson and the example of the Arab Revolt would inspire Arab nationalism, in the early 1920s language-based ethnic nationalism was less influential than was the Islamic reform movement Salafiyya. Salafiyya advocated Islamic renewal through education, and Salafi-inspired free schools became major competitors of the colonial schools. Theologically, Salafiyya opposed Morocco's heterodox folk practices involving reverence for *murabitin* (holy men) and the *turuq* (sing., *tariqa*, Sufi brotherhoods). Salafiyya was not itself a nationalist ideology, but in the Moroccan context nationalism and Salafiyya were mutually accommodating, if only because prominent *turuq* like the Kittaniyya had become some of the colonial state's most important collaborators.[24]

French Schools as Nests of Nationalists

The Moroccan nationalist movement was not solely a product of the French colonial schools. Many nationalist leaders had emerged from the traditional system or the Salafi schools, including Hassan Bouyad, a major contributor to the *Plan de réformes*, and Alal al-Fasi, who would lead the dominant nationalist faction after the Comité d'Action Marocaine split in 1936. Yet most of the nationalists who took the lead in shaping the nationalist agenda through *Maghreb*, *Action du Peuple*, and the *Plan de réformes* had studied at the *collèges musulmans*—most notably, Omar Abdeljalil (editor of *Maghreb*), Mohamed Hassan Ouazzani (editor of *Action du Peuple*), Ahmed Balafrej, Mohammed al-Kholti, and Mohamed Lyazidi.[25] Students who had received a French-sponsored education were also disproportionately represented in the political parties that succeeded the Comité d'Action Marocaine, including the parties led by Alal al-Fasi (Hizb al Watani and then Istiqlal) as well as the smaller parties created by Ouazzani (Hizb al-Amal al Watani and the Parti Démocratique de l'Indépendence).[26]

The prominence of French-educated Moroccans within the nationalist movement suggests an intimate relationship between DIP education for Muslims and nationalist dissidence. This relationship might be analyzed as a structural problem. The DIP created an allegedly elite educational track that provided students with a second-rate education and limited career opportunities; this led to discontent and eventually rebellion among former students. Unlike the *makhzan* officials, religious brotherhoods, and rural *qaïds* who shared power with the French, the *collège* students and Anciens élèves had little stake in continued collaboration with a regime that refused them access to such power. In this view, the nationalist movement represented an opportunity for the French-educated pseudo-elite to become the true ruling class in Morocco. However, such an analysis offers little insight into the ideas of the nationalist movement that emerged, that is, the discursive content that gave the movement cohesion and the power of persuasion.

The discourse of Moroccan nationalism was in some respects antagonistic to the official discourse of DIP pedagogy, as French–educated Moroccans drew upon republican, socialist, and Islamic ideas to react against what the schools taught them. However, there was also a complementary relationship between the conservative, ethnologically driven ideology promoted by the DIP and nationalism's emphasis on cultural unity and the denunciation of assimilation. In the early 1920s the French leadership in Morocco had believed that the primary threats to French hegemony were Bolshevism and pan-Islamism; pan-Arab nationalism was seen as a lesser danger, and the cultivation of a specifically Moroccan identity was seen as a bulwark against all three. Consequently, DIP pedagogical theory asserted that the assimilation of Moroccans to French culture was undesirable, that Moroccan culture and traditions ought to be protected, and even—despite the French Berber policy—that a distinct and unitary Moroccan character existed that was to be preserved and actively promoted by the state. On these matters, Morocco's emerging nationalists were in agreement with Hardy and Brunot. While some aspects of colonial discourse incited a nationalist counterreaction, others complemented and reinforced the nationalist conception of Morocco. Decades of anti-assimilationist French colonial discourse and education provided Moroccan nationalists with a repository of rhetorical devices that could be turned against the colonizers.

The anti-assimilationism of the educational system facilitated the alliance between French-educated Muslims and Muslims from traditional and Salafi educational backgrounds. Colonial education had trained students at the French *collège musulmans* in classical Arabic and had infused them with notions of a Moroccan identity tied to Arabic and Islam. *Collège* students had joined forces with the Salafi movement in the early 1920s, creating a situation quite different from that in Algeria at the time, where Young Algerians demanding the rights of Frenchmen stood apart from the Islamic reformers of the Association of Algerian Ulema. Salafi influence was evident when Morocco's Anciens élèves began to demand the expansion of schooling for Muslim girls, a sharp departure from the attitude of the previous generation of Moroccan elites. In addition, *collège* students had adopted the Salafi hostility to the *turuq*, and in 1928 *collège* students joined with reformist Qarawiyyin students to denounce Kittani and demand reform of the Qarawiyyin curriculum. As an Islamic movement that promoted modernization and attacked superstition,

Salafiyya had much appeal to young French-educated Moroccans who wanted to embrace a Muslim identity yet distinguish themselves from the "barbarous, savage practices" of the masses.[27]

The influence of Salafiyya among French-educated Muslims did not initially cause much alarm among the French. Paul Marty, who advocated a French-backed Islamic renaissance centered at the *collège* in Fez, was particularly pleased to see the interest that the Anciens élèves took in the Salafi *écoles rénovées*.[28] It is therefore unsurprising that in 1923, with Marty as the school director, Abdelqader Tazi believed that he could appeal to a French general by invoking "the Islamic spirit"; relations among the French rulers, Salafiyya, and youthful dissidence were still ambiguous.

The influence of French republicanism, socialism, and Arab nationalism among Moroccan students increased after Lyautey's departure in 1925, when a trickle of students were allowed to go to France to study. Although by 1931 there were still less than a dozen Moroccans studying there, among them were several future leaders of the nationalist movement: Ahmed Balafrej, Mohammed al-Fasi, Mekki Naciri, Mohamed al-Kholti, and Mohamed Hassan Ouazzani. The Moroccans in France remained in contact with the Anciens élèves groups and formed a link between Morocco's student movement and Tunisian and Algerian reformers and nationalists in Paris. Moroccan students in Paris also formed relationships with French socialists. Beginning in 1930, the socialist writer Daniel Guérin lent his support to the Moroccan anti-imperialist cause, and in 1932 Robert-Jean Longuet became the nominal editor of *Maghreb*. Although the French socialist establishment objected to the bourgeois and national characteristics of the Moroccan movement, the nationalist press reflected the influence of socialism as well as republicanism. Living in France did not necessarily bring a more secular orientation, however. Life in Paris brought these Moroccan students into personal contact with Shakib Arslan, who provided the young dissidents with a vital link to international anti-imperial Islamist movements.[29]

This analysis of the various "foreign" elements that shaped Moroccan nationalism should not, however, obscure the local nature of the grievances expressed in 1923 by Abdelqader Tazi. Although expressions of discontent were shaped by imported discourses, Morocco's budding nationalists were driven by grievances that were deeply personal. The imposition of a new racial hierarchy over the existing hierarchy in Morocco produced affronts to the dignity of Moroccan elites, who yearned for new idioms through which to express their discontent. The power and wealth of the Tazi family could not shield its scion from the insults of the lowliest Europeans, or from the psychic anguish that could make even a grand notable feel like "the wretched of the earth." This was certainly not a unique phenomenon in Morocco; similar affronts were producing similar responses throughout the colonized world. But the fires of discontent found their fuel locally, even as they were shaped by discourses that had become global.

The Nationalist Platform

The nationalist press of the early 1930s and the 1934 *Plan de réformes* addressed a wide range of topics, some of which have no obvious bearing on the role of French colonial education. Economic reforms were proposed to improve Moroccans' standard of living through tax reform and through economic growth, which was to be achieved by means of natural-resource exploitation and import tariffs. The nationalists called for an end to "budgetary and fiscal favoritism" that directed revenues from Moroccans toward expenditures that benefited the European community.[30] They also demanded that the colonial state bring an end to the expropriation of land for colonization and institute a variety of agricultural reforms designed to improve the condition of the Moroccan farmer. Not all of these items conflicted with the ideology of Lyautey and Hardy: Lyautey had always been wary of the impact of settler colonialism in Morocco, and Hardy had preached the development (*mise en valeur*) of Morocco's human resources. However, most of the nationalists' economic recommendations reflected the influence of European socialism, which they had become intimately acquainted with in France, not in the colonial schools. For example, the *Plan de réformes* called for social services for the poor, elderly, and unemployed as well as legislation on worker rights, including an eight-hour workday, annual vacations, improvements in salaries for Moroccan workers, the construction of worker housing, and the legalization of unions and mutual assistance organizations.[31]

Many of nationalists' political reforms directly attacked the fundamentals of Lyautism. In *Action du Peuple*, Ouazzani denounced a French colonial culture that betrayed the principles "de la France de la Révolution libératrice et humanitaire."[32] The *Plan de réformes* objected that French rule was "racial" in that the authorities made clear distinctions between Europeans and Moroccans. Denouncing the "politics of two weights and two measures," the *Plan* demanded that the French "renounce the politics of racial privilege which has inspired up to now all legislation and administrative organization."[33] This attacked the very foundation of colonial rule in Morocco, which was based on the maintenance of ethnic distinctions and the administrative separation of Europeans, Moroccan Jews, and arabophone and berberophone Moroccan Muslims. The *Plan* also called for an end to French rule through the collaboration of the *grands qaïds*, who had become the cornerstone of the French policy of political association (and who would become even more important as the sultan became sympathetic to the nationalists). The power of the *qaïds* was to be replaced by elected municipal councils and, in rural areas, by provisional advisory councils. A list of "private and public liberties" called for guarantees of freedom of movement, association, and expression and for prohibitions against corporal punishment and unwarranted search and seizure.[34] These republican political and legal reforms were anathema to the doctrines of Lyautey and Hardy.

Some of the nationalist educational proposals were likewise derived from republican models, in direct opposition to the policy and philosophy of the DIP. The nationalists called for an end to the "oil stain" approach to education, which aimed to influence Moroccan society through the education of a minority. Instead, the *Plan* demanded free and obligatory primary instruction for all Moroccan children. Recognizing that universal schooling could not be implemented all at once, the nationalists called for the establishment of regional teacher-training centers. Influenced by Salafiyya and by the Egyptian reformer Qasim Amin, the nationalists called for the construction of schools for Muslim girls in every city.[35] Similar goals would be soon be adopted by the DIP under the Noguès Residency (1936–43) and the Fourth Republic, although near-universal primary schooling for boys would not be realized until long after independence (and for girls, much longer).

In lieu of Lyautey's doctrine of segregating education according to social status in order to preserve the privileges of the traditional elites, the nationalists called for "the unification of the programs of modern instruction for all Moroccan Muslims, without territorial considerations, nor distinction based on social condition."[36] This would have eliminated the distinctions in education for Muslims between urban and rural schools and between the non-elite urban schools and the *écoles des fils de notables*. In *Action du Peuple*, Abdelqader Tazi demanded that European schools be open to Muslims and lamented the departure of Immarigeon, the *collège* director removed in 1922 for his desire to open the *lycées* to more Muslim students.[37] The nationalists thus sought to eliminate certain segregationist barriers that were fundamental to the DIP's commitment to preserving ethnic differences and traditional social hierarchies. The elimination of class and regional distinctions would be too radical even for the post-Lyautist policies of the Popular Front and the Fourth Republic, although these later French governments were willing to reduce the ethnic segregation of the Moroccan elite.

The nationalists not only pressed for the reform of the structure of protectorate education but also sought a liberalization of its content. The Hardy-Brunot approach was denounced as "obscurantist," a fairly accurate adjective for the DIP's policy of restricting the dissemination of knowledge to Moroccan Muslims.[38] Under Hardy and Brunot, curricular policy had always been as much about what was *not* to be taught as about what should be taught. *Action du Peuple* reiterated the demands of the Anciens élèves that education for Muslims lead to liberal professions such as medicine or engineering, and mocked Brunot's fears that post-secondary study in Europe might "alienate" Moroccans from their ancestral traditions, leading to atheism and miscegenation.[39] The *Plan de réformes* quoted Hardy's statement from 1920 (the same statement quoted by Brunot in his 1934 teacher's handbook) that "politics in the current European sense of the word is unsuitable for the work of progress(!) which is being accomplished here. Consequently, let us not think of the emancipation of the Moroccan citizen, nor of the slave, nor of the liberty of the woman."[40] The sarcastic exclamation point was added by the authors of the *Plan*. By presenting Hardy's statement as a piece of compromising evidence, the nationalists condemned the proscription of republican ideas from Morocco's schools, rejecting Hardy's notion that these ideas were dangerously alien to the Moroccan soul. The *Plan* also condemned the DIP's attempts to artificially maintain authentic Moroccan culture through the regulation of crafts production by the Service des arts indigènes. In crafts and in ideas, the nationalists claimed a right to change their society as they saw fit, in direct opposition to French attempts to define and mandate the preservation of "retrograde" characteristics.

However, while the nationalists denounced Hardy, they celebrated Lyautey. In fact, the *Plan de réformes* called for a renaissance of Lyautism. Despite the *Plan*'s criticisms of the racial basis of colonial policy and administrative organization, its authors overtly embraced the Lyautist doctrine that religious and ethnic traditions ought to be preserved. The nationalists (like the French) were very selective in their application of this doctrine of cultural preservation, but they explicitly called for a return to Lyautey's principles. The nationalists recognized that Lyautey had intended the *collèges* to teach an Arabic-based curriculum, although they neglected to mention the fact that this policy had been abandoned in the face of Moroccan demands for more French.[41] The *Plan* denounced French rule in Morocco in terms similar to those used by Lyautey and Hardy in their criticisms of French rule in Algeria: "IT IS ASSIMILATIONIST: it is inspired by direct rule and translates into an organized struggle, sometimes camouflaged, against our institutions, our Arab culture, and our traditions."[42] To the extent that this was true, it was so in opposition to the principles of Lyautey and Hardy, and the *Plan* quoted at length Lyautey's pledges to preserve the customs and religion of Morocco as well as the authority of the sultan. One may question the sincerity of the nationalists' apparent affection for Lyautey, of course. Nationalist discourse would later emphasize the gap between Lyautey's words and his actions.[43] Nevertheless, the nationalists agreed with Lyautey on a fundamental point: Arab and Muslim culture was to be preserved in Morocco through state intervention.

The nationalist platform tended to be illiberal with regard to questions of cultural and national identity, echoing the ideas of ethnic differentiation that Hardy had adopted from Maurice Delafosse. The *Plan de réformes* called for a prohibition of the acquisition of French citizenship by Moroccan Muslims and Jews, and it advocated the maintenance of ethnic differentiation in primary education.[44] Although some Moroccan children were to be allowed to attend schools for Europeans, the nationalists desired to maintain a segregated Muslim system in order to prevent the deracination of the Muslim population. The French baccalaureate had been made available in the *collèges* in 1930, but the nationalists called for a distinct Moroccan baccalaureate that would provide access to the French university system without sacrificing Moroccan culture. Omar Abdeljalil explained that this was necessary in order to fulfill Lyautey's dream of using the *collèges* to create a governing elite; Abdeljalil claimed that Lyautey himself had desired a Moroccan baccalaureate.[45] Proposals to merge the *collèges musulmans* with the *lycée* system had begun to appear in the leftist French press, but these proposals were vehemently opposed by the

Anciens Élèves organizations and by the nationalist press; a *Volonté du Peuple* article by Abdeljalil denounced this assimilationist "absorption" as an invitation to cultural "suicide."[46]

The nationalists were thus in agreement with the official DIP rejection of secular and universal schooling and with the desire to use the schools to maintain a distinct Moroccan Muslim identity through curricular differentiation. It was not difficult to see that the DIP had applied this policy imperfectly, however. Quranic instruction had been the one element of the curriculum that the French administration could not control; consequently, Islamic education had been marginalized. Arabic language arts were also underemphasized. Hardy had been brought in to increase the school system's commitment to the maintenance of traditional culture, but he had attempted this primarily through French-medium instruction, believing that a French-medium education could be divorced from cultural assimilationism. This was the assumption behind the formula "culture musulmane, instruction française."

The nationalists rejected this assumption but agreed that education ought not to turn "natives into Frenchmen." Colonial education had never attempted to convince them otherwise; on the contrary, DIP discourse was full of exhortations to Moroccan Muslims to maintain their traditional identity. So, too, was the nationalist press. In 1932 *Maghreb* accused the colonizers of seeking to turn Morocco into a "province of France" and declared that although Moroccans had accepted French "tutelage," "we are equally attached to our past, to our traditions; and if modernization should cost the sacrifice of our own personality, it is natural that we would not want it. In short, we are committed to modernize, even while remaining ourselves."[47] Lyautey could hardly have said it better himself.

The nationalists, however, accused the colonizers of offering an education that was assimilatory. This was true in a linguistic sense but not in terms of organizational structure or the social and political integration of graduates. Most importantly, the metacurriculum was anti-assimilatory. Simply put, the DIP taught students that assimilation was bad, and encouraged Muslim students in French-run schools to maintain a specifically Muslim and Moroccan identity. Even the few Muslims who attended the French schools for Europeans were encouraged to socialize with their Muslim peers and to join in the extracurricular life of the schools for Muslims rather than integrate into French student life.[48] This was very important for the development of the nationalist movement. There was no significant political element among French-educated Moroccan Muslims who opposed separatist nationalism and advocated political inclusion within France, as Ferhat Abbas had initially done in Algeria. *Maghreb*, *Action du Peuple*, and the *Plan de réformes* were largely the work of the most assimilated French-educated Muslims in Morocco—yet they opposed assimilationism.

In 1934 the nationalists set forth the goal that all education for Muslims eventually be conducted in Arabic, with French as a second language, although they recognized that such a reform could not be implemented immediately. They demanded that, in the meantime, Arabic and Islamic education be given an importance equal to that of the French-medium subjects.[49] This was not a new demand; the augmentation of Arabic education had been part of the agenda of the Anciens élèves organizations since the 1920s, along with their demands for increased opportunity for integration into French society. The DIP had been willing to make some concessions in terms of the allocation of instructional time in the non-elite schools, and in 1926 it increased the time for Arabic instruction in the urban primaries from three and a half hours (including religious instruction) to five hours per week. In the *collèges*, Arabic-medium instruction had always been given a larger role: eleven hours per week in the 1920 curriculum, although the quality of instruction was a point of contention. In the late 1920s, Arabic and Islamic studies had been introduced into some rural and professional schools, although it remained common for schools to operate without such instruction, despite complaints from Muslim parents.[50]

The Moroccan nationalists found such reforms far from adequate. In order to restore Arabic and Islam to their rightful place in the curriculum, the *Plan de réformes* challenged French authority over Muslim schooling, calling for the legalization of the recently banned "free schools" and the creation of a Vizirat of Public Instruction, a ministry under *makhzan* control that would oversee the education of Muslims. In order to promote the further separation of cultures, the *Plan* called for more schooling for girls, but stated that such schooling "should be based on Arabic and Islamic culture" and that it should be provided with assistance from Middle Eastern *institutrices* (schoolmistresses).[51] Unlike boys, girls did not merit a statement about the equal weighting of French and Arabic instruction; the priority was the maintenance of an Arabic and Muslim culture, reflecting the belief that girls, as future mothers, were the key to cultural preservation and therefore merited stricter controls (a belief common in both Western and Islamic societies).

The nationalists adopted the colonizers' belief that state-sponsored education could and should maintain authentic Moroccan culture and at the same time provide the skills necessary for the economic development of the country. "Muslim culture, French instruction," the slogan of the DIP in the Hardy-Brunot era, had created high expectations. Nationalists and Anciens élèves complained that the French schools had failed to achieve the stated goal of keeping students rooted in their traditional Arab-Muslim culture. These Muslim critics accepted Hardy's notion that education ought to be tied to the ethno-cultural characteristics of the students, and they called for a more rigorous application of the ethnic principle. At the same time, they sought the expansion of education to more Muslims and increased opportunity for themselves within French society.

The Berber Question
Thus the nationalists agreed with the colonial administration that Moroccan Muslims ought to maintain their distinct culture and identity. A more contentious question concerned what that culture and

identity consisted of, and whom it included and excluded. The dominant issue in the nationalist discourse and politics of the 1930s was the "Berber question." This issue underlay all of the nationalists' legal, political, administrative, and educational proposals.

In defining the traditional cultural identity of Moroccan Muslims, the policy of the Residency—but not the discourse of Hardy's DIP— made a clear distinction between Arabs and Berbers. Because the early nationalists were urban arabophones who were heavily influenced by Salafiyya, they envisioned a unitary Moroccan identity rooted in orthodox Islam and the Arabic language. This vision did not reflect the actual linguistic and cultic pluralism of Moroccan Muslims, but it was supported by the religious prestige of the Arabic language and the cultural prestige of urban Arab civilization. The nationalist assertion of a unitary political and cultural identity for all Moroccan Muslims was a direct challenge to the French Berber policy, which aimed to maintain cultural differences and political divisions between Berbers and Arabs.

French discourses about Berbers resonated both with discourses of French assimilationist colonialism and with the Lyautist version of "associationalism," which emphasized the preservation of cultural and social difference. In Lyautey's Morocco, French colonial officials were often forced to stifle their assimilationist tendencies. For many (Paul Marty, e.g.), the Berber policy seemed to present an opportunity to act on these inclinations. Nevertheless, the official Berber policy was rooted in Gallieni's *politique des races* and Lyautey's principle of respecting local traditions and institutions. The policy aimed to prevent the "arabization" of authentic Berber culture and was based on the idea that there was a fundamental difference between the traditions of the Berber areas and those of the arabophone cities, and that therefore the arabization of the Berbers had to be prevented. In response, Moroccan nationalists upheld the Lyautist principle of cultural preservation but denied that Berbers constituted a different culture that was worth preserving.

In 1930 a new edict, the Berber *dahir*, had provided Morocco's nationalists with a platform for public protest. Like the Dinshaway incident in Egypt, the Berber *dahir* of 1930 allowed educated dissidents to rally the masses and begin to create a popular nationalist movement. The 1930 *dahir* had established "customary tribunals" to administer justice according to "Berber customary law" in civil matters, along with appeals tribunals. The *dahir* also increased French legal authority over all the tribes and areas classified as "Berber," by decreeing that each of the customary tribunals was to be supervised by a French official. More radically, the *dahir* asserted that all serious criminal cases would fall under the jurisdiction, not of the Berber tribunals, but of French courts. The earlier Berber policy had claimed to preserve the status quo, threatened by the growing power of the centralized state, by allowing Berbers to live by their own customs, while the *makhzan* and the sultan had retained nominal sovereignty over the areas classified as Berber. The 1930 *dahir* officially severed these areas from the *makhzan* and the *sharia* (Islamic law) and placed them under French authority.[52]

The Berber *dahir* had been accompanied by the decree instituting the baccalaureate at the *collèges*. If this was intended to buy the complacency of the French-educated Muslims, it was woefully inadequate, as Mekki Merrouni has noted.[53] In order to stir up public opposition to the *dahir*, the nationalists organized the public recitation of *latif* prayers in mosques in Morocco's major cities. These prayers were normally reserved for natural disasters, but were altered to suit the situation: they finished with the words "protect us from ill treatment by fate and allow nothing to divide us from our brothers, the Berbers."[54] Street demonstrations followed. The authorities responded with repression; the leaders of the protests were arrested; several, including Ouazzani, were flogged by the pasha of Marrakesh.[55]

The nationalists responded with continued agitation, launching a press campaign in Paris and in the Spanish zone, where the authorities indulged a certain tolerance for anti-French propaganda. The Moroccan cause was also taken up in Geneva, where Shakib Arslan oversaw the journal *La Nation Arabe*, and in the pages of the anti-colonial papers of Syria and Egypt. Throughout the Muslim world, nationalists and Islamists (including Hassan al-Banna, founder of the Muslim Brotherhood) joined the Moroccan nationalist press in portraying Morocco's Berber question as a Christian assault on the Muslim *umma*. This interpretation of the Berber policy was lent credibility by the French Catholic press in Morocco, which had published articles calling for the conversion of the Berbers. Fears of Christian evangelism were further inflamed by rumors that Paul Marty had distributed Arabic-language translations of Renan's *Life of Jesus* in the Middle Atlas and by the highly unusual conversion of Omar Abdeljalil's brother, Mohamed, to Catholicism.[56]

The colonial authorities eventually reversed the most controversial aspect of the *dahir*: on 8 April 1934 the Residency revoked the jurisdiction of French criminal courts over the Berber populations, returning these areas to the ultimate jurisdiction of the sultan, although Berber customary law and the customary tribunals were maintained. The damage was done, however: the campaign against the *dahir* had transformed Moroccan nationalism into a political movement of international scope and mass appeal.

The nationalist platform articulated in the early 1930s was largely directed at the "stupid and detestable" Berber *dahir*.[57] The 1934 *Plan de réformes* asserted the sovereignty of the sultan over all Moroccans, Berber and Arab, Muslim and Jewish, in keeping with the Treaty of Fez. Consequently, the *Plan* implied, the French had no right to claim direct authority over the Berber territories. The authors quoted Lyautey's statement that "Morocco is an autonomous state, whose protection France has assured, but which rests under the sovereignty of the sultan with his own law."[58] For Lyautey this assertion had been the best defense against metropolitan republicans and assimilationists who, in 1914–15, had been prepared to offer French citizenship to Moroccans in exchange for military service. For the nationalists it was a statement that could be turned against the colonial regime.

However, the *Plan de réformes* did more than reassert the sultan's traditional authority over a complex network of social institutions and a diverse population. It also posited a unitary Moroccan people that was essentially arabophone and Muslim. The French policy was described as a campaign against "our Arab culture and our traditions"[59] and as a "policy of division among Moroccans themselves" that aimed "to directly assimilate the great majority of the Moroccan people." This assimilationist endeavor involved "a systematic and cunning campaign against Islam and Arab culture: it gravely compromises the authority of His Majesty the Sultan, the integrity of Moroccan justice, and the social union and territorial unity of Morocco."[60] In order to promote this putatively historical "social union," the nationalists proposed an assimilationist campaign of their own. Despite their demands that the French give up "all policies of privileges that favor one ethnic element to the detriment of another," the nationalists advocated the imposition of Arabic-language education for all Muslims; there were no proposals to maintain the Berber language or Berber traditions.[61]

No separate Berber nationalism developed during the colonial period after the failure of the Rif rebellion. In Benedict Anderson's terms, the regional scholastic "itineraries" of Middle Atlas students, who were not allowed to become students or teachers in arabophone schools, might be expected to have led French-educated Berbers to conceive of the Middle Atlas administrative region and its inhabitants as a nation. However, the impact of the schools for Berbers was limited in scope and in duration, because the development of such schools was delayed until after World War I. The itineraries of the Berber soldiers trained by the colonial state were not restricted to the Berber territories, and these soldiers were more influential and far more numerous than Berber teachers. Because French-run schools did not use the Berber language, no vernacular "print culture" of Berberism developed in the colonial period.[62] Meanwhile, and most importantly, Arabic print culture spread quickly, despite French policy to the contrary. These factors all discouraged the development of a Berber nationalism, although local resistance to centralized rule remained strong. Even the Berber culture movement that emerged in the 1980s has not taken on the discourse of territorial or ethnic nationalism. Although this recent Berberism has been "strongly condemnatory of the predominant monocultural order based on Islam and Arabism," the "Berber Manifesto" issued by berberophone Moroccan intellectuals in 2000 did not call for a Berber state but rather for "the advent of a *universal civilization* which is capable of integrating all the contributions of mankind."[63]

The Arabic-speaking Moroccan nationalists of the 1930s were not so accommodating in their attitudes toward cultural and institutional diversity. The French had invoked the preservation of Berber culture in an assault on the political sovereignty of the sultan; to defend Berberism while still defending the authority of the sultan would have been difficult, even if the nationalists had been so inclined, and they were not. The Arabic language had always been prestigious in Morocco, associated as it was with the awesome cultural weight of the Quran. There was also an element of social snobbery: urban Arabic speakers saw rural Berbers as rubes. Furthermore, the Salafi movement had been attacking heterodox religious culture as "superstition" for many years; as a result, the nationalists saw the Berber traditions as "primitive customs."[64] Such customs would inevitably be eradicated by the spread of true Islam. To this religious teleology, Ahmed Balafrej added a secular argument based on the growing economic integration of Morocco. "Sooner or later," argued Balafrej in *Maghreb*, "the Berber will descend to the plains and hear Arabic spoken. So why contrive to apply this nefarious policy [of isolating Berbers from Arabs]?"[65] Although the nationalists explicitly invoked Lyautey and his pledge to preserve Moroccan culture, their assertion of a unitary Moroccan identity threatened by French assimilationism precluded any concern for the decline of Berber culture.

The nationalist attack on the Berber policy accorded with the ethno-psychology of Hardy and the French-run schools, which had educated so many of the nationalist leaders. There had been no attempt to use the schools to convince the Arabic-speaking students of the cities that there were fundamental differences between Arabs and Berbers. Hardy's psychological approach to ethnology had produced a vision of Morocco at odds with the Berber policy, and his works remained recommended reading for DIP teachers long after Hardy was gone. In "Les caractères essentiels de la mentalité marocaine," and in *L'enfant marocaine*, Hardy and Brunot told teachers that all Moroccans shared a common mentality. Hardy's pedagogical history of Morocco, *Grandes étapes*, had portrayed Morocco as a single historical, cultural, and geographic unit. And in *L'âme marocaine* Hardy had argued that despite Morocco's diversity, "in this country there has lived and still lives a 'people.'"⁶⁶ This sentiment was echoed in the nationalist press, as *Action du Peuple* declared that "however different the practices, the mores, and the customs of elements of our population were and remain, the Moroccans constituted and still constitute a people like any other."⁶⁷

Hardy's vision of Moroccan identity was not adopted wholesale by Moroccan nationalists, of course. As Benita Parry writes,

> In the "hybrid moment" what the native rewrites is not a copy of the colonialist original, but a qualitatively different thing-in-itself, where misreadings and ambiguities expose the uncertainties and ambivalences of the colonialist text and deny it an authorizing presence. Thus a textual insurrection against the discourse of colonial authority is located in the natives' interrogation of the English [here, French] book within the terms of their own system of cultural meanings, a displacement which is read back from the record written by colonialism's agents and ambassadors.⁶⁸

For Hardy and for the nationalists, Morocco's berberophones and arabophones made up a single people, united by Islam, by geography, and by the authority of the sultan. However, the affluent, urban arabophone nationalists rejected Hardy's portrayal of classical Arabic as foreign to the Moroccan masses. They identified the Moroccan nation with "the powerful flame that Islam has planted in the heart of *Berbèrie*" but rejected the notion that Morocco's Berber heritage distanced Morocco from Arab culture.[69] For the nationalists, the "flame of Islam" had turned Berbers into Moroccans, and Moroccans were Arabs—or would be made Arabs through universal Arabic-language schooling.

Of course, the Moroccan Muslims of *collèges* did not need Georges Hardy to teach them an identity that was defined by geographical frontiers or the authority of a monarch, that embraced all Muslims, or that demanded the imposition of cultural unity through schooling. There were plenty of precedents for these ideas in the political discourse of the *makhzan*, in Salafiyya, and in European conceptions of the nation-state that Moroccan nationalists accessed through European sources and through the examples of other Arab nationalist movements. To assume that the nationalists could only have gotten these ideas from the DIP would be to subscribe to Hardy's false belief that culture and ideology could be controlled through the schools.

Nevertheless, the complementarity between the nationalist vision and that of the French educational leadership constituted an important part of the cultural and political landscape in Morocco. Anti-assimilationism, it seems, was highly assimilable. In contrast to Algeria and Senegal, no Moroccan group challenged French colonialism by demanding the rights of Frenchmen. A few French-educated Moroccan professionals urged patience and "cooperation"[70] as the nationalists became more confrontational in the postwar period, but Morocco's French-educated dissidents rallied around Alal al-Fasi's call for "the liberation of the Maghrib within the fold of its religion and its loyalty to the illustrious monarchy."[71] Mohamed Hassan Ouazzani was arguably an exception, but even though Ouazzani tended toward secularism and republicanism, he saw the protectorate not a step toward a desired assimilation but as a "Crime de Lèse-Nation." To the left of Ouazzani would later emerge Mehdi Ben Barka, who saw national political independence as a mere precursor to international revolution involving the "the radical destruction of semifeudal structures and colonial capital"—but Ben Barka embraced national liberation nonetheless.[72] There was no Moroccan counterpart to the young Ferhat Abbas in Algeria, who demanded political rights but denied that an Algerian nation had ever existed,[73] or to Senegal's Blaise Diagne, who had sought a solution to imperial injustice through the extension of French citizenship to natives—even in areas officially designated as "protectorates."

During the years in which many Moroccan nationalists had attended the French schools for arabophone Muslims, the schools reinforced the idea that there was a single Moroccan identity that needed to be defended and preserved. While the French-based curricula of the schools threatened to transform Moroccan culture, the administration urged students and teachers to preserve this culture. While the Berber *dahir* aimed to thwart the development of a unitary Moroccan identity, French pedagogical discourses encouraged an attachment to just such an identity. The anti-assimilationist colonial educational culture of the 1920s and early 1930s encouraged discourses of cultural essentialism, authenticity, tradition, and difference, creating a "nativist synergy,"[74] as French pedagogical discourses encouraged the conception of Morocco as a country inhabited by one distinct people who needed to defend themselves against threats to their imagined cultural unity.

9. Legacies and Reversals

We used to sing the praises of difference. We failed to foresee we'd be caught out when the advocates of withdrawal and closure sang the same song with different words. | Tahar Ben Jelloun, *French Hospitality*, 1999

A culture is not a prison-house, with its rules engraved in the souls of its participants. | Herman Lebovics, *Bringing the Empire Back Home*, 2004

The Hardy-Brunot era in protectorate education came to an end in the 1930s, as the nationalist movement shocked the protectorate leadership out of its complacency and forced the Direction de l'instruction publique to make concessions to the demands of its elite students and former students. Demands for educational parity and opportunity began to seem reasonable and modest, compared to the emerging movement for independence. Assimilation and hybridization were no longer seen as the gravest threats to the French colonial project in Morocco.

The election of the Popular Front in 1936 in France also contributed to a new outlook on colonial education. Although Louis Brunot remained head of Muslim Education until 1939 and continued to defend Hardy's approach, the ideas of Hardy and Brunot were incompatible with the political principles of the new government in Paris.

The Popular Front brought an increased commitment to egalitarianism and universal education, along with criticism of France's failure to bring education to more than a tiny fraction of the subject populations in North Africa. This political change was felt in Rabat with the appointment of Charles Noguès as resident-general in 1936.

The Noguès administration began a massive quantitative expansion of schooling. The administration began opening makeshift rural *écoles de goum* (soldiers' schools) and *écoles rurales élémentaires*, which allowed for the expansion of rudimentary French education where resources did not permit the construction of a fully staffed school offering the standard curriculum. In 1938–39, 130 new classes were opened, serving more than five thousand new students. This was a significant organizational accomplishment, although still inadequate to meet the needs of the swelling Moroccan population. In 1937 the French schoolteachers union (Syndicat national des instituteurs et institutrices de France et des colonies, section du Maroc) proposed that literate local Muslims be employed to provide elementary education in the native language of the students, with French as a second language. This rudimentary schooling would lead to a second level where a French teacher would supervise a staff of indigenous teachers; only at the third level would the best Muslim students receive instruction from actual French teachers, in preparation for work as functionaries. The union plan emphasized grassroots participation and the democratization of education rather than the tight central control of pedagogy that had been at the heart of the Hardy-Brunot approach. This plan was not adopted, but reforms implemented by Noguès and by the DIP beginning in 1936 nevertheless reflected the new ethos in colonial education. The *section normale* in the Rabat *collège* was expanded and renamed the Centre de formation pédagogique (Center for Pedagogical Training), and a plan was decreed in 1939 to train more Muslim auxiliary teachers at regional training centers.[1]

In Fez and Rabat the DIP sought to use the Anciens élèves as intermediaries between the administration and the Muslim elite, providing them with seats on the Council of Government where they could participate in discussions concerning the education budget. In response to pressure from the Anciens élèves, Arabic instruction was expanded, and the recently banned "free schools" were once again legalized, and placed under the authority of the sultan. The colonial state opened the exams for entrance into administrative positions (*concours administratif marocaines*) to *collège* graduates possessing the DESM or CESM. This effectively made these *collège* degrees equivalent to the baccalaureate and the *brevet élémentaire* within French Morocco (but not in France), partially fulfilling the Anciens élèves' demands of 1929.[2] Meanwhile, access to the French baccalaureate was improved; by 1940, fourteen hundred Moroccans had obtained the baccalaureate.[3] Muslim girls were also allowed access to the primary school certificate and to secondary education. At last, the DIP was striving to maximize the expansion of education for the Moroccan masses while offering the Moroccan elites increased opportunities for integration into French professions, instead of putting its energies and resources into the maintenance of cultural difference, structural separation, and discursive control.

Despite these changes, the nationalist leaders quickly became disenchanted with the Popular Front. The hope that French socialists might revolutionize the imperial order were soon frustrated. Educational expansion was accompanied by political repression, and the nationalists dismissed the Popular Front's reforms as too gradual, or recognized these reforms as attempts to preserve French domination rather than to overturn it. As Mohamed Hassan Ouazzani recalled in his memoirs, "In Morocco, French policy was very harsh. The colonial will manifested itself here with force. No concession had been made to the nationalist movement."[4]

Nevertheless, by 1939 the administration could claim that twenty-six thousand Muslims were enrolled in French-run schools. Once again, however, educational expansion was interrupted by world war. The scarcity of resources from 1939 to 1942 prohibited the construction of new schools, and Muslim enrollment remained flat during those years.[5]

Vichy

The Vichy regime brought a brief return to the rhetoric of ethnic identity and cultural separation within the educational service. In many ways, Vichy's glorification of action brought home to the motherland the virile anti-intellectualism of Lyautey's "colonial man" and the restrictive pedagogy of Hardy. Vichy brought about marked changes in metropolitan education, including the persecution of Jews and Freemasons, the abolition of the teachers unions, and the fusion of the upper primary with the *lycée* in an attempt to stamp out the republican culture of the primary school teaching corps.[6]

The Vichy government also recalled Georges Hardy to service in the colonies. Hardy had directed the École coloniale in Paris from 1926 to 1932 and then had served as rector of the Academy of Algiers from 1933 to 1937, before returning to France to become rector of his alma mater, the Faculty of Lille. Both the Vichy authorities and the German occupiers were apparently impressed with Hardy's life work promoting belief in ethnic psychological differences. Hardy had transformed the École coloniale into a prestigious institution of higher education and had reformed its curriculum to promote the use of ethnology in colonial administration. Under Vichy the school was allowed to keep its director, Robert Delavignette, and the majority of its faculty members; enrollment was even increased. (Jews were banned, of course.)[7] In 1940 the Vichy regime asked Hardy to return to his post as rector in Algiers, where he became an outspoken supporter of the Vichy regime.

In Algiers, Hardy applauded Marshal Pétain's National Revolution. Hardy once again advanced the critiques of rationalism and universalism that he had developed in the 1910s and 1920s. In short, he blamed the fall of France on Enlightenment republicanism, arguing in a radio address that "We have sinned through arrogance. We have accepted like a dogma the unlimited possibilities of human reason.... We have dreamed of tearing down frontiers, of organizing universal fraternity, of abolishing countries. . . . Let us restore the cult of the Homeland. . . . Let us find again the sense of authority, without which no society is possible."[8]

In Morocco, the *Bulletin de l'Enseignement* reprinted Hardy's speech, along with statements about the role of education in the National Revolution by Pétain and by his supporters in Algiers and in France. The *Bulletin* also printed a speech about Joan of Arc by a teacher at Rabat's Lycée Gouraud, and an article in support of Vichy's antifeminist natalism (explaining why large families were easier to raise than small ones).[9] Vichy policy led to the expulsion of Jewish students from the *lycées* and the removal of Jewish teachers from their posts at DIP schools. Noguès remained resident-general, however, and mitigated these policies by allowing AIU schools to remain open. Nevertheless, German, Polish, and Austrian Jews were incarcerated in labor camps.[10]

It is unclear whether France's National Revolution had much effect on policy toward Moroccan Muslims. There was little discussion of Muslim education in the educational bulletin between 1940 and 1942. Nor do DIP publications from the post-Vichy period offer any information on the subject; Lucien Paye reported only that budget limitations forced the DIP to stop opening new schools.[11] Alal al-Fasi, in his 1948 memoir, declared flatly that "the policies of the Residency-General in Morocco did not undergo any changes as a result of the German occupation of Paris and Marshal Pétain's seizure of power."[12] The years 1941 and 1942 brought plague and famine to Morocco, and it is possible that Noguès was too preoccupied to address educational reform of any kind. However, it is also likely that the DIP's silence regarding the Vichy years reflects the protective amnesia of the "Vichy syndrome" rather than mere inactivity.

Postwar

After the American landings in 1942, a republican reaction against Vichy brought about a wholesale rejection of Hardy's conservative and racialist ideas. In Algiers, Hardy himself was accused of collaboration. It was alleged that he "accepted important functions as the head of propaganda of the Legion in service of the policies of Vichy; that for political reasons he did nothing to attenuate the sanctions inflicted on the members of the teaching corps; and that on his own authority he aggravated the consequences of the racial laws, notably those concerning the attendance of Jewish students at educational establishments."[13] In February 1944, at the recommendation of the Commission d'épuration (Purge Commission), Charles de Gaulle dismissed Hardy from his post in Algiers, banned him from teaching, and stripped him of his pension.

In Morocco, however, Hardy's influence had already waned considerably, and consequently much continuity is evident between the late 1930s and the postwar period. Noguès's very republican head of primary education, Roger Thabault, had remained in his post under Vichy, and Michael Laskier suggests that Thabault's influence may have softened the impact of Vichy's anti-Semitic policies.[14] When Brunot had resigned as the head of Muslim Education in 1939, his interim replacement, A. Roux, had moved to reduce the influence of the Hardy-Brunot approach on the new generation of teachers. Roux replaced *Premiers conseils*, Brunot's 1934 handbook for teachers, with a new work, *Quelques conseils pratiques à l'usage du personnel suppléant des écoles musulmanes*. The 1939 guide was reissued in 1942 by Lucien Paye and again in 1946 by the postwar head of Muslim Education, Pierre Counillon.[15] This new guide emphasized procedural instructions and was notably short on ethnological generalizations. The handbook introduced new personnel to a pedagogical discourse that stressed the influence of the classroom environment on the individual pupil; there was no sign that the intellect or psychology of Moroccan students was limited by race or ethnicity.

After North Africa was "liberated" from Vichy in 1942, the DIP continued the expansion and democratization of education begun before the war. Between 1942 and 1944, Muslim enrollment increased to about thirty-three thousand, including seven thousand girls.[16] In 1944 a renewed commitment to educational expansion and economic development was affirmed at the Brazzaville conference. This commitment was reinforced by an increased awareness that the Moroccan birthrate was accelerating while literacy rates remained abysmal. Accordingly, the educational administration in Morocco abandoned the Lyautist doctrines of slow, gradual evolution and the preservation of traditional social structures. French policy now aimed for the total and rapid economic and social transformation of Morocco.

The protectorate's 1944 educational plan called for the extension of education to ten thousand new students per year for ten years. This would involve opening two hundred new classes per year and the recruiting or training of three hundred teachers, including Muslim *foqya*. To maximize the spread of literacy where the resources for more elaborate schools were lacking, the new resident-general, Erik Labonne, established rudimentary field schools (*écoles foraines*) to teach literacy and arithmetic. This literacy instruction could be in Arabic – even, theoretically, in Berber areas. Although Arabic instruction remained rare in the mountains, the policy of suppressing Arabic in Berber areas was recognized as an impediment to literacy development, despite ongoing concerns about the political influence of urban nationalists upon the Berbers.[17] The spread of education now took priority over the control of its content. According to official figures, the annual recruitment goals of the 1944 plan were regularly surpassed: by 1950, enrollment in Muslim schools was over 116,000, including more than 1,700 in the secondary classes of the *collèges*.[18] While some worried that the DIP was sacrificing quality for quantity, Muslim demand for French schooling still outstripped available DIP resources in urban areas, and even in most rural areas classroom space became scarce.

Roger Thabault, the new director of Public Instruction, recognized that despite its enormous growth, the school system was still inadequate to meet the needs of the growing Muslim population, still mostly illiterate. His responses to this problem were not restricted by a desire to preserve what he perceived as the existing social and psychological features of Moroccan society. While his new rural schools necessarily offered a rudimentary curriculum, the new prescriptions for the urban primary schools were much more ambitious than Hardy's 1920 programs. Not only were the *leçons des choses* much more scientifically oriented and the French language curriculum more complex, but the new history curriculum also included the French Revolution.[19] The DIP had finally abandoned its attempt to dam the flow of new knowledge.

Thabault echoed Hardy's emphasis on concrete, practical education, declaring his intention to "restrain, as much as possible without danger to education, the hold of a theoretical and verbal instruction over the youth of this land, in order to develop a practical instruction, pertaining to real things."[20] Yet he displayed none of Hardy's fear of the modernization of the Moroccan economy, nor did he speak of ethnic limitations. In Morocco as in the metropole, the progressive, pragmatic, anti-Scholastic educational reformism advocated by Claparède and the Compagnons de la université nouvelle was at last reunited with the meritocratic universalism of its origins. Thabault spoke of the need for Muslims to embrace "the infinite possibilities for economic and social progress" offered by French education. He celebrated the survival of universalist discourse as a "miracle": "The miracle is that this ideal of French thought, in its most profound, most intimate, most constant form, is also that of the people of France, who make no distinction between men according to race, color, or religion, who only distinguish them by the humanity they carry within them. . . . I am sure of the fertility of the ideas which it represents, and I am convinced that these ideas are necessary in a world that seeks to overcome so many errors and so many ruins."[21] Thus Thabault announced a break from not only the Vichy period but also from the policies of Georges Hardy.

Influenced by this post-Vichy commitment to republican universalism, and also by *collège* student participation in political demonstrations in January 1944,[22] Thabault's DIP took steps to reform elite Muslim education. Charles Sallefranques, the *collège* instructor whom Louis Vignon had attacked in 1923 for teaching French literature, now published an unabashedly republican French history textbook for use in the schools for Muslims.[23] The *collèges* were reshaped to provide something resembling equal opportunity. The administration abolished tuition payments and removed the excessive requirement that students seeking a baccalaureate carry a double load (*double culture*) including both the standard French curriculum and courses in Arabic and Moroccan culture. Henceforth, the *collèges* offered separate tracks: a *lycée*-style program leading to the French baccalaureate, and a "traditional" program leading to the DESM. Commercial and agricultural sections were also opened. In addition, the primary schools and *lycées* for Europeans were officially opened to all Moroccans who could meet the academic and age requirements. From this point onward, the *lycées* would be the real *écoles de fils de notables* for a large segment of the Moroccan commercial and political elite. Higher education was also made more accessible; a school of administration was opened in 1948, and the IHEM began accepting more Moroccan students: more than five hundred by 1951–52.[24] New opportunities were also opened to girls. Responding to the demands of the Anciens élèves and of Sultan Mohammed ben Youssef, the DIP mandated that curricula for girls resemble those for boys, and two *collèges* were created for Muslim girls between 1945 and 1947, in Rabat (complete with dormitory) and in Fez.

Predictably, the desire of elite Muslims for access to opportunities in French higher education and the professions meant that few opted for the "traditional" track in the *collèges* once the requirements for the baccalaureate were made less prohibitive: in October 1948, for example, only two students enrolled in the traditional track at the Fez *collège*. However, the disparity of opportunities between the two tracks was remedied in August 1948 with the creation of a *baccalauréat d'outre-mer* (overseas baccalaureate) by the metropolitan Direction of Public

Instruction, which allowed for a greater emphasis on indigenous language and culture than the standard degree. This was instituted in the *collèges* as the "Moroccan baccalaureate," replacing the DESM as the terminal degree for the traditional track and allowing access to higher education and the professions for the graduates of "adapted" education.[25] Those desiring educational assimilation were now permitted it, both within the *collèges* and within the *lycées*; on the other hand, those wanting a more "Moroccan" education were also allowed entry into the new baccalaureate elite.

This completed the metamorphosis of DIP policy from Hardy's pedagogy of restriction and ethnic separation to a policy of educational expansion and elite assimilation. Finally, the DIP had met the demands for integration and opportunity voiced by the Associations des Anciens élèves in the mid-1920s. This transformation would not save the protectorate, however. Although many elite Moroccan Muslims eagerly took advantage of the baccalaureate and the *lycée*, these were scant compensation for the humiliations of colonial rule. French-educated Muslim dissidents had long since turned to separatist nationalism, based on their own interpretation of Moroccan identity and cultural difference. These nationalists rejected the new DIP policies as an attack on their identity as Moroccan Muslims.

The End of Empire?
The nationalists triumphed. Beginning with the protests against the 1930 Berber *dahir*, Morocco's elite nationalists had gradually succeeded in rallying the impoverished, frustrated, undereducated masses. In 1944 the leaders of the Comité d'action marocaine formed a new nationalist party, Istiqlal, that called for full independence. It soon became clear that the sultan and Istiqlal had become allies. The French responded aggressively. After riots in December 1952, Istiqlal was outlawed, and in August 1953 the French authorities deposed the sultan, with the help of his rivals Abdelhay al-Kittani and Thami al-Glaoui. Morocco was soon torn by terrorist violence, rural rebellion, and urban insurrection. The French will and capacity to fight was sapped by

the 1954 defeat at Diên Biên Phû and the greater crisis of the revolutionary war in Algeria. In 1955 the French brought Mohammed ben Youssef back from exile in Madagascar in hopes that he might restore order amid chaos.[26] The end of the French protectorate in Morocco was declared on 2 March 1956, bringing to a close almost half a century of French rule.

Independence did not, however, signify the end of the story of French education in Morocco, or of the legacy of Hubert Lyautey, Georges Hardy, and Louis Brunot. The questions of power, culture, and identity that had been central to colonial relationships would remain central to the postcolonial Franco-Moroccan relationship and to politics in the new Morocco and in France. The joint declaration signed in March 1956 announced the beginning of a new era of cooperation in Franco-Moroccan relations "with respect for the sovereignty of the two States," not an end to the relationship.[27]

Such cooperation was vital to the future of education in Morocco. Independence notwithstanding, Morocco was to remain dependent on French schoolteachers. However flawed the DIP system may have been, its institutions and its teachers were to be the foundation upon which independent Morocco would build the schools of the future. No longer civil servants of the French state, French teachers were invited to stay as *coopérants*, employees of the Moroccan educational ministry who would teach in schools for Moroccans. These teachers were needed if Morocco was ever to achieve the 1934 *Plan de réformes*' goal of universal schooling. In 1959 the Institut des hautes études marocaines was transformed into the Université Mohammed V and began awarding Moroccan diplomas, but the majority of its faculty members were French until the 1970s. Meanwhile, the dichotomy between French-style and Islamic schooling remained. In 1940 the *makhzan* had claimed authority over the Salafi "free schools," and *makhzan* sponsorship had turned these private schools into an officially sanctioned parallel system. After independence, both the "free schools" and the Qarawiyyin continued to function alongside the former colonial schools, under the authority of a rector of Universités marocaines.[28]

At the primary and secondary levels, independent Morocco's Ministry of National Education, Youth, and Sports continued the DIP's postwar efforts to expand and democratize "modern" education. Shortly after independence, Morocco's first minister of education, Mohammed al-Fasi, acknowledged the DIP's belated efforts under the Fourth Republic but pointed out that a million and a half children of school age still received no formal education. He therefore announced a plan to open eighty new schools in October 1956 and to double the number of student teachers. In addition, a new department of "Basic Education and the Struggle against Illiteracy" was created, continuing the work of the postwar DIP's rudimentary *écoles foraines*.[29] There was a long road ahead, however: only 13 percent of children of primary school age attended school in 1956, and only 2.25 percent of secondary school age – and Morocco's population explosion had barely begun.[30] The missed opportunities of the Hardy-Brunot era had cost Morocco dearly.

Yet the quantitative expansion of education and literacy was only one of al-Fasi's priorities. Alongside the pressing need to expand schooling was the desire to accomplish what Eric Jennings has called "reculturation": the "disentanglement of colonial and decolonized cultures."[31] After the assimilationist interlude of the Fourth Republic, Morocco's schools were once again seen as tools to instill in pupils a putatively authentic and traditional identity. Ethnic identity and cultural authenticity were fundamental to the nationalist movement and generally constituted a strong current in twentieth-century global culture, anticolonial as well as colonial. After twenty-six years of nationalist struggle and a decade of assimilationist postwar educational policy, there was much public pressure to use public education to promote a Moroccan identity based in Arabic and Islam. Moroccan politics and the nationalist educational agenda would continue to be shaped by the reaction against the 1930 Berber *dahir*; the victory of the nationalists had not brought a divorce from the cultures of colonialism. The nationalists' ability to build a counterhegemony out of the elements of the colonial situation meant that the cultures and policies of "postcolonial" Morocco would be imbricated with those of the colonial administration.

Arabization, De-Arabization, and Re-Arabization
Minister of Education Mohammed al-Fasi had attended the Fez *collège* during Hardy's administration and had been an active contributor to the Hardy-era ethnographic project of documenting the traditional and authentic nature of Moroccan society. Before and after graduating from the *collège* in 1926, al-Fasi had published Moroccan folktales and poems in French publications. Like many other *collège* students, he had simultaneously studied at the Qarawiyyin and was thus exposed to traditionalist and Salafi influences. However, he went on to study at Lycée Henri IV in Paris, and eventually at the Sorbonne and the École des langues vivantes orientales. By the time the sultan appointed him rector of the Qarawiyyin in 1942, al-Fasi had been immersed in the discourse of French ethnology.

Yet Mohammed al-Fasi was also a committed nationalist, a member of the executive council of Istiqlal who had been a political prisoner of the protectorate regime. The choice of an educational minister with a background in both the French system and in the Qarawiyyin suggested that the policies of the new regime would bridge the gap between the traditional and the Western.[32] In Morocco, however, this gap was not so wide as is sometimes supposed. The appointment of al-Fasi in 1955 heralded a return to Hardy's attempt to use schools to prevent the assimilation of Moroccan Muslims to French culture.

The attempt to manufacture and maintain a static Moroccan identity would once again require certain sacrifices in terms of educational quality, quantity, and opportunity. Like the Hardy-Brunot attempts to preserve "the Moroccan" in the 1920s and 1930s, the postcolonial attempt to use schools as a tool of cultural control and to instill a preconceived cultural identity would require the expenditure of revenues and resources and would affect the economic utility of schooling for the individual child. This has been particularly evident in the case of language policy.

Al-Fasi's French-school background ensured that the new educational system would not entirely reject the French language or Western knowledge, and the new minister stated that French would be required as a second language for all students, and even that "French would really be the second national language."[33] Yet al-Fasi's traditionalist leanings, nurtured both in the Qarawiyyin and in the French schools, made him a staunch opponent of cultural hybridity or cosmopolitanism. Al-Fasi immediately reaffirmed the nationalist commitment to use the schools to promote a "Moroccan" culture and identity which was defined by the Arabic language and the Islamic religion. Morocco thus embarked on the project of "arabization" via the educational system.

At a press conference on 25 June 1956, al-Fasi announced that, beginning in October 1957, instruction in the first-year *cours préparatoires* would be given entirely in Arabic and that the first two years of the lower-primary *cours élémentaires* level would be divided equally between French and Arabic.[34] The long-term goal was to arabize all instruction from the primary to the baccalaureate, with French taught as a second language. Meanwhile, a Service of Higher Islamic Education was created, and al-Fasi announced plans to institute Arabic-language education for educational administrators. He also announced plans to begin the production of Arabic-language textbooks specifically designed for Morocco. Egyptian textbooks were declared inappropriate, in keeping with Hardy's declaration of the distinct natural unity of Morocco. In Morocco, arabization would never be synonymous with pan-Arabism, and a Moroccan textbook commission was convened to produce new Arabic-language reading and arithmetic texts. It was more difficult to produce teachers.

Al-Fasi initiated his policy of complete arabization of the *cours préparatoire* while at the same time pursuing a massive expansion of primary education, admitting two hundred thousand first-year pupils in 1957, more than a tenfold increase over the policies of Fourth Republic.[35] As Mohamed Hammoud has pointed out, al-Fasi's policies were implemented "without prior need assessment or provisions for adequately trained teachers well enough versed in Modern Standard Arabic (MSA) to be able to use it to teach basic arithmetic and natural science."[36]

Al-Fasi's bold policy of rapid arabization led the French to question whether there would be a future for French nationals in Moroccan public education. During this year of exploding enrollments, 150 French schoolteachers left Morocco, fearing that arabization would eventually lead to the elimination of their jobs. It was feared that others would soon join the exodus, for few were reassured by al-Fasi's offer that they would be kept on to teach the French language, even as math and other subjects were switched to Arabic-medium instruction.[37] Arabization in Moroccan public education also led French authorities to make alternative arrangements for the education of French children in Morocco. After lengthy negotiations, an agreement between the French and Moroccan states was reached in May 1957, and more than six thousand French teachers who had taught in the protectorate system would continue to be employed by the Moroccan state as *coopérants*. However, in exchange for educational assistance, French negotiators compelled the Moroccan government to permit a newly created Mission Universitaire Culturelle Française to use seven postprimary schools and more than a thousand primary classrooms for up to seven years. These French Mission schools were the legacy of the DIP schools for Europeans, which had also been educating a significant portion of the Moroccan elite since 1945. Instead of integrating these "European" schools into a postcolonial Moroccan system, the 1957 agreement removed them from the realm of Moroccan public education entirely. The buildings would eventually be handed over to the Moroccan state, but not the human resources or intellectual capital. This parallel educational arrangement fit the nationalist vision for a culturally and religiously segregated school system. Meanwhile, it allowed elite Moroccan families to escape the consequences of Moroccan educational policy (al-Fasi's own children attended French schools). However, the parallel Mission system preserved a structural redundancy that the new nation could ill-afford. The Mission schools ensured that French funds – and two thousand French teachers – that might have been used for mixed public education would instead be used to run a separate, private French system.[38]

For the Moroccan public and the new ruling elite, a more pressing problem was al-Fasi's inability to both arabize and universalize primary education, or even just the *cours préparatoire*, without a precipitous drop in the quality of schooling. This was an impossible task, as William Zartman has noted: "Only a public which felt that limited education was a colonialist plot with no practical reasons" would find this failure surprising or unacceptable.[39] The arabization ordered by al-Fasi was implemented inconsistently, since materials and trained personnel were often lacking. In order to maximize the reach of the available teaching staff, school hours were reduced for primary school pupils in the first three years, and class size swelled to an average of seventy pupils. To support the expansion of primary schooling and to replace French teachers lost to the Mission system, new normal schools were hastily created and teacher-training programs were accelerated. The teachers unions, both primary and secondary, denounced these efforts as deleterious to the quality of education. A newly constituted commission on educational reform argued that arabization, while a worthy goal, ought only to be implemented insofar as it could be done without sacrificing quality. Relentlessly committed to maximum arabization and universalization, however, al-Fasi deflected such concerns. In an attempt to solve staffing problems, Egyptian, Iraqi, and Lebanese teachers were recruited from abroad, at considerable expense.[40] As in the Hardy-Brunot era, this was seen as an unsatisfactory solution, not only because of the expense but also because of fears that foreign teachers were infecting Morocco with foreign political ideas.

Now, the threat was no longer pan-Islamism, French republicanism, or Bolshevism, but Nasserism. The new Moroccan regime, based as it was on the alliance of the bourgeois nationalist elite and the monarchy, was all too reminiscent of the one the Free Officers had overthrown in Egypt in order to bring Nasser to power. Consequently, the enthusiasm of the Egyptian teachers was unwelcome.

Amid what was widely seen a debacle, Mohammed al-Fasi was replaced as minister of national education in January 1958, although he was subsequently made rector of Universités marocaines. His two immediate successors, Omar Abdeljalil (1958) and Abdelkrim Benjelloun Touimi (December 1958 to 1961), were also graduates of the Fez *collège* who had gone on to study in France. However, their post-secondary education in agricultural engineering and law, respectively, gave them a more pragmatic orientation than al-Fasi had gained through his Parisian studies in oriental languages. Under the new leadership, arabization would be pursued more cautiously.

Abdeljalil's ministry concluded that full universalization and arabization had to be postponed in favor of maintaining quality and training a technical and administrative elite. Hours of attendance for primary school classes were increased, and class size was capped at fifty. Students who had attended classes in the first three primary grades the previous year were required to repeat the year. Only the *cours préparatoire* remained fully arabized. Math and science instruction were to remain in French after the first year of schooling. Benjelloun Touimi extended Arabic-medium math and science to the second year, but the emphasis was on increasing school enrollments; there was no plan to pursue full primary arabization in the short term.[41]

As Mohamed Elbiad has put it, "arabization of education has been the stumbling block of every Moroccan government since independence."[42] However, after the death of King Mohammed ben Youssef (Mohammed V) in 1961 and the accession of Hassan II, arabization was further deprioritized. Hassan II had received a private bilingual education under the tutelage of French and Moroccan instructors, including Mehdi Ben Barka. Hassan II's approach to education accorded with Ben Barka's; both advocated bilingualism and the education of girls. In other matters, however, Ben Barka was perceived as a threat to the regime. The leader of Istiqlal's left wing, Ben Barka founded the Union nationale des forces populaires in 1959. Consequently, Ben Barka played no role in Hassan II's educational ministry. In 1963 Ben Barka was condemned by the state, and in 1965 he was murdered in France at the behest of Minister of the Interior Mohammed Oufkir. However, Hassan II's educational leadership, including ministers Youssef Ben Abbès (1961–65) and Mohammed Ben Hima (1965–67), shared the pragmatism and acceptance of bilingualism that Ben Barka had expressed during the education debates of the late 1950s. Ben Abbès was a French-educated lawyer; Ben Hima had attended the Rabat *collège* but then had studied medicine in France. Ben Abbès brought in thousands of new French teachers to support the continuing expansion of education and to replace the remaining Egyptian and Middle Eastern *coopérants*. Nevertheless, enrollment continued to outstrip capacity, and concerns persisted about the effect of expansion on the quality of schooling. In a move reminiscent of Louis Brunot in the 1930s, Ben Hima in 1965 sought to manage enrollment by imposing age restrictions at the secondary level, summarily ending the educational careers of numerous students. This time, however, students in Casablanca and elsewhere responded by rioting in March 1965.[43]

Oufkir, a graduate of the French military academy for Moroccan officers at Meknes, put down the riots by force. Hassan II blamed the disturbance on teachers and "the so-called intellectual."[44] Ben Hima blamed arabization for the high failure rates and poor instruction in the schools that had led to the student unrest. In 1966 he ordered that science instruction be reconverted to French throughout the primary levels, a change that was implemented in the fall of 1967. Meanwhile, the advocates of arabization accused Ben Hima of a lack of patriotism, and Istiqlal proposed a plan for full arabization of primary and secondary schooling within eight years. Although Hassan II rejected this proposal, the pressure for arabization from Istiqlal and from the public was sufficient to prompt him to replace Ben Hima. Ben Hima's replacement, Abdelhadi Boutaleb, declared that arabization could proceed only insofar as qualified instructors became available. The first two years of primary schooling again reverted to a fully Arabic-medium program, but both math and science were taught in French for the remaining three. Secondary schooling continued in French, although Arabic was eventually introduced in the humanities.[45]

Meanwhile, arabization had gained political and cultural momentum. The World Bank and UNESCO had begun to promote arabization, based on the sound pedagogical notion that literacy is best spread when the language of instruction is the language of the home. The teaching corps in Morocco, now largely moroccanized, began to lobby for arabization. In 1971 the Union of Higher Education and the National Association of Moroccan Writers jointly endorsed full arabization at all levels and condemned "bilingualism and biculturalism" for depleting the budget, creating "pedagogical and psychological problems," and depriving Arabic of its "natural role."[46] Istiqlal, the trade unions, and the Moroccan press rallied to the cause.

In the late 1970s, Hassan II responded to this pressure by restoring arabization as an educational priority, appointing Azeddine Laraki as minister of education. In 1978, Hassan II declared that "arabization should be the irreversible point of departure for educational reform."[47] By the 1990s, Laraki and his successors achieved the complete arabization of the public primary and secondary schools, with French taught only as a second language. Science, math, and engineering instruction continued in French only at the university level and at numerous private schools.

The Costs of Reculturation

These false starts and reversals obviously entailed costs for students, for teachers, and for the society as a whole. The repeated reversals of the late 1950s and early 1960s meant that some students began primary school in Arabic, then were required to repeat a year, but with math and science in French; later they might again find themselves in math and science classes that had been arabized, especially if they were required to redouble again due to poor performance. The next generation of students made their way through a fully arabized primary system, only to be faced with math and science instruction in French at the secondary or, as is currently the case, tertiary level. In post-independence Morocco the transitional costs of arabization were exacerbated by administrative inexperience, the legacy of a colonial regime that had denied Moroccans real governing responsibility since 1912. Other costs were intrinsic to the decision to alter the main language of schooling. As linguist Beverly Seckinger has put it, "In the course of the changeover from one system of language-use to another — a change officially considered to be for the (eventual) good of Moroccan society — a great many individuals unfortunately fall between the cracks created by these changing systems. Either they are trained in one language, then expected to work in another, or they are partially trained to work in one language, then expected to continue their training in another, without sufficient preparation."[48]

For the arabophone Moroccan nationalist these costs are worth bearing, because arabization is seen, as Elbiad has put it, as a "cultural reaction against European civilization" and "a way of self-assertion and a means of establishing one's law (of language) by leading a life one's own way."[49] Such costs may sometimes be worth bearing from the point of view of the cultural and political goals of the policy maker or of the public, but these costs are often hidden and unpredictable, or at any rate unpredicted. Moreover, as Seckinger has recognized, these are more than mere transitional costs, unfortunate but temporary. They are hazards endemic to cultural policy: "Both problems stem from a gap between tidy theory and an untidy world, where languages can't be classed into separate boxes, nor people's use of them be guided into restricted paths."[50] Language policy, unlike other sorts of cultural policy such as the French crafts policy, is unavoidable. The state must make linguistic choices, because public education inevitably entails putting state money and power behind chosen languages. However, such choices are rarely made based on a cost-benefit analysis.

Nationalist elites throughout North Africa saw arabization as a "return to the authentic Arab identity as it was known formerly, that is, before the Ottoman and European influence, in such a way as to enable the Arab individual to recover his Arabic identity and to save him from the ambivalence which he suffers vis-à-vis the modern world."[51] Newspapers declared that arabization was the "people's choice" and that "citizens are burdened with this Frenchification that is alienating them in their own country."[52] Yet many Moroccans, of various classes, continued to see French-language education as the key to economic success. In the late 1970s the Moroccan Left began to criticize the government for an "arabization of the poor," for maintaining French as a language for the upper class, not only in social life but also in business, law, and administration.[53] Morocco's political and economic elite continued to send their children to French Mission schools, which had been opened to them during the Fourth Republic. The rich thus avoided the difficulties encountered by "arabized" students when entering higher education in science, mathematics, and engineering in Morocco or when pursuing opportunities in Europe.

Meanwhile, precious state resources were diverted to efforts at "corpus arabization," the attempt to designate and promote words of Arabic origin to fill perceived gaps in Arabic's lexical corpus. In 1960 the Institut d'études et recherches pour l'arabisation was founded in Rabat, directed by Ahmed Lakhdar-Ghazal.[54] Like similar institutions in Cairo, Damascus, and Baghdad, Lakdar-Ghazal's institute encouraged the writers of textbooks and newspapers to use approved Arabic words instead of borrowings from European languages, "turning into Arabic all that which is foreign."[55] The corpus arabization project sought to create a culturally pure version of Arabic, while obstructing the universal linguistic phenomena of code switching, code mixing, and lexical borrowing – all strongly present in Moroccan oral language use. The effect, insofar as this project has been successful, has been to maximize the distance between language-as-spoken and the written text — certainly unhelpful for literacy development, but that was not the point.

Ultimately, the argument for arabization was based not on financial or pedagogical concerns but on the ideal of the monocultural nation-state and the belief that the Arabic language was an essential element of Moroccan nationhood, and therefore that French-language instruction constituted a betrayal of the Moroccan self. The fear of hybridization long promoted by the colonizers was transformed into the argument that French borrowings in Arabic represent linguistic colonialism, and that decolonization therefore requires cleansing the "national" tongue of colonial influences for the sake of political liberation or psychological well-being. The notion that speaking the colonizer's language represents the "colonization of consciousness" is predicated on the so-called Whorf-Sapir hypothesis, the idea that the language spoken permanently determines the nature of cognition. This theory, although popular, has not won a consensus within linguistics. The equation of decolonization with a rejection of language change might be better understood as a historically developed concept, a legacy of both the colonizers' discourse of cultural preservation and the nationalist inversion thereof.

Nationalist claims about the "natural role" of a language become problematic when the state governs a linguistically diverse population — as is almost always the case. As Florian Coulmas has pointed out, "The monolingual state and, by consequence, the true nation state, has always been the odd exception rather than the rule. It is by no means self-evident, therefore, why linguistic pluralism is generally regarded as a problem."[56]

In postcolonial India, linguistic pluralism had precluded the assertion of Hindi as a national language. Despite attempts by the Congress Party to implement a "three-language formula" in which each citizen would speak both Hindi and English in addition to his or her native tongue, English has remained the lingua franca of education and commerce in India. For pan-Indian nationalists, however, this was no tragedy; Gandhi had envisioned an Indian identity that transcended both language and religion, and since partition this concept has fared well against competition from more particularistic nationalisms. In Morocco, however, the Arab-Islamic orientation of the nationalist elite, fostered in the colonial schools as well as in traditional and "free" schools, precluded such a supra-ethnic nationalism.

Arabization came at a cost. Mohammed al-Fasi and his successors recognized that, because of the shortage of appropriate Arabic-language books and qualified personnel, there was a tension between their goal of cultural management and the need to drastically increase enrollment. Unlike Georges Hardy, however, they did not seriously consider the gap between Moroccan Arabic dialects and the written version when evaluating the merits of arabization. Nor did they acknowledge the fact that a large percentage (probably a majority) of Moroccan children spoke Berber at home, a fact with major educational ramifications. The legacy of the French Berber policy's attempt to "divide and rule" meant that Moroccan nationalism allowed no mention of Berber identity or rights, or of the possible advantages of teaching beginning literacy in the first language of the students.[57] As Mustapha El Qadéry has argued, Moroccan nationalism's "negation" of the French Berber policy was shaped by colonial discourse in its portrayal of Berbers as mere primitives "to be assimilated and arabized."[58] The erstwhile Collège Berbère in Azrou was renamed the Collège Musulman Tarik ben Ziyad.

Arabization meant that Berber-speaking children would have to learn two new languages in school (French and Arabic) instead of one (French). This was true to a lesser extent for Arabic-speaking children, due to the distance between Moroccan Arabic dialects and the Modern Standard Arabic embraced by the educational system. More use of French, on the other hand, would have made it easier for public school graduates to do business with Europeans, both in Morocco and while working in Europe.

However, the continued use of French would have entailed great costs and sacrifices, for Berber speakers as well as Arabic speakers. French was spoken natively by almost no Moroccans (although more French-language education might have led to more widespread use of French in public life, thus mitigating its unfamiliarity to schoolchildren). If French-medium schooling had been maintained, the post-independence expansion of education would have required the state to hire more teachers from Europe – at European salaries. A more francophone Morocco might have had weaker political and economic ties with the Arabic-speaking Middle East, and might have received less educational aid from Saudi Arabia. Worst of all, the ghettoization of Morocco's poor, rural Berber population might have been exacerbated if they had not been schooled by the Moroccan state in the language of the urban elites. However, independent Morocco's arabization policies were not inspired by such an analysis of costs and benefits, but rather by the concepts of culture and identity developed within the colonial embrace during the decades of the protectorate.

Conclusion

In the early twentieth century, cracks had appeared in the facade of republican imperialism. The *mission civilisatrice* had threatened to betray the empire, as colonial subjects became increasingly adept at articulating resistance in ways that were effective within the imperial context. Francophone elites had begun to challenge the dichotomy of domination and subordination, colonizer and colonized, turning the colonizers' own words against them. The empire had therefore required a new theory and a new language of imperialism. Lyautey, Delafosse, Hardy, and Brunot were appointed to positions of authority in the empire because they were able to offer this new language, this new culture of colonialism.

Once the ideas of these men converged in Morocco, they came up against the political, social, institutional, and discursive constraints of a particular colonial situation. For Hardy, this meant the pressure of constructing "adapted," ethnographically informed curricula and policies in a short period of time, when the available ethnological scholarship offered little concrete guidance for pedagogy. It also meant harmonizing his own impressions of Morocco with the ideas of the IHEM and of the protectorate's political-military establishment, while simultaneously trying to live up to Lyautey's vision of a vigorous new approach to colonial life. Meanwhile, this colonial agenda was challenged by the responses of the colonized population. Hardy believed that schools could control and shape society and culture, but Morocco's inhabitants were not pliable subjects who accepted the roles he envisioned for them. Elite and non-elite Muslims consistently resisted his attempts to dictate their cultural and economic options, and persistently used the French schools and the French language for their own purposes.

The colonial discourse of the French protectorate produced a distorted vision of Moroccan life that was closed off to counterevidence and complicating empiricism and which prevented adroit adaptation of policy to changing circumstances and to the aspirations of Moroccan Muslims. Such distortion may be an inevitable consequence of "seeing like a state," that is, of collecting and interpreting information and converting it into policy. However, this distortion was exacerbated by particular ideas endemic to the colonial culture of Morocco: the valuation of action as an end in itself; the belief that true knowledge can come only through an emotional communion with the Other; the belief that dispassionate reflection withers human potential. These ideas were fundamental to the colonial doctrines of Lyautey and Hardy and also to the metropolitan discourse of educational reform and the search for cultural renewal after World War I. In Morocco these ideas were combined with the equally pernicious notion that human beings are distinctly divided into groups with discrete moral, social, and psychological characteristics, groups that are easily identifiable by their language, religion, parentage, social role, or phenotype. This notion is inherently hostile to individual variation, whether in the context of colonial education, anticolonial nationalism, or postcolonial racism.

It is also inherently ill-suited to comprehend the complexities and fluidity of human behavior, especially in an era of change. Worst of all, it is inherently ill-suited to the peaceful coexistence of those who affirm their membership in different groups.

Alas, the end of empire did not bring an end to the fundamental ingredients of Hardy's failures: Lyautey's masculine glorification of action and Delafosse's "respectful" affirmation of authentic ethnic characteristics. Hardyism would live on in the culture and politics of France, despite the humiliation of Vichy. Hardy himself sought to rescue his reputation, and his pension, by making use of a 1944 law that allowed government employees dismissed for political reasons to seek compensation. Although this law had originally been intended for the victims of the Vichy regime, not its supporters, Hardy was able, in 1950, to persuade the Conseil d'état to annul de Gaulle's decree declaring him a collaborator; Hardy's pension was restored, and he received a portion of his back pay. Thus rehabilitated, Hardy resumed his role as a spokesman for empire, singing the praises of colonialism in Catholic and conservative circles, even as Morocco celebrated its independence.[59]

As the empire crumbled, the Gaullist regime re-tasked the ethnologists and administrators of the colonial service to service in the metropolitan Ministry of Culture, where they were to employ their skills in defense of a definition of French culture that could serve as an "adhesive" for a fractured postcolonial France.[60] Yet there was still much imperialist sentiment in France, especially on the Right. Fifty-seven deputies had voted against ratifying Moroccan independence in 1956. They were outvoted, but the loss of Morocco only increased the desire to retain Algeria, where the Front de libération nationale had been fighting for independence since 1954. As Stéphane Bernard put it, "The extreme Right had finally bowed to reality, but its defeat was paltry reward for victory, since events showed that it had implicitly bartered Morocco and Tunisia for assurance that no stone would be left unturned to keep Algeria."[61] In 1962, when Algeria lay in ruins, a million embittered settlers and defeated soldiers were forced to seek refuge in a France that no longer believed in empire.

The discontents of these *coloniaux déracinés* would eventually find an intellectual and political voice in the postcolonial New Right. The discourse of the New Right offered a renaissance of the colonial philosophy developed between 1900 and 1930 by men like Hubert Lyautey and Georges Hardy. The new metropolitan discourse, like the colonial discourse, used "cultural, social, and anthropological terms" to critique "the cosmopolitanism, atomization, rootlessness, and anomie of the modern age . . . through the celebration of all authentic cultures in a purportedly xenophile, 'differentialist' spirit."[62] Thus the New Right adapted colonial philosophy to the metropole. The discourse of "respect" and "difference" allowed the racism of Jean-Marie Le Pen and the Front de libération nationale to utilize the language of multiculturalism, just as Hardy and Brunot were able to draw upon the language of democratic educational reform to support their pedagogy of ethnic separation and curricular restriction. Little may remain of Brunot's "sympathetic sensitivity toward the indigenes," but the masculinist and anti-universalist intellectual heritage of Lyautism has continued to resonate in French culture.[63] The power of such ideas is magnified in France by the failures of the main countervailing discourse, an "unreconstructed Jacobin republicanism" that refuses to allow the least accommodation of differences in language, culture, or background.[64] This uncompromising universalism has led to educational failure and explosive social unrest in the French suburbs populated by the children and grandchildren of France's former colonial subjects.

Meanwhile, in Morocco, nationalists have made use of colonial ideas of ethno-cultural essentialism in the construction of an anticolonial counterhegemony. For the subordinated elites of the French empire, cultural essentialism was a tool for rallying a diverse public, for rescuing personal dignity from the humiliation of imperialism, and for manufacturing and enforcing a consensus that would bring stability to the postcolonial society. Of course, the nationalism of the colonial period was distinguished from the racism of the colonial regime and of the New Right by the relations of power: the difference between resistance and domination. Postcolonial Moroccan nationalism is more ambiguously situated, however, depending on whether one considers it in relation to the looming cultural and economic power of the West or from the vantage point of Morocco's ethnic and religious subalterns: Berbers, Saharans, the few remaining Jews, and now also South Asian and West African immigrants and their Moroccan-born children. For them, the statement that "in this country there has lived and still lives a 'people'" is fraught with painful omissions.[65]

Notes

Abbreviations

ANF	Archives nationales de France, Paris
BEAOF	*Bulletin de l'Enseignement de l'Afrique Occidentale Française*
BEPM	*Bulletin de l'Enseignement Public du Maroc*
CADNM	Centre des archives diplomatiques de Nantes, Morocco collection
CAOM	Centre des archives d'outre-mer, Aix-en-Provence
CHEAM	Centre des hautes études d'administration musulmane
DIP	Direction de l'instruction publique, des beaux-arts et des antiquités
FRAAS	Fondation du Roi Abdul-Aziz Al Saoud pour les études islamiques et les sciences humaines, Casablanca
JOAOF	*Journal Officiel de l'Afrique Occidentale Française*

Note: In references to archival documents, the archive abbreviation is followed by the collection, microfilm number and/or series, the box number, then (except in the case of loose papers) the name or number of the folder, and then, where applicable, the document number.

1. Empire and Education

1. Cooper, *Colonialism in Question*, 16; see also Comaroff and Comaroff, *Ethnography*, 29.
2. Eickelman, *Knowledge and Power*, 62; see also Boulahcen, *Sociologie de l'éducation*, 12–16.
3. Paul, "Professionals and Politics," 84–88.
4. Laskier, *Alliance Israélite Universelle*, 93; see also Roland, "Alliance Israélite Universelle."
5. Pennell, *Morocco*, 84–134; see also Burke, *Prelude*.
6. Pennell, *Morocco*, 134–57.
7. Halstead, *Rebirth*, 35–37; Hoisington, *Lyautey*, 48–49.
8. Abu-Lughod, *Rabat*, 137.
9. Saada, "*Regards croisés*," 2.
10. Cooper, *Colonialism in Question*, 28.
11. Gramsci, *Selections*, 12.
12. Betts, *Assimilation and Association*.
13. Ha, "From 'Nos Ancêtres, les Gaulois,'" 102.
14. Daughton, *Empire Divided*, 9.
15. Cooper, *Colonialism in Question*, 28.
16. Suret-Canale, *French Colonialism*, 84.
17. Wilder, *French Imperial Nation-State*, 6–10.
18. Rabinow, *French Modern*, 105.
19. Daughton, *Empire Divided*, 261.
20. Laroui, *L'histoire du Maghreb*, 9.
21. Lyautey, 4 February 1897, in *Lettres*, 142.
22. Lyautey, 12 February 1897, in *Lettres*, 146–47.
23. Vicompte E. M. de Vogue to Lyautey, 2 October 1898, qtd. in Lyautey, 3 January 1899, in Lyautey, *Lettres*, 267.
24. Lyautey, *Rôle colonial*, 2.
25. Qtd. in Hoisington, *Lyautey*, 52.
26. "C'est un Maréchal Lorrain," *Le Chef: Revue Mensuelle de Scoutism*, no. 71 (1930): 104–5.
27. Lyautey to Foreign Affairs, 15 June 1915, ANF 475 Archives privées [hereafter cited as AP] 84, doc. 5.
28. Rabinow, *French Modern*, 239.

29. Lyautey qtd. in Abu-Lughod, *Rabat*, 143.
30. Daughton, *Empire Divided*, 22.
31. Blanckaert, "Of Monstrous Métis?" 49.
32. Burke, "First Crisis of Orientalism," 217–18; Burke, "Creation," 3–4; Jadda, *Bibliographie analytique*, 15–16.
33. Conklin, "New 'Ethnology,'" 31.
34. Burke, "First Crisis of Orientalism," 217.
35. Sibeud, "Ethnographie africaniste," 14–16.
36. Valensi, "Maghreb vu du centre," 242.
37. Burke, "First Crisis of Orientalism," 222.
38. Wilder, *French Imperial Nation-State*, 63–64.
39. Conklin, "New 'Ethnology,'" 39.
40. Conklin, "New 'Ethnology,'" 30.
41. Mitchell, *Colonising Egypt*, 140.
42. Lebovics, *True France*, 9.
43. Burke, "Creation," 7–8.
44. Scott, *Seeing Like a State*, 2, 89, 340–44.
45. Bouche, "L'enseignement," 882.
46. Zartman, *Morocco*, 195.
47. N. Thomas, *Colonialism's Cultures*.
48. Cooper, *Colonialism in Question*, 17.
49. Lyautey, 17 May 1921, ANF 475AP 171/2/26.
50. Kelly, *French Colonial Education*, 28.
51. Ha, "From 'Nos Ancêtres, les Gaulois,'" 106. See also Kelly, *French Colonial Education*, 1–21; Kelly, "Franco-Vietnamese Schools," 9–18; Lebovics, *True France*, 11, 98–134.
52. Ageron, *Algériens musulmans*, 1:317–25.
53. R. Robinson, "Non-European Foundations," 122.
54. Vermeren, "La formation des élites," 47–50; Colonna, *Instituteurs algériens*, 50; Ageron, *Modern Algeria*, 75–76.
55. Lyautey to Foreign Affairs, 15 June 1915, ANF 475AP box 84, doc. 5.
56. Perkins, *Modern Tunisia*, 34–43, 62–64.
57. Vermeren, "La formation des élites," 30, 57; Paye, "Introduction et évolution," 16; Perkins, *Modern Tunisia*, 66–67.
58. Suret-Canale, *French Colonialism*, 370; Harrison, *France and Islam*, 57–67, 79; Bouche, "L'enseignement," 703–57.

59. Thompson, *Colonial Citizens*, 1.

60. Burrin, *France under the Germans*, 2.

61. Katz, *Murder in Marrakesh*, 276.

62. Scott, *Weapons of the Weak*, 29.

63. Saada, "*Regards croisés*," 1–3; Balandier, "La situation coloniale," 4–10.

64. Burke, "Middle Eastern Societies," 16.

2. An Uncertain Beginning

1. Gaston Loth, "Rapport," BEPM, no. 9 (1917): 49. This document is also the source of the present chapter's second epigraph.

2. Loth, "Rapport," 9–10, 25, 44–51; DIP, *Historique*, 53, 249. Official enrollment statistics should be understood as suggestive rather than accurate.

3. Loth, "Rapport," 50.

4. Qtd. in Vermeren, "La formation des élites," 57.

5. Loth, "Rapport," 51.

6. Lyautey to Foreign Affairs, 15 June 1915, ANF 475AP 84, doc. 5; Lyautey, "Au sujet des troupes," n.d., ANF 475AP 84, doc. 30.

7. Paye, "Introduction et évolution," 390. See also Loth, "Entretien avec Si El Hajoui," 6 November 1912, CADNM DIP 43/folder "Karaouiyine I"; Mohamed Nehlil, "Rapport sur l'Université Qaraouiyin," n.d., ANF 475AP 171/6/7; Eickelman, *Knowledge and Power*, 86–87.

8. "Les bases politiques," 28 October 1915, CADNM Direction des affaires chérifiennes [Direction of Sharifian Affairs, hereafter cited as DACH] 112/folder "Collèges Musulmans: P.V. . . . 1917–1920."

9. "Les bases politiques," 28 October 1915.

10. Loth, "Rapport," 37–38.

11. Lyautey, 4 December 1913, CADNM DACH 112/folder T1113C "Collèges Musulmans: Correspondence et Notes"; Halstead, *Rebirth*, 105.

12. Loth, "Rapport," 37–38, 50.

13. "Les bases politiques," 28 October 1915.

14. "Les bases politiques," 28 October 1915.

15. Neigel, "Note sur le fonctionnement du collège," n.d., CADNM DACH 112/folder "Collèges Musulmans: P.V. . . . 1917–1920"; Neigel, "Rapport," 28 December 1915, ANF 475AP 171/7/90.

16. "Les bases politiques," 28 October 1915.

17. Lyautey et al., correspondence, 1919–1924, ANF 475AP 171/5, docs. 3, 9, 10, 15, 17; Gershovich, *French Military Rule*, 193–98.

18. Mohammed Hajoui, "Texte du Discours," 23 November 1913, CADNM DACH 112/folder TIII1. This document is also the source of the present chapter's first epigraph.

19. Mokri, "Note," 27 August 1918, CADNM DACH 112/folder "Collèges Musulmans: P.V. . . . 1917–1920"; Merrouni, "Collège musulman," 146–53.

20. Neigel, "Note sur le fonctionnement du collège," n.d.

21. Lyautey, "Note," 12 August 1917, CADNM DACH 112/folder "Collèges Musulmans: P.V. . . . 1917–1920." On the terms "Service des renseignements" and "Affaires indigènes," see Bidwell, *Morocco under Colonial Ruile*, xi.

22. Commission des collèges musulmans, "Note," 17 September 1917, CADNM DACH 112/folder "Collèges Musulmans: P.V. . . . 1917–1920."

23. Commission des collèges musulmans, "Note," 17 September 1917; Neigel, "Note" to Loth, 21 October 1917; "Programmes des Collèges Musulmans," 1918; all in CADNM DACH 112/folder "Collèges Musulmans: P.V. . . . 1917–1920."

24. Mokri, "Note," 27 August 1918.

25. Direction de l'enseignement, "Programme des études secondaires," *Bulletin Officiel*, no. 345 (1919): 532–42.

26. Commission des collèges musulmans, "Séance du 2 Septembre 1918," 1918, CADNM DACH 112/folder "Collèges Musulmans: P.V. . . . 1917–1920."

27. Louis Brunot, "Le haut enseignement musulman," 23 June 1920, CADNM DIP 43/folder "Karaouiyine I."

28. Rivet, *Maghreb à l'épreuve*, 28.

29. Eickelman, *Knowledge and Power*, 58.

30. Neigel, "Rapport," 28 December 1915.

31. Louis Brunot, "Karaouiyine et le collège," 12 February 1918, CADNM DIP 43/folder "Karaouiyine I."

32. Direction des Affaires Indigènes [signature illegible], 5 March 1918, CADNM DACH 112/folder "Collèges Musulmans: P.V. . . . 1917–1920."

33. "Situation de l'enseignement au 1er Octobre 1912," 1912, CADNM DACH 112/folder TIII4.

34. Ageron, *Modern Algeria*, 72–73.

35. Lorcin, *Imperial Identities*, 27–34, 165.

36. Burke, "Image," 175–99; see also Lafuente, *Politique berbère*, 42–54.

37. Burke, "Image," 175–99; Hoisington, *Lyautey*, 71–72; Ageron, "La politique berbère," 62–65; Lafuente, *Politique berbère*, 80–84.

38. "Note du Secrétariat Gl. du Gt. chérifien," 1913, CADNM Direction des affaires indigènes [Direction of Indigenous Affairs, hereafter cited as DAI] 101/folder "Instructions Politiques et Directions Générales, 1913."

39. Conseil de Politique Indigène, "Procès-Verbal de la douzième séance," 16 March 1922, ANF 475AP 171/2/38.

40. Qtd. in Ageron, "La politique berbère," 62.

41. Loth, "Rapport," 52; Bidwell, *Morocco under Colonial Rule*, 242; Bertschi, 15 June 1914, CADNM DAI 63/folder "Écoles Berbères 1914–1915."

42. Clancy-Smith, "Envisioning Knowledge," 99–100.

43. Loth, "Rapport," 48.

44. Clancy-Smith, "Envisioning Knowledge," 102; see also Perkins, *Modern Tunisia*, 63.

45. Loth, "Rapport," 53.

46. Qtd. in Irbouh, *Art in the Service of Colonialism*, 107–8.

47. Irbouh, *Art in the Service of Colonialism*, 112–22.

48. Bouillot, "L'Enseignement Professionel indigène à Salé," 1913, CADNM DACH 112/folder T1114.

49. Qtd. in Loth, "Rapport," 55–56.

50. Laskier, *Alliance Israélite Universelle*, 156.

51. DIP, *Historique*, 239–41.

52. Georges Hardy, 5 September 1923, ANF 475AP 171/2/51; see also Laskier, *Alliance Israélite Universelle*, 156–64.

53. Pennell, *Morocco*, 171. There were more than 100,000 Europeans in Morocco by 1925, and about 219,000 (160,000 in the French zone) by 1930. Paul, "Professionals and Politics," 193; Rivet, *Maghreb à l'épreuve*, 274.

54. Loth, "Rapport," 6–9; DIP, *Historique*, 39; "Situation de l'Enseignement . . . Juin 1913," 1913, CADNM DAI box 100.

55. Gaudefroy-Demombynes, *L'oeuvre française*, 215–22; Vermeren, "La formation des élites," 63.

56. Baina, *Systèm*, 1:153; Loth, "Rapport," 42–43; DIP, *Historique*, 249; DIP, *Bilan 1945–1950*, 63–64. Budget figures are rounded from Paye, "Introduction et évolution," 477.

57. "Services de L'Instruction Publique," 1912, CADNM DAI 101/folder "Organisation du Protectorat-1912."

58. Gaudefroy-Demombynes, *L'oeuvre française*, 56.

59. Loth, "Rapport," 6.

60. Loth, "Rapport," 6; DIP, *Historique*, 39.

61. Lyautey to Foreign Affairs, 27 January 1920, ANF 475AP 171/1/44.

62. W. P. Schaefer, "Franco-Moroccan and Italo-Libyan Schools," 15–16.

63. Gaudefroy-Demombynes, *L'oeuvre française*, 57–59.

64. Lyautey to Foreign Affairs, 27 January 1920.

65. Lyautey to Foreign Affairs, 27 January 1920.

3. The West African Connection

1. Throughout the present chapter I have made use of Bouche, "L'enseignement"; Johnson, *Emergence of Black Politics*; Genova, *Colonial Ambivalence*; and Conklin, *Mission to Civilize*.

2. Ponty to Cor, 27 August 1913, CAOM 1 Affaires politiques [hereafter cited as AFFPOL] 170/folder 3.

3. Ponty, 1910, qtd. in Suret-Canale, *French Colonialism*, 78.

4. Conklin, *Mission to Civilize*, 109–10.

5. Ponty, 1908, qtd. in Bouche, "L'enseignement," 807.

6. Conklin, *Mission to Civilize*, 114.

7. Ponty, *Justice indigène*, 53.

8. Crowder, *West Africa*, 284; Bouche, "L'enseignement," 777; Hardy, *Conquête morale*, 42–44.

9. Bouche, "L'enseignement," 523, 531–32. An earlier École supérieure commerciale Faidherbe in Saint-Louis had been established to replace a Catholic secondary school for Africans but had closed in 1907.

10. Georges Hardy, "Sur la situation . . . juin 1911 à novembre 1912," 1912, ANF 200Mi 1145/J13/78.

11. Bouche, "L'enseignement," 812–14.

12. William Ponty and Georges Hardy, "Circulaire [1 May 1914]," *JOAOF* 10, no. 494 (1914): 462.

13. Ponty and Hardy, "Circulaire [1 May 1914]," 471.

14. Ponty and Hardy, "Circulaire [1 May 1914]," 473, 471.

15. Ponty and Hardy, "Circulaire [1 May 1914]," 476.

16. Georges Hardy, "En passant," BEAOF, no. 10 (December 1913): 276–77.

17. Qtd. in Conklin, *Mission to Civilize*, 132.

18. Crowder, *West Africa*, 360.

19. Ponty and Hardy, "Circulaire [1 May 1914]," 462.

20. Ponty and Hardy, "Circulaire [1 May 1914]," 462.

21. Ponty and Hardy, "Circulaire [1 May 1914]," 466–67. The 1914 curriculum has been adroitly summarized in Conklin, *Mission to Civilize*, 133–35.

22. Georges Hardy, "En passant," BEAOF, no. 3 (1913): 74–75.

23. Hardy, *Conquête morale*, 57. This book is also the source for this chapter's first epigraph.

24. William Ponty, "Politique agraire," BEAOF, no. 3 (1913): 88–89.

25. Conklin, *Mission to Civilize*, 137.

26. Conklin, *Mission to Civilize*, 152–53; Johnson, *Emergence of Black Politics*, 81–84, 165–69.

27. Johnson, *Emergence of Black Politics*, 217–18.

28. Qtd. in Johnson, *Emergence of Black Politics*, 168, 164.

29. Conklin, *Mission to Civilize*, 150–5; Genova, *Colonial Ambivalence*, 24–42; Johnson, *Emergence of Black Politics*, 185–91.

30. "Remobilisation," *L'AOF: Echo de la Côte Occidental d'Afrique*, no. 1029 (1917). In CAOM 1AFFPOL 534/folder 1.

31. Qtd. in Johnson, *Emergence of Black Politics*, 175.

32. Conklin, *Mission to Civilize*, 148.

33. François-Joseph Clozel in Hardy, *Conquête morale*, iii.

34. Clozel to Lt. Gov. of Haut-Senegal-Niger, n.d., ANF 200Mi 1145/J13/45.

35. Conklin, "'On a semé la haine,'" 69–72.

36. William Ponty, "Questions scolaires," BEAOF, no. 1 (1913): 21–22; Delafosse, *Les nègres*, 9–12.

37. Conklin, "'On a semé la haine,'" 69; Conklin, *Mission to Civilize*, 118.

38. Conklin, "'On a semé la haine,'" 66–71.

39. "Conseil supérieur de l'enseignement primaire," BEAOF, no. 23 (1916): 166.

40. Jezequel, "Maurice Delafosse," 90–104.

41. Hardy, *Conquête morale*, 26.

42. Hardy, "Nos élèves," BEAOF, no. 3 (1913): 78.

43. Hardy, *Conquête morale*, 290–97.

44. Hardy, "Discours," in *Maurice Delafosse*, 15.
45. Hardy, *Conquête morale*, 14–15.
46. Hardy, *Conquête morale*, 31–33.
47. Hardy, "Rapport," *BEAOF*, no. 33 (1916): 225–26.
48. Joost Van Vollenhoven, "Circulaire au sujet des chefs indigènes," 15 August 1917, in Vollenhoven, *Une âme du chef*, 191; Vollenhoven, "Circulaire au sujet d'un plan d'action scolaire," 5 October 1917, in Vollenhoven, *Une âme du chef*, 178–79.
49. Hardy, *Conquête morale*, 297–98.
50. Hardy, *Conquête morale*, 297–336.
51. Hardy, *Conquête morale*, 193.
52. Hardy, *Conquête morale*, 187.
53. Hardy to Gov. Gen., August 1916, ANF 200Mi 1170/J63/1, 79.
54. "École Faidherbe, programme," 1916, ANF 200Mi 1170/J63/15.
55. Georges Hardy, "Rapport sûr le fonctionnement du service," 18 February 1918, ANF 200Mi 1147/J16/46–49.
56. Correspondence of Government General with Compagnie française de l'Afrique occidentale, 9 August, 25 October 1918, ANF 200Mi 1171/J63, docs. 228, 330, 334; Bouche, "L'enseignement," 863.
57. Qtd. in Clozel to Min. of Colonies, 24 August 1915, CAOM IAFFPOL 597/folder 1.
58. Johnson, *Emergence of Black Politics*, 189.
59. Antonetti's complaints were paraphrased in Gabriel Angoulvant, "A.S. des Écoles," to Antonetti, 20 June 1918, ANF 200Mi 1147/J16/68.
60. Raphael Antonetti, "Extrait d'une lettre personelle," 1918, ANF 200Mi 1147/J16/63.
61. Hardy to Angoulvant, June 1918, ANF 200Mi 1147/J16/67.
62. "Objet: Au sujet de l'attitude incorrecte de divers élèves," to Hardy, 26 October 1918, ANF 200 Mi 1168/J57/119.
63. Hardy, "L'après guerre," *BEAOF*, no. 42 (1919): 59–63.
64. Hardy, "En passant," *BEAOF*, no. 39 (1918): 106–7.
65. Hardy, "L'École normale William Ponty," *BEAOF*, no. 20 (1916): 74.
66. Hardy, *Conquête morale*, 60.
67. Hardy, "En passant," *BEAOF*, no. 39 (1918): 106–7.
68. Hardy, *Deux routes*, 5–6.
69. Hardy, *Deux routes*, 6.

70. Hardy, *Deux routes*, 37.

71. Hardy, "L'après guerre," 59–63.

72. "Extraits d'articles," 1919, ANF 200Mi 1147/J16/83.

73. *Democratie*, 16 March 1919, qtd. in "Extraits d'articles," 1919, ANF 200Mi 1147/J16/83. This is also the source for this chapter's second epigraph.

74. Kelly, *French Colonial Education*, 46–63.

75. Service du personnel to Hardy, 18 March 1919, ANF 200Mi 1168/J57/119.

76. Henri Simon, 8 May 1919, qtd. in Bouche, "L'enseignement," 869.

77. Henri Simon, "Rapport au Président," 20 June 1919, ANF 200Mi 1181/J82/102.

78. "École Normale William Ponty: Rapport Annuel 1919," ANF 200Mi 1168/J57/214.

79. "Le Conseil Supérieur de l'Enseignement Primaire," 2 June 1919, ANF 200Mi 1148/J17, docs. 83, 96.

80. Qtd. in Conklin, *Mission to Civilize*, 166.

81. Bouche, "L'enseignement," 868–77, 889. See also Sabatier, "Educating a Colonial Elite."

82. Genova, *Colonial Ambivalence*, 111–21.

4. A New Pedagogy for Morocco?

1. Hardy, "L'éducation française," 774.

2. Hardy, "L'éducation française," 774.

3. William Ponty and Georges Hardy, "Circulaire [1 May 1914]," *JOAOF* 10, no. 494 (1914): 464–66.

4. Hardy, "Note sur l'enseignement des indigènes," 10 April 1921, ANF 475AP 171/2/24, p. 5. Emphasis in original. This is also the source for the present chapter's epigraph.

5. Hardy, "L'après guerre," *BEAOF*, no. 42 (1919): 59–63.

6. Hardy, "En passant: Les leçons de la guerre," *BEAOF*, no. 24 (1916): 198.

7. Hardy, "En passant," *BEAOF*, no. 27 (1916): 52; Hardy, "Quelques leçons," *BEAOF*, no. 41 (December 1918–January 1919): 38–40.

8. Hardy, "Quelques leçons," 43.

9. Hardy, "Plan d'études et programmes de l'enseignement des indigènes," *BEPM*, no. 24 (1920): 393.

10. Watson, "Politics of Educational Reform," 82–83; Talbott, *Politics of Educational Reform*, 10–11.

11. Louis Legrand qtd. in Talbott, *Politics of Educational Reform*, 26.
12. Talbott, *Politics of Educational Reform*, 27.
13. Alaimo, "Shaping Adolescence," 420–21.
14. Charles Bayet, 1897, qtd. in Alaimo, "Adolescence, Gender, and Class," 1031.
15. Claparède, *Experimental Pedagogy*, 85, 189.
16. Hardy and Brunot, *L'enfant marocain*, 7.
17. Alaimo, "Adolescence, Gender, and Class," 1051.
18. Talbott, *Politics of Educational Reform*, 34–36.
19. F. Jean-Desthieux, "L'application de la methode: La crise de l'apprentissage et l'école primaire," *L'Opinion*, 3 August 1918, 78–79; Decaunes and Cavalier, *Réformes*, 233.
20. Talbott, *Politics of Educational Reform*, 112–15.
21. Decaunes and Cavalier, *Réformes*, 60.
22. Compagnons, "Nos idées et les pouvoirs publics," *L'Opinion*, 3 August 1918, 76–77.
23. Compagnons, *L'université nouvelle: La doctrine*, 16–17, 29.
24. Claparède, *Experimental Pedagogy*, 55.
25. Compagnons, *L'université nouvelle: La doctrine*, 28.
26. Compagnons, *L'université nouvelle: Les applications*, 61, 28.
27. Claparède, *Experimental Pedagogy*, 287; Compagnons, *L'université nouvelle: La doctrine*, 36–40.
28. Roorda, *Le pédagogue n'aime pas les enfants*, 101.
29. Hardy, "Note sur l'enseignement des indigènes," 10 April 1921, p. 10.
30. Commission des collèges musulmans, "Réunion du 16 juillet 1920," 1920, CADNM DACH 112/folder "Collèges Musulmans: P.V. . . . 1917–1920."
31. Hardy, "Note au sujet des instituteurs," 1920, ANF 475AP 171/2/19; Affaires indigènes, "Note," n.d., ANF 475AP 171/2/31; Hardy, "Plan d'action," 1920, ANF 475AP 171/3/15.
32. Hardy, "Plan d'études," 398–99, 406–11.
33. Edict of 17 May 1919, qtd. in Merrouni, "Collège musulman," 157.
34. Hardy, "Plan d'études," 397.
35. Hardy, "Plan d'études," 404.
36. Commission interministérielle des affaires musulmanes, "Compte rendu," 1921, ANF 475AP 171/2/42.

37. See chapter 7.
38. Hardy, "Plan d'études," 407.
39. Hardy, "Plan d'études," 410–11.
40. Hardy, "Plan d'études," 409.
41. Hardy, "Plan d'études," 412.
42. Hardy, "Plan d'études," 410–15.
43. Hardy, "Plan d'études," 410.
44. Brunot, *Premiers conseils*, 5.
45. DIP, *Historique*, 51.
46. Gaudefroy-Demombynes, *L'oeuvre française*, 66, 68.
47. Gaudefroy-Demombynes, *L'oeuvre française*, 68–70; Paye, "Introduction et évolution," 111.
48. Hardy, "Plan d'études," 398–99, 406–11.
49. Hardy, "Plan d'études," 395–97.
50. Hardy, "Plan d'études," 413.
51. Hardy, "Plan d'études," 412–13.
52. Marty to Hardy, 16 March 1923, ANF 475AP 171/7/52.
53. Hardy, "Circulaire . . . écoles de filles," 1925, CADNM DACH 112/folder T1111; Abd el-Ouahad, 27 Moharrem 1339, received 3 November 1920, CADNM DACH 112/folder T1114.
54. Hardy, "Directions pour les écoles-ouvroirs," BEPM, no. 27 (1921): 21–22.
55. Ponty and Hardy, "Circulaire [1 May 1914]," 477.
56. Bouche, "L'enseignement," 755–77.
57. Qtd. in Brunot, *Premiers conseils*, 5–6.
58. Paye, "Introduction et évolution," 281.
59. Figure for 1920–21 from DIP, *Historique*, 240–45.
60. Hardy, "Plan d'études franco-israélite," BEPM, no. 24 (1920): 420.
61. Laskier, *Alliance Israélite Universelle*, 160–65.

5. A Psychological Ethnology

1. According to Burke, Lyautey snubbed Alfred Chatelier, who had hoped that Lyautey would bring the scholars of the Mission Scientifique to lead these research efforts. Burke, "First Crisis of Orientalism," 223–24; see also Burke, "Image," 195–96.
2. Burke, "Image," 78; Zniber, "Présentation," 4.

3. Simon, "Les études berbères au Maroc," 10.

4. Zniber, "Présentation," 4.

5. Loth, "Rapport," BEPM, no. 9 (1917): 13.

6. "Comptes rendus des séances mensuelles de l'Institut des hautes-études marocaines," *Hespéris* 1, no. 4 (1921): 463.

7. Hardy, "Discours," *Hespéris* 1, no. 4 (1921): 430; Jean Célérier, "L'année géographique," *Hespéris* 1, no. 4 (1921): 453.

8. DIP, *Historique*, 18.

9. Hardy qtd. in Lyautey, "Discours," *Hespéris* 1, no. 4 (1921): 439.

10. Lyautey, "Discours," 440.

11. Hardy, "Discours," 436.

12. Hardy, "Discours," 436.

13. Célérier, "L'année géographique," 456. On the different approaches of Hardy and Célérier, see Naciri, "Géographie coloniale."

14. Hardy, "Discours," *Hespéris* 2, no. 4 (1922): 429.

15. DIP, *Historique*, 67–69.

16. Hardy, *Mon frère le loup*, 1.

17. Hardy, *L'âme marocaine*, 1.

18. Hardy, *L'âme marocaine*, 4–5.

19. Hardy, *L'âme marocaine*, 5–13.

20. Hardy, *L'âme marocaine*, 1.

21. Hardy, "L'éducation française," 774.

22. Hardy, "L'éducation française," 774.

23. Louis Brunot, "Les caractères essentiels," BEPM, no. 53 (1923): 35–39.

24. Hardy and Brunot, *L'enfant marocain*, 1.

25. Hardy and Brunot, *L'enfant marocain*, 1.

26. Brunot, "Les caractères essentiels," 36.

27. "Comptes rendus des séances mensuelles de l'Institut des hautes-études marocaines," *Hespéris* 1, no. 4 (1921): 465.

28. Hardy, "Plan d'études et programmes de l'enseignement des indigènes," BEPM, no. 24 (1920): 401.

29. Brunot, "Les caractères essentiels," 35.

30. Brunot, "Les caractères essentiels," 47, qtd. in Hardy, *L'âme marocaine*, 21.

31. Brunot, "Les caractères essentiels," 45, qtd. in Hardy, *L'âme marocaine*, 25.

32. Henri Terasse, "Le sens artistique des Marocains," BEPM (1924), qtd. in Hardy, *L'âme marocaine*, 46.

33. Brunot, "Les caractères essentiels," 48–50.
34. Hardy and Brunot, *L'enfant marocain*, 10.
35. Brunot, "Les caractères essentiels," 47, qtd. in Hardy, *L'âme marocaine*, 36.
36. Hardy and Brunot, *L'enfant marocain*, 10.
37. Lloyd Morgan qtd. in Claparède, *Experimental Pedagogy*, 90.
38. Claparède, *Experimental Pedagogy*, 91.
39. Brunot, "Les caractères essentiels," 38.
40. Hardy, *L'âme marocaine*, 181.
41. Brunot, "Les caractères essentiels," 40, qtd. in Hardy, *L'âme marocaine*, 43.
42. Hardy, "Plan d'études," 409.
43. Hardy, "Note sur l'enseignement des indigènes," 10 April 1921, ANF 475AP 171/2/24, p. 13; Hardy, "Quelques rémarques," 9 February 1924, ANF 475AP 171/2/91.
44. Proponents of the all-Berber thesis included Captain Victor Piquet, Georges Surdon, and even Marcel Mauss. Lafuente, *Politique berbère*, 86–89; Valensi, "Maghreb vu du centre," 244.
45. Hardy, "L'éducation française," 774.
46. Hardy, "Plan d'action," 1920, ANF 475AP 171/3/15; Affaires indigènes, "Note," n.d., ANF 475AP 171/2/31.
47. Hardy and Aurès, *Grandes étapes*, 11.
48. Hardy and Aurès, *Grandes étapes*, 103.
49. Maurice Le Glay, "L'école française et la question berbère," BEPM, no. 33 bis (1921): 1–14.
50. D. Robinson, *Paths of Accommodation*, 71.
51. Hardy, *Conquête morale*, 107–8.
52. Marty, 1913, qtd. in Harrison, *France and Islam*, 116.
53. Georges Hardy, "A/s des écoles en pays berbères," 9 November 1923, ANF 475AP 171/2/52; Paye, "Introduction et évolution," 258; Feugeas, "L'enseignement dans le Moyen Atlas," CHEAM, 19 May 1948, FRAAS microfilm, p. 4.
54. Marty to Hardy, 5 June 1923, ANF 475AP 171/7/55.
55. Hardy, 1921, qtd. in Rivet, *Lyautey et l'Institution du Protectorat*, 277–78; see also Georges Hardy, "Plan d'action," 1920, ANF 475AP 171/3/15.
56. Lorcin, *Imperial Identities*, 11–12.
57. Hardy, *L'âme marocaine*, 14.

58. Brunot, "Les caractères essentiels," 37.

59. In 1929 Le Glay was involved in the suppression of a book manuscript by a teacher, René Euloge, who echoed Hardy's views about the unifying force of Islam among Moroccans. Lafuente, *Politique berbère*, 114. On the relation between Berber customs and Islamic law, see Ben-Layashi, "Secularism in the Moroccan Amazigh Discourse," 159.

60. A. Coudry, "Le problème de l'enseignement," CHEAM, 29 October 1951, FRAAS microfilm, pp. 1–12.

61. Hardy, *Mon frère le loup*, 3.

62. Hardy, "Discours," 430.

63. Hardy, *Mon frère le loup*, 3.

64. Hardy, *Mon frère le loup*, 12.

65. Hardy, *Mon frère le loup*, 31–32.

66. Hardy, *Mon frère le loup*, 2.

67. Hardy, *Mon frère le loup*, 10.

68. Hardy, *Mon frère le loup*, 11.

69. Hardy, *Mon frère le loup*, 12.

70. Hardy, "Plan d'études," 393.

6. "A Worker Proletariat with a Dangerous Mentality"

1. Pennell, *Morocco*, 203.

2. Gaudefroy-Demombynes, *L'oeuvre française*, 102–3.

3. DIP, *Historique*, 249.

4. DIP, *Historique*, 4, 259.

5. Irbouh, *Art in the Service of Colonialism*, 100.

6. "Du souq à l'usine: Procès-verbal," BEPM *Numéro décennal 1920–1930* (1930): 34.

7. "Du souq à l'usine: Procès-verbal," BEPM *Numéro décennal 1920–1930* (1930): 34.

8. "Du souq à usine: Procès-verbal," BEPM, no. 72 (1926): 35, qtd. in Gaudefroy-Demombynes, *L'oeuvre française*, 77 n. 1.

9. Paye, "Introduction et évolution," 216; Gaudefroy-Demombynes, *L'oeuvre française*, 87–88.

10. Marty, *Le Maroc de demain*, 152–53.

11. Gaudefroy-Demombynes, *L'oeuvre française*, 83–84; Pennell, *Morocco*, 201–2.

12. Gaudefroy-Demombynes, *L'oeuvre française*, 94–95, 99.

13. Irbouh, *Art in the Service of Colonialism*, 37, 48–49.

14. Irbouh, *Art in the Service of Colonialism*, 49–59.

15. Marty, *Le Maroc de demain*, 157.

16. Prosper Ricard, "Arts marocains," *Hespéris* 2, no. 4 (1922): 444–47.

17. Gabriel Rousseau, "L'enseignement professionel," BEPM 43 (1922): 20.

18. Ricard, "Arts marocains," 447.

19. Alfred Bel, "Proposition," 1915, CADNM DACH 112/folder T1114; Gaudefroy-Demombynes, *L'oeuvre française*, 87, 103; Marty, *Le Maroc de demain*, 156–57.

20. Rousseau, "L'enseignement professionel," 20.

21. Gaudefroy-Demombynes, *L'oeuvre française*, 105.

22. Pennell, *Morocco*, 222.

23. Gaudefroy-Demombynes, *L'oeuvre française*, 107.

24. DIP, *Historique*, 258–59.

25. Gaudefroy-Demombynes, *L'oeuvre française*, 99–104.

26. "Du souq à l'usine: Procès-verbal," BEPM *Numéro décennal 1920–1930* (1930): 34–38.

27. DIP, *Historique*, 61.

28. "Les vocations de nos élèves," BEPM, no. 67 (1924): 255–313.

29. Louis Brunot, "Circulaire relative à l'enseignement de l'agriculture," 183–85, 1920, reprinted in Brunot, *Premiers conseils*; Paye, "Introduction et évolution," 215–16; Gaudefroy-Demombynes, *L'oeuvre française*, 109–14; DIP, *Historique*, 62–63.

30. Louis Brunot, "Circulaire," 4 May 1920, CADNM DACH 112/folder T1111.

31. Brunot, "Circulaire," 4 May 1920.

32. Brunot, "Circulaire relative à l'enseignement de l'agriculture," 183–85; Paye, "Introduction et évolution," 215–16; Gaudefroy-Demombynes, *L'oeuvre française*, 109–14; DIP, *Historique*, 62–63.

33. "Du souq à usine: Procès-verbal," BEPM, no. 72 (1926), qtd. in Gaudefroy-Demombynes, *L'oeuvre française*, 78 n. 1.

34. Brunot, "Circulaire relative à l'enseignement de l'agriculture," 188. See also Gotteland, "Circulaire no. 317," 17 June 1931, CADNM Rabat 250/folder "Enseignement agricole."

35. DIP, *Historique*, 60.

36. Rothstein, "Out of Balance," 1.

37. Brunot, "Les caractères essentiels," BEPM, no. 53 (1923): 40, qtd. in Hardy, *L'âme marocaine*, 43.

38. Camille Mattieu, "Le Dessin, le travail manuel et les écoles indigènes," BEPM, no. 95 (1929): 113–14.

39. Gaudefroy-Demombynes, *L'oeuvre française*, 98–99.

40. L. Massignon qtd. in Paye, "Introduction et évolution," 215.

41. DIP, *Historique*, 61.

42. Rivet, *Maghreb à l'épreuve*, 238.

43. Pennell, *Morocco*, 198–203; Rivet, *Maghreb à l'épreuve*, 299.

44. DIP, *Historique*, 3–4, 249; Paye, "Introduction et évolution," 467, 477. The budget for Muslim instruction was 2,970,390 francs in 1921, rising to 9,844,000 in 1924 and peaking in 1934 at 24,241,350 "Poincaré" francs (after Poincaré's 1928 devaluation). In 1930 the total education budget was 106 million Poincaré francs. Inflation makes these budgetary figures difficult to interpret, and Paye notes that they are approximations.

45. DIP, *Historique*, 249; Paye, "Introduction et évolution," 217, 476–77. The figure of 1,200 rejected applicants in 1933, cited by Paye, was from the nationalist newspaper *Maghreb*.

46. W. P. Schaefer, "Franco-Moroccan and Italo-Libyan Schools," 19.

47. "Circulaire au sujet de l'age de recrutement des élèves dans les écoles musulmanes [1 June 1933]," in Brunot, *Premiers conseils*, 126.

48. DIP, *Historique*, 55–56.

49. Conseilleur du Gouvernement Chérifien to Directeur Général de l'Instruction Publique, 7 April 1939, CADNM DIP box 85, doc. 3368.

50. Abdallah Ben Brahim to Directeur de l'Enseignement, 20 March 1939, CADNM DIP box 85, p. 5.

7. Elite Demands

1. Mohammed Ben Abd el-Ouahad, "Discours," BEPM, no. 26 (1920): 511–12.

2. Mokri, "Note," 27 August 1918, CADNM DACH 112/folder "Collèges Musulmans: P.V. . . . 1917–1920"; Hardy to M. le Délégué à la Residence Générale, 14 April 1920, CADNM 112/folder T1113C.

3. Hardy to M. le Délégué à la Residence Générale, 14 April 1920; see also Bidwell, *Morocco under Colonial Rule*, xi, 94–96.

4. Hardy, "Note sur l'enseignement des indigènes," 10 April 1921, ANF 475AP 171/2/24, p. 8.

5. Hardy, "Pour le cas où le Général demanderait," August 1920, ANF 475AP 2/folder 17, p. 9.

6. "Projet d'organisation d'un enseignement supérieur musulman," n.d., CADNM DIP 51/folder 100.

7. Hardy, "Pour le cas où le Général demanderait," August 1920, p. 9; Hardy, "Note sur l'enseignement des indigènes," 10 April 1921, p. 3; Hardy, "Circulaire au sujet de l'orientation," 8 June 1921, CADNM DACH 112/folder T1113, p. 3.

8. Lyautey, Huot, and Immarigeon, correspondence, 1919, ANF 475AP 171/7/40–42; see also Abdelqader Tazi, "La vérité sur le collège musulman," *Action du Peuple*, 27 October 1933.

9. Marty, "Rapport . . . sur le fonctionnement," 1923, ANF 475AP 171/7/61, p. 30.

10. Marty, "Rapport . . . sur le fonctionnement," 1923, pp. 13–16.

11. Louis Vignon, "Maroc d'aujourd'hui," excerpt from *Correspondant*, 25 August 1923, ANF 475AP 171/7/79, p. 597.

12. Charles Sallefranques to Vignon, 5 December 1923, ANF 475AP 171/7/80; see also "La visite de M. Roustan au collège musulman," *Volonté du Peuple*, 15 December 1933, 2.

13. Marty, "Rapport . . . sur le fonctionnement," 1923, p. 4.

14. Abd el-Ouahad, "Discours," 511.

15. DIP, *Historique*, 226; Merrouni, "Collège musulman," 382.

16. DIP, *Historique*, 233–45; Paye, "Introduction et évolution," 227–28.

17. Brunot, "Récrutement des écoles," *BEPM* 26 (1920): 509.

18. Brunot, "Récrutement des écoles," 507.

19. Brunot, "Récrutement des écoles," 508.

20. Paye, "Introduction et évolution," 228.

21. DIP, *Historique*, 234–38; Paye, "Introduction et évolution," 228–29.

22. Marty, *Le Maroc de demain*, 136–41; Damis, "Free-School Movement," 45, 74–79; Lafuente, *Politique berbère*, 119–31; Pennell, *Morocco*, 141–43; Paye, "Introduction et évolution," 224–34; Brown, *People of Salé*, 194.

23. Rivet, *Maghreb à l'épreuve*, 333; Merrouni, "Collège musulman," 252–53.

24. DIP, *Historique*, 245; Damis, "Free-School Movement," 74, 78.

25. "Statuts de l'Association Indigène," 1920, CADNM DACH 112/folder T111B; Conseilleur p.i. du Gouvernement Chérifien to Hardy, 20 September 1920, CADNM DACH 112/folder T111B.

26. Hardy, "Note au sujet des Anciens élèves," 1920, ANF 475AP 171/7/33.

27. Hardy, 29 June 1922, CADNM DACH 112/folder T111I0.

28. Marty, *Le Maroc de demain*, 170–71.

29. Hardy, "Circulaire au sujet de l'orientation," 8 June 1921; Marty, "Note sur l'enseignement sécondaire," June 1922, CADNM DIP box 51; Robert Montagne, "Enseignement indigène," May 1922, CADNM DIP box 51; P. Cellier, "Note sur l'enseignement," n.d., CADNM DIP box 51; Hardy, "Les jeunes marocaines," 17 November 1924, ANF 475AP 171/2/81.

30. Gaudefroy-Demombynes, *L'oeuvre française*, 148–49; Merrouni, "Collège musulman," 345; Halstead, *Rebirth*, 147.

31. Ageron, "L'Association des étudiants," 26–27; Paye, "Introduction et évolution," 312–14; Halstead, *Rebirth*, 172–73; Merrouni, "Collège musulman," 345.

32. Hardy and Brunot, *L'enfant marocain*, 10; Louis Brunot, "Propos sur le bilinguisme," BEPM, no. 96 (1929): 160–61.

33. Gaudefroy-Demombynes, *L'oeuvre française*, 170–71.

34. Brunot, *Premiers conseils*, 5–6.

35. E.-F. Gautier, "L'instituteur chez les indigènes," BEPM, no. 92 (1928): 369.

36. Brunot, "Propos sur l'éducation," BEPM, no. 85 (1928): 12.

37. Brunot, "Propos sur l'éducation," 15.

38. Brunot, "Propos sur le bilinguisme," 160–61.

39. Brunot, "Propos sur l'éducation," 18.

40. Brunot, "Propos sur l'éducation," 18.

41. "Commençons par le commencement," BEPM, no. 83 (1927): 34.

42. *L'École et la Vie*, 22 July 1927, qtd. in Brunot, "Propos sur l'éducation," 13–14.

43. Brunot, "Propos sur l'éducation," 14.

44. Brunot, "Propos sur l'éducation," 15.

45. Rothstein, "Out of Balance," 1.

46. DIP, *Historique*, 226; Merrouni, "Collège musulman," 180–201; Paye, "Introduction et évolution," 245, 317.

47. Le Tourneau, "L'enseignement franco-marocaine," CHEAM, 10 November 1945, FRAAS microfilm, p. 6.

48. Brunot, *Premiers conseils*, 7–9; Merrouni, "Collège musulman," 195–98.

8. Nests of Nationalism

1. Paul Marty to Hardy, 10 September 1923, ANF 475AP 171/7/63.
2. Colonna, *Instituteurs algériens*, 153.
3. Decherf to Lyautey, 16 October 1923, ANF 475AP 171/7/74.
4. Abdelqader Tazi to Decherf, 5 October 1923, trans. from Arabic to French, ANF 475AP 171/7/75.
5. Decherf to Lyautey, 16 October 1923.
6. Qtd. in Vermeren, "La formation des élites," 62.
7. Prochaska, *Making Algeria French*, 10.
8. Emphasis in the French translation.
9. Halstead, *Rebirth*, 166–69. I have made use of Halstead throughout this chapter, as well as Pennell, *Morocco*; Lafuente, *Politique berbère*; and Ageron, "L'Association des Étudiants."
10. Brunot to Neigel, Salenc, et al., 13 March 1934, and Gotteland, "Note au sujet des associations d'anciens élèves," to Neigel, Salenc, et al., 16 March 1934, both in CADNM DIP 38/folder "Féderation des Associations d'Anciens Élèves."
11. Barbari, *Tempête*, 14; see also El Maghrebi, "Les aspirations du 'Maghreb,'" *Maghreb*, July 1932, 3.
12. Al-Khabir, "L'assemblée déliberante," *Maghreb*, March 1933, 25.
13. Al-Fasi, *Independence Movements*, 139.
14. Comité d'action marocaine, *Plan de réformes*, v.
15. Examples of the latter include Laroui, *Origines*, and Cagne, *Nation*.
16. Anderson, *Imagined Communities*, 163.
17. Langhor, "Educational 'Subcontracting,'" 48.
18. Balandier, "La situation coloniale," 7.
19. Bhabha, "Signs," 35.
20. Parry, "Problems in Current Theories," 43.
21. Bhabha, "Signs," 32.
22. Paul Marty, 14–17 July 1923, ANF 475AP 171/13/31.
23. Brown, *People of Salé*, 196–97; Lafuente, *Politique berbère*, 135–37.

24. Halstead, *Rebirth*, 161.

25. Halstead, *Rebirth*, 213–14, 278–80; see also Aouchar, *Presse marocaine*, 40.

26. Al-Fasi's faction included prominent French-educated nationalists such as Ahmed Balafrej, Omar Abdeljalil, Mohammed al-Kholti, Mohamed Diouri, and Mohammed Lyazidi. See Rivet, *Maghreb à l'épreuve*, 347; Aouchar, *Presse marocaine*, 34.

27. "L'interdiction des Aissaouas et des confréries similaires," *Action du Peuple*, 25 August 1933, 3. See also Merrouni, "Collège musulman," 348–49; Gaudefroy-Demombynes, *L'oeuvre française*, 159; Pennell, *Morocco*, 164, 207.

28. Paul Marty, "Note sur les écoles rénovées," 31 March 1922, ANF 475AP 171/8/83; Marty to Hardy, 10 September 1923, ANF 475AP 171/7/63.

29. Ageron, "L'Association des étudiants," 26–7; Halstead, *Rebirth*, 129, 172–73.

30. Comité d'action marocaine, *Plan de réformes*, viii.

31. Comité d'action marocaine, *Plan de réformes*, 99–105.

32. Mohamed Hassan Ouazzani, "À nos lecteurs," *Action du Peuple*, 1 August 1933, 1.

33. Comité d'action marocaine, *Plan de réformes*, 23, 41.

34. Comité d'action marocaine, *Plan de réformes*, 47–48, 52–55.

35. Comité d'action marocaine, *Plan de réformes*, 83–91.

36. Comité d'action marocaine, *Plan de réformes*, 84; see also "Le IIIe congrès des étudiants musulmans nord-africains," *Action du Peuple*, 29 September 1933, 1.

37. Abdelqader Tazi, "La vérité sur le collège musulman," *Action du Peuple*, 27 October 1933, 1.

38. Comité d'action marocaine, *Plan de réformes*, viii.

39. "Étudiants marocaines en Europe et en Orient," *Action du Peuple*, 1 August 1933, 2.

40. Comité d'action marocaine, *Plan de réformes*, viii; Brunot, *Premiers conseils*, 5–6.

41. Omar Abdeljalil, "L'enseignement secondaire musulman: III," *Volonté du Peuple*, 20 January 1934, 1.

42. Comité d'action marocaine, *Plan de réformes*, x.

43. For example, Ouazzani, *Protectorat*, 71; Al-Fasi, *Independence Movements*.

44. Comité d'action marocaine, *Plan de réformes*, 56–57.

45. Abdeljalil, "L'enseignement secondaire musulman: III," 1.

46. Omar Abdeljalil, "L'enseignement secondaire musulman: I," *Volonté du Peuple*, 12 January 1934, 1. See also Brunot, "Karaouiyine et le Collège," 12 February 1918, CADNM DIP 43/folder "Karaouiyine I"; Merrouni, "Collège musulman," 346.

47. El Maghrebi, "Les aspirations du 'Maghreb,'" 4.

48. Brunot, "Rapport sur la réorganisation," 11 June 1934, CADNM DIP 28/folder "Féderation des Anciens Élèves."

49. Omar Abdeljalil, "L'enseignement secondaire musulman: II," *Volonté du Peuple*, 19 January 1934, 1; Comité d'action marocaine, *Plan de réformes*, 84.

50. Gaudefroy-Demombynes, *L'oeuvre française*, 70, 74; Merrouni, "Collège musulman," 117, 167, 359; Paye, "Introduction et évolution," 246.

51. Comité d'action marocaine, *Plan de réformes*, 88–89.

52. Halstead, *Rebirth*, 68–75; Ageron, "La politique berbère," 62–77. See also "La justice indigène avant la Protectorat," n.d., ANF 475AP III/4 bis/16.

53. Merrouni, "Collège musulman," 389.

54. Halstead, *Rebirth*, 181.

55. Halstead, *Rebirth*, 181–83; Pennell, *Morocco*, 212–14.

56. Lafuente, *Politique berbère*, 102–12; Julien, *Maroc face aux impérialismes*, 159–60.

57. Ouazzani, "À nos lecteurs," 1.

58. Comité d'action marocaine, *Plan de réformes*, 12.

59. Comité d'action marocaine, *Plan de réformes*, x, 30.

60. Comité d'action marocaine, *Plan de réformes*, 30.

61. Comité d'action marocaine, *Plan de réformes*, xiii.

62. Anderson, *Imagined Communities*, 121.

63. Maddy-Weitzman, "Ethno-politics and Globalization," 74.

64. Protest poster, 1930, qtd. in Pennell, *Morocco*, 214.

65. Ahmed Balafrej, "Et maintenant?" *Maghreb*, May–June 1933, 52.

66. Hardy, *L'âme marocaine*, 14.

67. "Précisions sur la question berbère," *Action du Peuple*, 24 November 1933, 1.

68. Parry, "Problems in Current Theories," 42.

69. El Maghrebi, "Les aspirations du 'Maghreb,'" 4.

70. Paul, "Professionals and Politics," 255.

71. Al-Fasi, *Independence Movements*, 170.

72. Ben Barka, *Political Thought*, 63.

73. Abbas, "On the Margins of Nationalism," 219–22.

74. Jennings, "Conservative Confluences," 602.

9. Legacies and Reversals

1. Paye, "Introduction et évolution," 488–94.

2. Paye, "Introduction et évolution," 241–44; Merrouni, "Collège musulman," 350–52.

3. Pennell, *Morocco*, 228.

4. Ouazzani, *Combats*, 1:69; see also M. Thomas, *French Empire*, 277.

5. Paye, "Introduction et évolution," 494.

6. Jennings, "Vichy à Madagascar"; Jennings, *Vichy in the Tropics*; Ginio, "'Marshal Pétain Spoke'"; Ginio, "Enfants africains"; Hellman, *Knight-Monks of Vichy*; Barreau, "Vichy, idéologue de l'école"; Barreau, "Abel Bonnard"; Atkin, "Church and Teachers"; Decaunes and Cavalier, *Réformes*.

7. Cohen, *Rulers of Empire*, 143–44.

8. Georges Hardy, "La Légion française," BEPM, no. 168 (1941): 162–63.

9. Henri-Philippe Pétain, "Message du Maréchal Pétain," BEPM, no. 173 (1942): 260–64; Jean Courtarvel, "L'école et la nation," BEPM, no. 168 (1941): 168–71.

10. Laskier, *Alliance Israélite Universelle*, 179–82; Rivet, *Maghreb à l'épreuve*, 357.

11. Paye, "Introduction et évolution," 494–95.

12. Al-Fasi, *Independence Movements*, 201.

13. Conseil d'état, "Sieur Hardy, séance," 13 May 1949, ANF F 17/27552 (Dossier de Georges Hardy)/17 (no. 84.344).

14. Laskier, *Alliance Israélite Universelle*, 179–82.

15. Achille, Lamine, and Magne, *Quelques conseils pratiques*.

16. Paye, "Introduction et évolution," 495, 499; DIP, *Bilan 1945–1950*, 12.

17. A. Coudry, "Le problème de l'enseignement," CHEAM, 29 October 1951, FRAAS microfilm, pp. 10–11; Feugeas, "L'enseignement dans le Moyen Atlas," CHEAM, 19 May 1948, FRAAS microfilm, p. 10.

18. DIP, *Bilan 1945–1950*, iii, 66.

19. Hivernaud, *Aide-mémoire de l'instituteur au Maroc*, 199–203.

20. Roger Thabault, "Allocution radiodiffusée le 5 Juin 1945," BEPM, no. 182 (1945): 163.

21. Thabault, "Allocution radiodiffusée le 5 Juin 1945," 165.

22. Merrouni, "Collège musulman," 203.

23. Sallefranques, *Douze leçons d'histoire de France*.

24. Jadda, *Bibliographie analytique*, 38–39.

25. Merrouni, "Collège musulman," 212.

26. Pennell, *Morocco*, 282–91; Bernard, *Franco-Moroccan Conflict*, 356–69.

27. "Reconnaissance de l'indépendance du Maroc 2 mars 1956," reproduced in Alaoui, *Le Maroc*, 267.

28. Vermeren, "La formation des élites," 469–70; Paye, "Introduction et évolution," 360–73.

29. Mohammed al-Fasi, "Conference de presse," BEPM, no. 237 (1956): 11–25.

30. Baina, *Systèm*, 1:153.

31. Jennings, "Conservative Confluences," 602.

32. Vermeren, "La formation des élites," 459; Lakhdar Ghazal, ed., *Melanges Mohammed El Fasi*, 1–2.

33. Qtd. in Zartman, *Morocco*, 164.

34. Al-Fasi, "Conference de presse," 11–25.

35. Vermeren, "La formation des élites," 460.

36. Hammoud, "Arabicization in Morocco," 41.

37. Zartman, *Morocco*, 164–65.

38. Zartman, *Morocco*, 165–67, 194; Baina, *Systèm*, 2:502, 515, 525; Paul, "Professionals and Politics," 300–301.

39. Zartman, *Morocco*, 162.

40. Zartman, *Morocco*, 166–71; Hammoud, "Arabicization in Morocco," 41; Vermeren, "La formation des élites," 460.

41. Zartman, *Morocco*, 172–88.

42. Elbiad, "Sociolinguistic Study," 101.

43. Vermeren, "La formation des élites," 455–65; Paul, "Professionals and Politics," 301–4.

44. Pennell, *Morocco*, 323.

45. Hammoud, "Arabicization in Morocco," 48–51; Vermeren, "La formation des élites," 465–66.

46. Qtd. in Hammoud, "Arabicization in Morocco," 52. Hammoud cites *Al Alam*, 9 April 1971, and *Annuaire de l'Afrique du Nord*, 1971.

47. *L'Opinion*, 11 December 1978, quoted in Elbiad, "Sociolinguistic Study," 102.

48. Seckinger, "Implementing Morocco's Arabization Policy," 1–2.

49. Elbiad, "Sociolinguistic Study," 87.

50. Seckinger, "Implementing Morocco's Arabization Policy," 2.

51. Elbiad, "Sociolinguistic Study," 92.

52. *Al-Alam*, 11 June 1972, qtd. in Hammoud, "Arabicization in Morocco," 52.

53. Mohamed al-Majdoubi, member of parliament for the Union socialiste des forces populaires, qtd. in Hammoud, "Arabicization in Morocco," 56.

54. Elbiad, "Sociolinguistic Study," 98–103.

55. Qtd. in Elbiad, "Sociolinguistic Study," 86.

56. Coulmas, *What Are National Languages Good For?* 18.

57. The injustice of depriving Berber-speaking children of the opportunity to read in their mother tongue has been a central complaint of the Berber culture movement that emerged in the 1980s.

58. Qadéry, "Les Berbères," 428–29.

59. Ministère de l'éducation nationale, "Dossier de Georges Hardy," 1940–1956, ANF F 17/27552, docs. 2–25. Hardy's claim that he attempted to mitigate the impact of Vichy's anti-Semitic laws has been contradicted by Daniel Rivet, who argues that these laws were enforced with greater rigor in Algeria than in the metropole. Rivet, *Maghreb à l'épreuve*, 356.

60. Lebovics, *Bringing the Empire Back Home*, 59.

61. Bernard, *Franco-Moroccan Conflict*, 369.

62. Griffin, "Plus ça change!" 221–23.

63. Brunot, "Les caractères essentiels," BEPM, no. 53 (1923): 36.

64. Lebovics, *Bringing the Empire Back Home*, 179.

65. Hardy, *L'âme marocaine*, 14.

Bibliography

Archives and Depositories
Archives nationales de France, Paris
Centre des archives diplomatiques de Nantes
Centre des archives d'outre-mer, Aix-en-Provence
Fondation du Roi Abdul-Aziz Al Saoud pour les études islamiques et les sciences humaines, Casablanca

Books, Articles, and Theses
Abbas, Ferhat. "On the Margins of Nationalism: I Am France!" In *Sources in the History of the Modern Middle East*, edited by Akram Khater, 219–22. Boston: Houghton Mifflin, 2005.
Abu-Lughod, Janet. *Rabat: Urban Apartheid in Morocco*. Princeton: Princeton University Press, 1980.
Achille, M., Lamine, and Magne. *Quelques conseils pratiques à l'usage du personnel suppléant des écoles musulmanes*. 3rd ed. Rabat: École du livre, 1946.
Adas, Michael. "Contested Hegemony: The Great War and the Afro-Asian Assault on the Civilizing Mission Ideology." *Journal of World History* 15, no. 1 (2004): 31–63.
Ageron, Charles-Robert. *Les algériens musulmans et la France*. 2 vols. Paris: Presses universitaires de France, 1968.
——. "L'Association des étudiants musulmans nord-africains en France durant l'entre-deux-guerres." *Revue Française d'Histoire d'Outre-Mer* 70 (1983): 25–56.

———. *Modern Algeria: A History from 1830 to the Present.* Translated by Michael Brett. 9th ed. London: Hurst, 1990.

———. "La politique berbère du protectorat marocain de 1913 à 1934." *Revue d'Histoire Moderne et Contemporaine* 18 (1971): 50–90.

Alaimo, Kathleen. "Adolescence, Gender, and Class in Education Reform in France: The Development of Enseignement Primaire Supérieur, 1880–1910." *French Historical Studies* 18, no. 4 (1994): 1025–55.

———. "Shaping Adolescence in the Popular Milieu: Social Policy, Reformers, and French Youth, 1870–1920." *Journal of Family History* 17, no. 4 (1992): 419–38.

Alaoui, Moulay Abdelhadi. *Le Maroc du traité de Fes à la libération, 1912–1956.* Rabat: Éditions la porte, 1994.

Al-Fasi, Alal. *The Independence Movements in Arab North Africa.* Translated by Hazem Zaki Nuseibeh. New York: Octagon Books, 1970.

Al-Sayyid, Afaf Lutfi. *Egypt and Cromer: A Study in Anglo-Egyptian Relations.* London: John Murray, 1968.

Altbach, Philip, and Gail Paradise Kelly, eds. *Education and Colonialism.* New York: Longman, 1978.

Amselle, Jean-Loup, and Emmanuelle Sibeud, eds. *Maurice Delafosse: Entre orientalisme et ethnographie: L'itinéraire d'un africaniste (1870–1926).* Paris: Maisonneuve et Larose, 1998.

Anderson, Benedict. *Imagined Communities: Reflections on the Origin and Spread of Nationalism.* New York: Verso, 1991.

Aouchar, Amina. *La presse marocaine dans la lutte pour l'indépendance (1933–1956).* Casablanca: Wallada, 1990.

Arendt, Hannah. *The Origins of Totalitarianism.* New York, 1951.

Ashcroft, Bill, Gareth Griffiths, and Helen Tiffin, eds. *The Post-Colonial Studies Reader.* New York: Routledge, 1995.

Association universelle des amis de Jeanne d'Arc. *Patrie française et principes chrétiens.* Paris: Nouvelles éditions latines, 1956.

Atkin, Nicholas. "Church and Teachers in Vichy France, 1940–1944." *French History* 4 (1990): 1–22.

Baina, Abdelkader. *Le systèm de l'enseignement au Maroc.* 3 vols. Casablanca: Éditions maghrébines, 1981.

Balafrej, Ahmed. "Allal al-Fassi." In *Les Africains*, 12:43–59. Paris: Jeune Afrique, 1983.

Balandier, Georges. "La situation coloniale: Ancien concept, nouvelle réalité." *French Politics, Culture, and Society* 20, no. 2 (2002): 4–10.

Barbari, Mouslim. *Tempête sur le Maroc ou les erreurs d'une "politique berbère."* Paris: Éditions Rieder, 1931.

Barreau, Jean Michel. "Abel Bonnard, ministre de l'éducation nationale sous Vichy, ou l'éducation impossible." *Revue d'Histoire Moderne et Contemporaine* 43 (1996): 464–78.

———. "Vichy, idéologue de l'école." *Revue d'Histoire Moderne et Contemporaine* 38 (1990): 590–616.

Bel, Alfred. *Les industries de la céramique à Fès*. Algiers and Paris: Carbonel/A. Leroux, 1918.

———. *La religion musulmane en berbérie: Esquisse d'histoire et de sociologie religieuses*. Vol. 1. Paris: Librairie orientaliste Paul Geuthner, 1938.

Bell, Daniel. *The Cultural Contradictions of Capitalism*. New York: Basic Books, 1978.

Benabdi, Linda C. "Arabization in Algeria: Processes and Problems." PhD diss., Indiana University, 1980.

Ben Barka, Mehdi. *The Political Thought of Ben Barka*. Havana: Tricontinental, 1968.

Benhabib, Seyla. *The Claims of Culture: Equality and Diversity in the Global Era*. Princeton: Princeton University Press, 2002.

Benhaddou, Ali. *Maroc: Les élites du royaume: Essai sur l'organisation du pouvoir au Maroc*. Edited by Jean-Paul Chagnollaud, *Histoire et perspectives méditerranéennes*. Paris: Harmattan, 1997.

Ben Jelloun, Tahar. *French Hospitality: Racism and North African Immigrants*. Translated by Barbara Bray. New York: Columbia University Press, 1999.

Ben-Layashi, Samir. "Secularism in the Moroccan Amazigh Discourse." *Journal of North African Studies* 12, no. 2 (2007): 158–71.

Bentahila, Abdelâli. *Language Attitudes among Arabic-French Bilinguals in Morocco*. Avon, UK: Multilingual Matters, 1983.

Bernard, Stéphane. *The Franco-Moroccan Conflict, 1943–1956*. Translated by Marianna Oliver, Alexander Baden Harrison Jr., and Bernard Phillips. New Haven: Yale University Press, 1968.

Berque, Jacques. *Le Maghreb entre deux guerres*. 3rd ed. Paris: Éditions du seuil, 1962.

Betts, Raymond. *Assimilation and Association in French Colonial Theory, 1890–1914*. New York: Columbia, 1961.

———. *France and Decolonisation, 1900–1960*. New York: St. Martin's, 1991.

Bhabha, Homi K. "Signs Taken for Wonders." In *The Post-Colonial Studies Reader*, edited by Bill Ashcroft, Gareth Griffiths, and Helen Tiffin, 29–35. New York: Routledge, 1995.

Bidwell, Robin. *Morocco under Colonial Rule: French Administration of Tribal Areas, 1912–1956*. London: Frank Cass, 1973.

Blanckaert, Claude. "Of Monstrous Métis? Hybridity, Fear of Miscegenation, and Patriotism from Buffon to Paul Broca." In *The Color of Liberty*, edited by Sue Peabody and Tyler Stovall, 42–70. Durham NC: Duke University Press, 2003.

Bonnell, Victoria E., and Lynn Hunt, eds. *Beyond the Cultural Turn: New Directions in the Study of Society and History*. Berkeley: University of California Press, 1999.

Bouche, Denise. "L'école rurale en Afrique occidentale française de 1903 à 1956." In *The Making of Frenchmen*, edited by Donald Baker and Patrick Harrigan, 207–19. Waterloo, Ontario: Historical Reflections Press, 1980.

———. "L'enseignement dans les territoires français de l'Afrique occidentale de 1817 à 1920: Mission civilisatrice ou formation d'une élite?" Thesis, Université de Paris I, 1975.

Boulahcen, Ali. *Sociologie de l'éducation: Les systèmes éducatifs en France et au Maroc; Étude comparative*. Casablanca: Afrique Orient, 2002.

Bourdieu, Pierre, and J. C. Passeron. *Reproduction in Education, Society, and Culture*. London: Sage, 1977.

Brown, Kenneth. *People of Salé: Tradition and Change in a Moroccan City, 1830–1930*. Manchester: Manchester University Press, 1976.

Brunot, Louis. *Premiers conseils: Collection d'instructions et de manuels pédagogiques pour les maîtres des écoles musulmanes*. Rabat: École du livre, 1934.

Brunschwig, Henri. *French Colonialism, 1871–1914: Myths and Realities*. Translated by William G. Brown. New York: Praeger, 1964.

Burke, Edmund, III. "The Creation of the Moroccan Colonial Archive, 1880–1930." *History and Anthropology* 18, no. 1 (2007): 1–9.

———. "First Crisis of Orientalism, 1890–1914." In *Connaissances du Maghreb: Sciences sociales et colonisation*, edited by Jean-Claude Vatin, 213–26. Paris: Éditions du CNRS, 1984.

———. "France and the Classical Sociology of Islam, 1798–1962." *Journal of North African Studies* 12 (2007): 551–61.

———. "The Image of the Moroccan State in French Ethnological Literature: A New Look at the Origins of Lyautey's Berber Policy." In *Arabs and Berbers*, edited by Ernest Gellner and Charles Micaud, 175–99. Lexington: D. C. Heath, 1972.

———. "Middle Eastern Societies and Ordinary People's Lives." In *Struggle and Survival*, edited by Edmund Burke III, 1–27. Berkeley: University of California Press, 1993.

———. *Prelude to Protectorate in Morocco: Precolonial Protest and Resistance, 1860–1912*. Chicago: University of Chicago Press, 1976.

Burrin, Phillippe. *France under the Germans: Collaboration and Compromise*. Translated by Janet Lloyd. New York: New Press, 1996.

Cagne, Jacques. *Nation et nationalisme au Maroc: Aux racines de la nation marocaine*. Rabat: Dar Nachr al Maarifa, 1988.

Cameron, Deborah. "Linguistic Relativity: Benjamin Lee Whorf and the Return of the Repressed." *Critical Quarterly* 41, no. 2 (1999): 153–56.

Chanet, Jean-François. *L'école républicaine et les petites patries*. Paris: Aubier, 1996.

Clancy-Smith, Julia. "Envisioning Knowledge: Educating the Muslim Woman in Colonial North Africa, c. 1850–1918." In *Iran and Beyond*, edited by Rudi Matthee and Beth Baron, 99–118. Costa Mesa: Mazda Publishers, 2000.

Clancy-Smith, Julia, and Frances Gouda, eds. *Domesticating the Empire: Race, Gender, and Family Life in French and Dutch Colonialism*. Charlottesville: University Press of Virginia, 1998.

Claparède, Edouard. *Experimental Pedagogy and the Psychology of the Child*. Translated by Mary Louch and Henry Holman. Bristol, UK: Thoemmes Press, 1998.

Coe, Cati. "Educating an African Leadership: Achimota and the Teaching of African Culture in the Gold Coast." *Africa Today* 49, no. 3 (2002): 23–44.

Cohen, William. *Rulers of Empire: the French Colonial Service in Africa*. Stanford: Hoover Institution Press, 1971.

Colonna, Fanny. *Instituteurs algériens, 1883–1939*. Travaux et recherches de science politique no. 36. Paris: Presses de la fondation nationale des sciences politiques, 1975.

Comaroff, John, and Jean Comaroff. *Ethnography and the Historical Imagination*. Boulder: Westview, 1992.

Comité d'action marocaine. *Plan de réformes marocaines*. Paris: Imprimerie Labor, 1934.

Compagnons, Les. *L'université nouvelle: La doctrine*. 3rd ed. Vol. 1. Paris: Librairie Fischbacher, 1919.

———. *L'université nouvelle: Les applications de la doctrine*. 3rd ed. Vol. 2. Paris: Librairie Fischbacher, 1919.

Conklin, Alice. *A Mission to Civilize: The Republican Idea of Empire in France and West Africa, 1895–1930*. Stanford: Stanford University Press, 1997.

———. "The New 'Ethnology' and 'La Situation Coloniale' in Interwar France." *French Politics, Culture, and Society* 20, no. 2 (2002): 29–46.

———. "'On a semé la haine': Maurice Delafosse et la politique du gouvernement général en AOF, 1915–1936." In *Maurice Delafosse*, edited by Jean-Loup Amselle and Emmanuelle Sibeud, 65–77. Paris: Maisonneuve et Larose, 1998.

Conklin, Alice L., and Julia Clancy-Smith. "Introduction: Writing Colonial Histories." *French Historical Studies* 27, no. 3 (2004): 497–505.

Cooper, Frederick. *Colonialism in Question: Theory, Knowledge, History*. Berkeley: University of California Press, 2005.

Cooper, Frederick, and Ann Laura Stoler, eds. *Tensions of Empire: Colonial Cultures in a Bourgeois World*. Berkeley: University of California Press, 1997.

Coulmas, Florian, ed. *What Are National Languages Good For? Papers Presented at a Workshop of the Linguistics Society of America Institute*. Washington DC, 1985.

Crowder, Michael. *West Africa under Colonial Rule*. Evanston: Northwestern University Press, 1968.

Damis, John. "The Free-School Movement in Morocco, 1919–1970." PhD diss., Fletcher School of Law and Diplomacy, 1970.

Daughton, J. P. *An Empire Divided: Religion, Republicanism, and the Making of French Colonialism, 1880–1914*. New York: Oxford University Press, 2006.

Decaunes, Luc, and M. L. Cavalier, eds. *Réformes et projets de réforme de l'enseignement français de la Révolution à nos jours (1789–1960)*. Vol. 16 of *Mémoires et documents scolaires*. Paris: Institut pédagogique national, 1962.

Delafosse, Maurice. *Les nègres*. Paris: Éditions Rieder, 1927.
Direction générale de l'instruction publique, des beaux-arts et des antiquités. *Bilan 1945–1950*. Rabat: École du livre, 1950.
———. *Historique (1912–1930)*. Rabat: École du livre, 1930.
Eickelman, Dale. *Knowledge and Power in Morocco: The Education of a Twentieth-Century Notable*. Princeton: Princeton University Press, 1985.
Elbiad, Mohamed. "A Sociolinguistic Study of the Arabization Process and Its Conditioning Factors in Morocco." PhD diss., State University of New York at Buffalo, 1985.
El Mansour, Mohamed. "Salafis and Modernists in the Moroccan Nationalist Movement." In *Islam and Secularism in North Africa*, edited by John Ruedy. New York: St. Martin's, 1996.
Fanon, Frantz. *The Wretched of the Earth*. New York: Grove Press, 1963.
Flood, Christopher, and Hugo Frey. "Questions of Decolonization and Post-Colonialism in the Ideology of the French Extreme Right." *Journal of European Studies* 28 (1988): 69–89.
Fondation Mohammed Hassan Ouazzani. *Mohammed Hassan Ouazzani*. Casablanca: Imprimière rapide, 1980.
Fraser, W. R. *Education and Society in Modern France*. New York: Humanities Press, 1963.
Fysh, Peter, and Jim Wolfreys. *The Politics of Racism in France*. New York: MacMillan, 1998.
Garcia, Luc. "L'organisation de l'instruction publique au Dahomey, 1894–1920." *Cahiers d'études africaines* 10, no. 1 (1971): 59–100.
Gaudefroy-Demombynes, Roger. *L'oeuvre française en matière d'enseignement au Maroc*. Paris: Librairie orientaliste Paul Geuthner, 1928.
Geertz, Clifford. *The Interpretation of Cultures: Selected Essays*. New York: Basic Books, 1973.
Genova, James. "Les Chefs Naturels: The Politics of Cultural Authenticity in the Making of Post-Colonial France and West Africa, 1914–1956." PhD diss., State University of New York at Stony Brook, 2000.
———. *Colonial Ambivalence, Cultural Authenticity, and the Limitations of Mimicry in French-Ruled West Africa, 1914–1956*. New York: Peter Lang, 2004.
Gershovich, Moshe. *French Military Rule in Morocco: Colonialism and Its Consequences*. London: Frank Cass, 2000.

Gesell, Arnold. In *A History of Psychology in Autobiography*, vol. 4, edited by Edwin Boring, Herbert Langfeld, Heinz Werner, and Robert Yerkes, 123–42. New York: Russell & Russell, 1952.

Gharbi, Khaddouj. *Lexique et enseignement français au Maroc*. Casablanca: Afrique Orient, 1994.

Ginio, Ruth. "Les enfants africains de la révolution nationale: La politique vichyssoise de l'enfance et de la jeunesse dans les colonies de l'AOF (1940–1943)." *Revue d'Histoire Moderne et Contemporaine* 49, no. 4 (2002): 132–53.

———. "'Marshal Pétain Spoke to Schoolchildren' – Vichy Propaganda in French West Africa, 1940–1943." *International Journal of African Historical Studies* 33 (2000): 291–312.

Gloster-Coates, Patricia. "Historical Patterns of Higher Education for Women in Morocco since Independence." In *Views from the Edge*, edited by Neguin Yavari, Lawrence G. Potter and Jean-Marc Ran Oppenheim. New York: Columbia University Press, 2004.

Gramsci, Antonio. *Selections from the Prison Notebooks of Antonio Gramsci*. Edited by Quintin Hoare and Geoffrey Nowell Smith. New York: International Publishers, 1992.

Griffin, Roger. "Plus ça change! The Fascist Pedigree of the Nouvelle Droite." In *The Development of the Radical Right in France*, edited by Edward J. Arnold, 217–52. New York: St. Martin's Press, 2000.

Ha, Marie-Paule. "From 'Nos Ancêtres, les Gaulois' to 'Leur Culture Ancestrale': Symbolic Violence and the Politics of Colonial Schooling in Indochina." *French Colonial History* 3 (2003): 101–17.

Halpern, Manfred. "Emile Durkheim: Analyst of Solidarity but Not of Transformation." In *Connaissances du Maghreb: Sciences sociales et colonisation*, edited by Jean-Claude Vatin, 245–47. Paris: Éditions du CNRS, 1984.

Halstead, John P. "The Changing Character of Moroccan Reformism, 1921–1934." *Journal of African History* 3 (1964): 435–47.

———. *Rebirth of a Nation: The Origins and Rise of Moroccan Nationalism, 1912–1944*. Cambridge: Harvard University Press, 1969.

Halttunen, Karen. "Cultural History and the Challenge of Narrativity." In *Beyond the Cultural Turn*, edited by Victoria E. Bonnell and Lynn Hunt, 165–81. Berkeley: University of California Press, 1999.

Hammoud, Mohamed Salah-Dine. "Arabicization in Morocco: A Case Study in Language Planning and Language Policy Attitudes." PhD diss., University of Texas at Austin, 1982.

Hannoui, Abdelkhalek. "Diglossia, Medial Arabic, and Language Policy in Morocco." DA diss., State University of New York at Stony Brook, 1987.

Hardy, Georges. *L'âme marocaine d'après la littérature française*. Bulletin de l'enseignement public du Maroc no. 73. Paris: Émile Larose, 1926.

———. *Une conquête morale: L'enseignement en A.O.F.* Paris: Librairie Armand Colin, 1917.

———. *Les deux routes: Conseils pratiques aux jeunes fonctionnaires indigènes*. Bulletin de l'enseignement de l'AOF no. 40 (November 1918). Gorée, 1919.

———. "L'éducation française au Maroc." *Revue de Paris* 28 (1921): 773–89.

———. *Géographie de l'Afrique occidentale française*. Bulletin de l'enseignement en Afrique occidentale française nos. 8–9. Gorée, 1913.

———. *Mon frère le loup: Plaidoyer pour une science vivante*. Bulletin de l'enseignement public du Maroc no. 69. Paris: Émile Larose, 1925.

Hardy, Georges, and Paul Aurès. *Les grandes étapes de l'histoire du Maroc*. Bulletin de l'enseignement public du Maroc no. 29. Paris: Émile Larose, 1921.

Hardy, Georges, and Louis Brunot. *L'enfant marocain: Essai d'ethnographie scolaire*. Bulletin de l'enseignement public du Maroc no. 63. Paris: Émile Larose, 1925.

Harrison, Christopher. *France and Islam in West Africa, 1860–1960*. New York: Cambridge University Press, 1988.

Hellman, John. *The Knight-Monks of Vichy France: Uriage, 1940–1945*. Montreal: McGill-Queen's University Press, 1993.

Hivernaud, A. *Aide-mémoire de l'instituteur au Maroc*. Casablanca: Imprigema, 1955.

Hoisington, William. *The Casablanca Connection: French Colonial Policy, 1936–1943*. Chapel Hill: University of North Carolina Press, 1984.

———. *Lyautey and the French Conquest of Morocco*. Scranton PA: Macmillan, 1995.

Irbouh, Hamid. *Art in the Service of Colonialism: French Art Education in Morocco 1912–1956*. London: Tauris, 2005.

———. "French Colonial Art Education in Morocco." *Ijele: Art eJournal of the African World* 2, no. 1 (2001).

Jadda, M'Hamed. *Bibliographie analytique des publications de l'Institut des hautes études marocaines (IHEM): 1915–1959*. Rabat: Faculté des lettres, 1994.

Jennings, Eric. "Conservative Confluences, 'Nativist' Synergy: Reinscribing Vichy's National Revolution in Indochina, 1940–1945." *French Historical Studies* 27, no. 3 (2004): 601–35.

———. "Vichy à Madagascar: La 'Révolution Nationale,' l'enseignement et la jeunesse, 1940–1942." *Revue d'Histoire Moderne et Contemporaine* 1999 (1999): 729–46.

———. *Vichy in the Tropics: Pétain's National Revolution in Madagascar, Guadeloupe, and Indochina, 1940–1944*. Stanford: Stanford University Press, 2001.

Jezequel, Jean-Hervé. "Maurice Delafosse et l'émergence d'une littérature africaine à vocation scientifique." In *Maurice Delafosse*, edited by Jean-Loup Amselle and Emmanuelle Sibeud, 90–104. Paris: Maisonneuve et Larose, 1998.

Johnson, G. Wesley. *Double Impact: France and Africa in the Age of Imperialism*. Westport CT: Greenwood Press, 1985.

———. *The Emergence of Black Politics in Senegal: The Struggle for Power in the Four Communes, 1900–1920*. Stanford: Stanford University Press, 1971.

———. "The Impact of the Senegalese Elite upon the French, 1900–1940." In *Double Impact*, edited by G. Wesley Johnson, 154–78. Westport CT: Greenwood Press, 1985.

———. "William Ponty and Republican Paternalism in French West Africa (1866–1915)." In *African Proconsuls*, edited by L. H. Gann and Peter Duignan, 127–56. New York: Free Press, 1978.

Julien, Charles-André. *Le Maroc face aux impérialismes, 1415–1956*. Paris: Éditions J.A., 1978.

Katz, Jonathan G. *Murder in Marrakesh: Émile Mauchamp and the French Colonial Adventure*. Bloomington: Indiana University Press, 2006.

Kelly, Gail Paradise. "Colonial Schools in Vietnam: Policy and Practice." In *Education and Colonialism*, edited by Philip Altbach and Gail Paradise Kelly, 96–121. New York: Longman, 1978.

———. "Franco-Vietnamese Schools, 1918–1938." PhD diss., University of Wisconsin–Madison, 1975.

———. *French Colonial Education: Essays on Vietnam and West Africa*. Edited by David H. Kelly. New York: AM Press, 2000.

———. "The Presentation of Indigenous Society in the Schools of French West Africa and Indochina, 1918 to 1938." *Comparative Studies in Society and History* 26, no. 3 (1984): 523–42.

Klein, Martin. *Slavery and Colonial Rule in French West Africa*. Cambridge: Cambridge University Press, 1998.

Knibiehler, Yvonne. "L'enseignement au Maroc pendant le protectorat (1912–1956): Les 'fils de notables.'" *Revue d'Histoire Moderne et Contemporaine* 41, no. 3 (1994): 489–98.

Knibiehler, Yvonne, Geneviève Emmery, and Françoise Leguay. *Des français au Maroc: La présence et la mémoire (1912–1956)*. Paris: Denoël, 1992.

Kodish, Bruce. "What We Do with Language – What It Does with Us." *ETC: A Review of General Semantics* 60 (2003): 383–95.

Lafuente, Giles. *La politique berbère de la France et le nationalisme marocain*. Paris: Harmattan, 1999.

Lahlou-Alaoui, Zakia. "Lyautey ou le 'père du protectorat' français du Maroc: Le double et son langage." In *Maroc: Littérature et peinture coloniales (1912–1956)*, 19–26. Rabat: Publications de la Faculté des lettres, 1996.

Lakhdar Ghazal, Ahmed, ed. *Mélanges Mohammed El Fasi: Publiés à l'occasion du dixième anniversaire de l'Université Mohammed V, 1957–1967*. Rabat: Université Mohammed V, 1967.

Langhor, Vickie. "Educational 'Subcontracting' and the Spread of Religious Nationalism: Hindu and Muslim Nationalist Schools in Colonial India." *Comparative Studies of South Asia, Africa, and the Middle East* 21, nos. 1–2 (2001): 42–49.

Laroui, Abdallah. *L'histoire du Maghreb: Un essai de synthèse*. Casablanca: Centre culturel arabe, 1995.

———. *The History of the Maghrib: An Interpretive Essay*. Translated by Ralph Manheim. Princeton Studies on the Near East. Princeton: Princeton University Press, 1977.

———. *Les origines sociales et culturelles du nationalisme marocain (1830–1912)*. Paris: François Maspero, 1980.

Laskier, Michael. *The Alliance Israélite Universelle and the Jewish Communities of Morocco, 1862–1962*. Albany: State University of New York Press, 1983.

Lebovics, Herman. *Bringing the Empire Back Home: France in the Global Age*. Durham NC: Duke University Press, 2004.

———. *True France: The Wars over French Cultural Identity, 1900–1945*. Ithaca: Cornell University Press, 1992.

Léon, Antoine. *Histoire de l'éducation technique*. 2nd ed. Vol. 938 of *"Que sais-je?" Le point de connaissances actuelles*. Paris: Press universitaires de France, 1968.

Lévy-Bruhl, Lucien. *Les fonctions mentales dans les sociétés inférieures*. Paris: Alcan, 1910.

Lorcin, Patricia. *Imperial Identities: Stereotyping, Prejudice, and Race in Colonial Algeria*. New York: I. B. Tauris, 1995.

Loti, Pierre. *Morocco (Au Maroc)*. Translated by W. P. Baines. New York: Stokes, 1930.

Lyautey, Louis-Hubert. *Lettres du Tonkin et du Madagascar*. Vol. 2. Paris: Armand Colin, 1920.

———. *Paroles d'action*. Edited by Georges Duby. Paris: Éditions la porte, 1995.

———. *Du rôle colonial de l'armée*. Paris: Armand Colin, 1900.

———. "Du rôle social de l'officier." *Revue des Deux Mondes* 104 (1891): 443–59.

Maddy-Weitzman, Bruce. "Ethno-politics and Globalization in North Africa: The Berber Culture Movement." *Journal of North African Studies* 11, no. 1 (2006): 71–83.

Mann, Gregory. *Native Sons: West African Veterans and France in the Twentieth Century*. Durham NC: Duke University Press, 2006.

Marty, Paul. *Le Maroc de demain*. Paris: Comité de l'Afrique française, 1925.

———. "La politique indigène du Gouverneur Général Ponty en Afrique occidentale française." *Revue du Monde Musulman* 31 (1915): 1–22.

Maurice Delafosse, 1870–1926. Paris: Société d'éditions géographiques, maritimes, et coloniales, 1928.

McFerren, Margaret. "Special Report: Arabization in the Maghreb." Washington DC: Center for Applied Linguistics, December 1984.

Memmi, Albert. *The Colonizer and the Colonized*. Translated by Howard Greenfeld. Boston: Beacon Press, 1965.

Merrouni, Mekki. "Le collège musulman de Fès (1914 à 1956)." PhD diss., Université de Montréal, 1981.

Michel, Marc. "Maurice Delafosse et l'invention d'une africanité nègre." In

Maurice Delafosse, edited by Jean-Loup Amselle and Emmanuelle Sibeud, 78–89. Paris: Maisonneuve et Larose, 1998.

Mitchell, Timothy. *Colonising Egypt*. Berkeley: University of California Press, 1988.

Mommsen, Wolfgang J. *Theories of Imperialism*. Translated by P. S. Falla. Paperback ed. Chicago: University of Chicago Press, 1982.

Montagne, Robert. *Révolution au Maroc*. Paris: France-Empire, 1953.

Naciri, Mohamed. "La géographie coloniale: Une 'science appliquée' à la colonisation; Perceptions et interprétations du fait colonial chez J. Célerier et G. Hardy." In *Connaissances du Maghreb: Sciences sociales et colonisation*, edited by Jean-Claude Vatin, 309–33. Paris: Éditions du CNRS, 1984.

Ouardighi, Abderrahim. *L'itinéraire d'un nationaliste: Mehdi ben Barka 1920– 1965 une biographie*. Rabat: Éditions Moncho, 1982.

Ouazzani, Mohamed Hassan. *Combats d'un nationaliste marocain: 1933–1937*. Edited by Izarab Ouazzani. 2 vols. Fez: Fondation Mohamed Hassan Ouazzani, 1987.

———. *Le protectorat – Crime de lèse-nation: Le cas du Maroc*. Fez: Fondation Mohamed Hassan Ouazzani, 1992.

Oved, Georges. *La gauche française et le nationalisme marocain, 1905–1955*. Vol. 2, *Tentations et limites du réformisme colonial*. Paris: Harmattan, 1984.

Parry, Benita. "Problems in Current Theories of Colonial Discourse." In *The Post-Colonial Studies Reader*, edited by Bill Ashcroft, Gareth Griffiths and Helen Tiffin, 36–44. New York: Routledge, 1995.

Parti de l'Istiqlal. *Bref aperçu sur le Maroc avant le protectorat, sous le protectorat et les aspirations du peuple marocain*. Rabat: Bureau de documentation et d'information, 1952.

Paul, James A. "Professionals and Politics in Morocco: A Historical Study of the Mediation of Power and the Creation of Ideology in the Context of European Imperialism." PhD diss., New York University, 1975.

Paye, Lucien. "Introduction et évolution de l'enseignement moderne au Maroc." Thesis, Université de Paris Sorbonne, 1957.

Peabody, Sue, and Tyler Stovall, eds. *The Color of Liberty: Histories of Race in France*. Durham NC: Duke University Press, 2003.

Pennell, C. R. *Morocco since 1830: A History*. London: Hurst, 2000.

Perkins, Kenneth J. *A History of Modern Tunisia*. Cambridge: Cambridge University Press, 2004.

Ponty, William. *Justice indigène: Instructions aux administrateurs sur l'application du décret du 16 août 1912.* Dakar: Imprimerie Ternaux, 1913.

Porter, Geoff. "At the Pillar's Base: Islam, Morocco, and Education in the Qarawiyin Mosque, 1912–2000." PhD diss., New York University, 2002.

Pratt, Mary Louise. *Imperial Eyes: Travel Writing and Transculturation.* New York: Routledge, 1992.

Prochaska, David. *Making Algeria French: Colonialism in Bône, 1870–1920.* New York and Paris: Cambridge University Press/Éditions de la Maison des sciences de l'homme, 1990.

Qadéry, Mustapha El. "Les Berbères entre le mythe colonial et la négation nationale: Le cas du Maroc." *Revue d'Histoire Moderne et Contemporaine* 45, no. 2 (1998): 425–50.

Rabinow, Paul. *French Modern: Norms and Forms of the Social Environment.* Cambridge: MIT Press, 1989.

Rivet, Daniel. "École et colonisation au Maroc: La politique de Lyautey au début des années 20." *Cahiers d'Histoire* 21 (1976): 173–97.

———. *Lyautey et l'institution du protectorat français au Maroc, 1912–1925.* Vol. 2. Paris: Harmattan, 1988.

———. *Le Maghreb à l'épreuve de la colonisation.* Paris: Hachette, 2002.

Robinson, David. "France as a Muslim Power in West Africa." *Africa Today* 46, nos. 3–4 (1999): 105–27.

———. *Paths of Accommodation: Muslim Societies and French Colonial Authorities in Senegal and Mauritania, 1880–1920.* Athens: Ohio University Press, 2000.

Robinson, Ronald. "Non-European Foundations of European Imperialism: Sketch for a Theory of Collaboration." In *Studies in the Theory of Imperialism,* edited by Roger Owen and Bob Sutcliffe, 117–42. New York: Longman, 1972.

Roland, Joan Gardner. "The Alliance Israélite Universelle and French Policy in North Africa, 1860–1918." PhD diss., Columbia University, 1969.

Roorda, Henri. *Le pédagogue n'aime pas les enfants.* Lausanne: Librairie Payot, 1918.

Rothstein, Richard. "Out of Balance: Our Understanding of How Schools Affect Society and How Society Affects Schools." Chicago: The Spencer Foundation, 2002.

Russell, Mona. "Competing, Overlapping, and Contradictory Agendas: Egyptian Education under British Occupation, 1882–1922." *Comparative Studies of South Asia, Africa, and the Middle East* 21 (2001): 50–60.

Saada, Emmanuelle. "*Regards Croisés*: Transatlantic Perspectives on the Colonial Situation." *French Politics, Culture, and Society* 20, no. 2 (2002): 1–3.

Sabatier, Peggy. "Educating a Colonial Elite: The William Ponty School and its Graduates." PhD diss., University of Chicago, 1977.

Saïd, Edward. *Orientalism*. New York: Vintage Books, 1979.

Sallefranques, Charles. *Douze leçons d'histoire de France à usage des maîtres de l'enseignement musulman*. Rabat: École du livre, 1950.

Schaefer, Wayne Peter. "Franco-Moroccan and Italo-Libyan Schools, 1912–1940: A Comparison." PhD diss., University of Illinois at Chicago, 1987.

Schaefer, Wolf. "Global Civilization and Local Cultures: A Crude Look at the Whole." *International Sociology* 16 (2001): 301–19.

Scham, Alan. *Lyautey in Morocco*. Berkeley: University of California Press, 1970.

Scott, James C. *Seeing Like a State: How Certain Schemes to Improve the Human Condition Have Failed*. New Haven: Yale University Press, 1998.

———. *Weapons of the Weak: Everyday Forms of Peasant Resistance*. New Haven: Yale University Press, 1985.

Seckinger, Beverly. "Implementing Morocco's Arabization Policy: Two Problems of Classification." In *What Are National Languages Good For?* edited by Florian Coulmas, 1–29. Washington DC: Linguistic Society of America, 1985.

Segalla, Spencer D. "French Colonial Education and Elite Moroccan Muslim Resistance, from the Treaty of Fes to the Berber Dahir." *Journal of North African Studies* 11, no. 1 (2006): 85–106.

———. "Georges Hardy and Educational Ethnology in French Morocco, 1920–1926." *French Colonial History* 4 (2003): 171–90.

Sherman, Daniel J. "'People's Ethnographic': Objects, Museums, and the Colonial Inheritance of French Ethnology." *French Historical Studies* 27, no. 3 (2004): 669–703.

Sibeud, Emmanuelle. "Ethnographie africaniste et 'inauthenticité' coloniale." *French Politics, Culture, and Society* 20, no. 2 (2002): 11–28.

Simon, Colonel H. "Les études berbères au Maroc." In *Les Archives Berbères . . . 1915–1916*, 7–10. Rabat: Al Kalam, 1987.

Singer, Barnett. "Lyautey: An Interpretation of the Man and French Imperialism." *Journal of Contemporary History* 26 (1991): 131–57.

Sinha, Mrinalini. *Colonial Masculinity: The "Manly Englishman" and the "Effeminate Bengali" in the Late 19th Century*. Manchester: Manchester University Press, 1995.

Slavin, David. "French Colonial Film before and after *Itto*: From Berber Myth to Race War." *French Historical Studies* 21 (1998): 125–55.

Sonolet, L., and A. Pérès. *Le livre du maître africain: À l'usage des écoles de village*. 2nd ed. Paris: Armand Colin, 1923.

Soucy, Robert. *French Fascism: The First Wave, 1924–1933*. New Haven: Yale University Press, 1986.

———. *French Fascism: The Second Wave, 1933–1939*. New Haven: Yale University Press, 1995.

Spivak, Gayatri Chakravorty. "Can the Subaltern Speak?" In *The Post-Colonial Studies Reader*, edited by Bill Ashcroft, Gareth Griffiths, and Helen Tiffin, 24–28. New York: Routledge, 1995.

Stoler, Ann Laura. *Capitalism and Confrontation in Sumatra's Plantation Belt, 1870–1979*. New Haven: Yale University Press, 1985.

———. *Carnal Knowledge and Imperial Power: Race and the Intimate in Colonial Rule*. Berkeley: University of California Press, 2002.

———. *Race and the Education of Desire: Foucault's History of Sexuality and the Colonial Order of Things*. Durham NC: Duke University Press, 1995.

Stoler, Ann Laura, and Frederick Cooper. "Between Metropole and Colony: Rethinking a Research Agenda." In *Tensions of Empire*, edited by Frederick Cooper and Ann Laura Stoler, 1–56. Berkeley: University of California Press, 1997.

Suret-Canale, Jean. *Afrique noire occidentale et centrale*. 3rd ed. Paris: Éditions sociales, 1968.

———. *French Colonialism in Tropical Africa*. Translated by Till Gottheiner. New York: Pica Press, 1971.

Swearingen, Will D. *Moroccan Mirages: Agrarian Dreams and Deceptions, 1912–1986*. Princeton: Princeton University Press, 1987.

Talbott, John. *The Politics of Educational Reform in France, 1918–1940*. Princeton: Princeton University Press, 1969.

Taylor, Charles. "The Politics of Recognition." In *Multiculturalism and "The

Politics of Recognition," edited by Amy Gutmann, 25–73. Princeton: Princeton University Press, 1992.

Thomas, Martin. *The French Empire between the Wars: Imperialism, Politics, and Society.* Manchester: Manchester University Press, 2005.

Thomas, Nicholas. *Colonialism's Cultures: Anthropology, Travel, and Government.* Princeton: Princeton University Press, 1994.

Thompson, Elizabeth. *Colonial Citizens: Republican Rights, Paternal Privilege, and Gender in French Syria and Lebanon.* New York: Columbia University Press, 2000.

Tlili, Bechir. "Le mouvement national marocain à la veille de la deuxième guerre mondiale (1932–1937)." *Les Cahiers de Tunisie* 34, no. 1–2 (1986): 15–110.

Valensi, Lucette. "Le Maghreb vu du centre: Sa place dans l'école sociologique française." In *Connaissances du Maghreb: Sciences sociales et colonisation*, edited by Jean-Claude Vatin, 227–44. Paris: Éditions du CNRS, 1984.

Vermeren, Pierre. "La formation des élites par l'enseignement supérieur au Maroc et en Tunisie au XXème siècle." Thesis, Université de Paris VIII Saint-Denis, 2000.

Vollenhoven, Joost Van. *Une âme du chef: Le Gouverneur Général J. Van Vollenhoven.* Paris: Imprimerie Henri Diéval, 1920.

Watson, D. R. "The Politics of Educational Reform in France during the Third Republic, 1900–1940." *Past and Present*, no. 34 (1966): 81–99.

Whitehead, Clive. *Colonial Educators: The British Indian and Colonial Education Service, 1858–1983.* New York: I. B. Tauris, 2003.

Whorf, Benjamin Lee. *Language, Thought, and Reality.* Edited by John B. Carrol. Cambridge: MIT Press, 1956.

Wilder, Gary. *The French Imperial Nation-State: Negritude and Colonial Humanism between the Two World Wars.* Chicago: University of Chicago Press, 2005.

Young, Robert. *Colonial Desire: Hybridity in Theory, Culture, and Race.* New York: Routledge, 1995.

Zartman, I. William. *Morocco: Problems of New Power.* New York: Prentice Hall, 1964.

Zniber, Mohamed. "Présentation de la deuxième édition." In *Les Archives Berbères . . . 1915–1916*, 3–5. Rabat: Al Kalam, 1987.

Index

Abbas, Ferhat, 226, 235
Abd al-Karim, Muhammad bin, 172
Abdelaziz, Moulay (sultan), 5
Abdelhafid (sultan), 5–6
Abdeljalil, Larbi ben, 205–6
Abdeljalil, Omar, 217, 224, 225, 230, 253, 285n26
Abd el-Ouahad, Mohammed ben, 177–78, 185, 187
Abderrahmane (sultan), 3
Abduh, Muhammed, 189
accommodation, 11, 28–29, 43–44, 56, 153–54, 158, 167, 211–12
Action du Peuple, 211, 217, 221, 223, 226, 233
Afghani, Jamal al-Din al-, 189
L'Afrique occidentale française (AOF). *See* French West Africa
age restrictions, 174, 188, 254
agronomy schools, 167
Algeria, 4, 36–37, 226, 262; Berbers in, 15, 47, 49, 118, 140, 142; education policy in, 24–25, 50, 155; political resistance in, 214, 218, 226, 235, 247, 262–63
Alliance française, 4
Alliance israélite universelle (AIU), 4, 54, 112, 241. *See also* Moroccan Jews: education of
"Amadou l'Artilleur," 61, 84–85
L'âme marocaine d'après la littérature française (Hardy), 124–25, 130–31, 142, 233

Amin, Qasim, 109, 222
Anciens Élèves. *See* Associations des Anciens Élèves
Anglo-French Entente Cordiale, 5
Angoulvant, Gabriel, 71, 80
anti-assimilationism. *See* assimilationism
anti-intellectualism, 99, 144–45; and Lyautey's colonial philosophy, 13, 19, 90, 145
Antonetti, Raphael, 80, 81
apprenticeships, 64, 104, 161–62, 165–66, 168; and European businesses, 155, 157, 176. *See also* vocational education
apprivoisement, 63, 76, 87, 92. *See also* colonialism theories
Arabic language instruction, 91, 225, 239, 243; in the *collèges*, 40, 43, 44–47, 102, 201, 223–24; and corpus arabization, 257–58; and nationalism, 223–24, 226–27, 231, 234, 257–59; in postcolonial Morocco, 250–51, 259–60; and the Quran, 3, 24; in rural schools, 108, 138, 143, 226; in urban and elite schools, 105–6, 107–8. *See also* language instruction
arabization, 30–31, 47, 143, 228; in postcolonial Morocco, 250–60. *See also* Berbers
Arab Revolt, 216
Archives Berbères, 48, 117–18
Archives Marocaines, 16

Arslan, Shakib, 211, 219, 229–30
assimilationism, 87, 101, 237; in Algeria, 24–25; and the Berbers, 141–42, 144, 228, 230–31; in French West Africa, 63, 68, 69, 70–71, 78; and Lyautey's anti-assimilationism, 15, 25, 27, 36–37, 183–85, 188, 230; and nationalism, 224–26, 230–31, 234–35, 249; and pedagogy, 9–10, 55, 92, 103, 191, 218, 235; in Tunisia, 25–26. *See also* colonialism theories
associationalism, 9, 17, 23, 178, 228. *See also* colonialism theories
L'association des étudiants musulmans nord-africains en France (AEMNAF), 195, 201
Association du commerce, industrie, et agriculture (ACIA), 155
Association of Muslim North African Students in France (AEMNAF), 195, 200
Associations des Anciens Élèves, 191–93, 207; and nationalism, 211, 216, 217, 218–19; and reform, 193–96, 200–201, 210, 226, 238–39, 245. See also *collèges*
Atlas Mountains. *See* Middle Atlas
Au Maroc (Loti), 126
Aurès, Paul, 124, 138–39

baccalaureate: French, 44, 45, 101–2, 178, 183–84, 188, 193–95, 200–201, 224, 239; overseas, 245–46
Balafrej, Ahmed, 217, 219, 232, 285n26
Banna, Hassan al-, 230
Basset, Henri, 118, 122, 126–27, 128
Basset, René, 16
Bel, Alfred, 34, 52, 53, 58
Ben Abbès, Youssef, 254
Ben Barka, Mehdi, 234–35, 254
Ben Brahim, Abdallah, 175
Ben Hima, Mohammed, 254–55
Ben Jelloun, Tahar, 237
Benjelloun Touimi, Abdelkrim, 253
Berber *dahir*, 48, 139, 229–30, 235, 246, 248. *See also* nationalism
Berber policy, 47–50, 77, 211, 228–30, 232–33, 259. *See also* Berbers
Berbers, 2, 243, 278n44, 289n57; and arabization, 228, 259–60; and Berber-Arab dichotomy, 137–44; and Berber policy, 47–50, 77, 211, 228–30, 232–33, 259; Kabyle, 15, 47, 49, 118, 140; and nationalism, 227–34; schools for, 47–50, 77, 100, 140–44, 183, 259
Berber Studies Committee, 117–18, 119. *See also* Institut des hautes études marocaines (IHEM)
Berriau, Henri, 42
Bolshevism, 19, 144, 218
Bouillot, Louise, 51–52, 53
Boutaleb, Abdelhadi, 255
Bouyad, Hassan, 216
Brazzaville conference, 243
Brunot, Louis, 18–19, 53, 89, 90, 106, 172, 183, 237, 242; and Associations des Anciens Élèves, 195–98, 200; and Berber-Arab dichotomy, 142–43; and *collèges* commission, 42–47; and enrollment, 174, 186–88; and ethnology, 20, 123, 130, 131–34, 135–36, 149, 154, 179, 198–200, 201–2; as head of Fez *collège*, 40; and nationalists, 211, 223; and rural schools, 166–67
— Works: "Les caractères essentiels de la mentalité marocaine," 127, 128, 129, 135–36, 233; *Premiers conseils*, 197, 242
budget, education system, 55, 57, 152, 163, 173, 176, 241, 281n44
Bulletin de l'Enseignement Public du Maroc, 20, 123, 124, 127, 139–40, 142, 144, 165, 170, 178, 197, 199, 201, 241
business community, European, 154–55, 157, 159, 164, 165, 168, 176. *See also* vocational education

"Les caractères essentiels de la mentalité marocaine" (Brunot), 127, 128, 129, 135–36, 233
Casablanca, 5, 40, 57
Célérier, Jean, 121
Centre de formation pédagogique, 238
certificat d'études secondaire musulmanes (CESM), 186, 239
Le Chatelier, Alfred, 16, 17, 276n1
citizenship, French, 36, 68–70, 84, 224, 235
Claparède, Edouard, 97, 99–100, 135, 198–99, 244

Clozel, François-Joseph, 17, 71–72, 75–76, 78, 79
Cochinchina, 23
Collège Alaoui, 26
Collège Berbère, 141, 259
Collège de France, 16
Collège Moulay Idriss, 39, 140, 201
Collège Moulay Youssef, 39
Collège Musulman Tarik ben Ziyad, 259
collèges, 58, 96, 141, 217, 238; creation of, 39, 40–47; and curriculum, 41, 43–45, 102–3, 122, 183–85, 223–24, 226; employment for graduates of, 178–82; enrollment in, 39, 55, 173, 185–88, 189, 190–91, 243; equivalency of, to French baccalaureate, 44, 45, 101–2, 178, 183–84, 188, 193–95, 200–201, 224, 239; and nationalism, 217, 223–25; and postwar reform, 245–46. *See also* Associations des Anciens Élèves; *écoles des fils de notables*; elites (Muslim Moroccan)
Collège Sadiqi, 25–26, 194–95
collèges arabes. See *collèges*
collèges musulmans. See *collèges*
colonial administration: and Berbers, 48, 49, 77, 137–40, 211; employment in, 43, 65, 79–80, 81–82, 181, 186, 201; Lyautey's philosophy of, 11–15, 29, 36–37, 52, 90, 95, 112–13, 120, 153–54, 213, 230; under the Popular Front, 237–40; postwar, 241–44; training institutions for, 117, 118–19, 122, 178. *See also* colonialism theories; *makhzan*
colonialism theories, 8–11, 148; *apprivoisement*, 63, 76, 87, 92; associationalism, 9, 17, 23, 178, 228; and hybridization, 213–15, 237, 258; Lyautism, 11–15, 36–37, 213, 221–23, 263. *See also* assimilationism; colonial administration
colonizer-colonized relationship, 7–8, 12, 13–14, 20, 22, 28–31, 179; and language difficulties, 132–33; and nationalism, 213; postcolonial, 247–48, 260; and racial hierarchy, 147–48. *See also* colonialism theories
Comité des études historiques et scientifiques, 17
Compagnons de l'université nouvelle, 98–101, 244

companies, European. *See* business community, European
Congrès de l'enseignement professionnel indigène, 168
conservatism, 26, 169–70; and female education, 50, 110; Lyautey's attachment to, 12, 13, 14, 25, 106
corpus arabization, 257–58. *See also* Arabic language instruction
Counillon, Pierre, 242
craft industry, 5, 159–63, 223; and training courses, 51–53, 155, 161–62. *See also* vocational education
Crémieux, Adolphe, 4
cultural identity, 52, 120, 218, 223–28, 231, 233–35, 246, 261, 278n44; and arabization, 248–60; French, 262–63. *See also* nationalism
curriculum, 35–36, 39, 101, 104–5, 118–19, 196; in *collèges*, 41, 43–45, 102–3, 122, 183–85, 223–24, 226; female education, 51–52, 53; of "free schools," 190; French metropolitan, 95–96, 100; in French West Africa, 64–65, 67, 72, 78, 81; and Moroccan character, 130, 134, 137; and nationalism, 222–23, 226; postwar, 244; and professional education, 154–55, 164–65. *See also* pedagogy

Dakar, 27, 68, 69, 70, 83–84, 85
dar al-muallimat, 51–52. *See also* female education
de Gaulle, Charles, 242
Delafosse, Maurice, 17, 83, 87, 94, 113, 224; influence of, on Hardy, 62, 72–74, 75, 77, 90–91, 144
Delavignette, Robert, 240
La Démocratie du Sénégal, 69, 84
Les deux routes (Hardy), 82–83, 84–85, 86
Diagne, Blaise, 79, 83–84, 85, 86–87, 101, 214, 235; election of, 69–70; influence of, on Hardy, 62
Diouf, Galandou, 69
diplôme d'études secondaire musulmanes (DESM), 186, 193–94, 200–201, 239, 246
Direction de l'enseignement, 54, 56, 89. *See also* Direction de l'instruction public (DIP)

Direction de l'instruction public (DIP), 34, 89, 125, 132, 153–54, 237; and budget, 55, 57, 152, 163, 173, 176, 241, 281n44; and connection between knowledge and policy, 123–24; and curriculum, 134, 136, 137; and enrollment, 151, 153; and ideology, 169–70, 175–76, 179–80; in independent Morocco, 248; and postwar education expansion, 242–46, 248; and professional schools, 155–56, 163–72

Direction de l'instruction public, des beaux arts et des antiquités (DIP). *See* Direction de l'instruction public (DIP)

Doukkali, Bouchaib, 38, 40

Doutté, Edmond, 16

École coloniale, 22, 72, 90, 172, 240

École des langues orientales, 16, 51, 72

École des pupilles mécaniciens de la marine, 63

École Faidherbe, 79–80, 81, 86

École industrielle et commerciale de Casablanca, 155, 163

École normale (École William Ponty), 63–64, 80, 81, 86

écoles de fortune, 23

écoles de goum (soldiers' schools), 238

écoles des fils de notables, 39–40, 95, 165, 195, 222; enrollment in, 189, 191; and language instruction, 102–3, 107–8. See also *collèges*; elites (Muslim Moroccan)

écoles franco-israélites, 54, 110–11

écoles primaires supérieures, 96, 141

écoles rurales élémentaires, 238

École supérieure de langue arabe et de dialectes berbères (ESLADB), 117, 118–19, 126–27. *See also* Institut des hautes études marocaines (IHEM)

École supérieure professionnelle Pinet-Laprade, 63–64

école unique, 98, 112

economy: French West African, 76; and modernization, 19, 34, 76, 130, 151–53, 158, 172–73, 176, 244; and reform, 220

educational theory. *See* pedagogy

"L'education française au Maroc" (Hardy), 126

educators. *See* teachers

Egypt, 3, 19–20, 44, 46, 215

elites, Vietnamese, 23

elites (Muslim Moroccan), 19, 217, 260–61; collaboration with, 13–14, 19, 29–30, 33–34, 37–39, 41–44, 53, 89, 178–82, 192–93, 206–9, 217; and postcolonial education, 251–52, 257; and reform demands, 178–82, 185–92, 200, 237–39, 245–46; and vocational education, 164–65. See also *collèges*; *écoles des fils de notables*

El Mokri (grand vizier), 159–60, 178–79, 191–92, 214; and Islamic education, 42, 44, 180–81

L'enfant marocain (Hardy), 124, 127, 132, 142, 233

enrollment, 34–35, 52–53, 137, 151, 152, 173–74, 180, 238, 239–40; in AIU schools, 4; in *collèges*, 39, 55, 173, 185–88, 189, 191, 243; in *écoles des fils de notables*, 189, 191; of European settlers, 54; and female education, 52–53, 110, 174–75, 242–43; in French-run Algerian schools, 25; in French West Africa, 63–64, 80; of Moroccan Jews, 54; postcolonial, 254; postwar, 242–43; in primary schools, 34, 152, 153, 174, 188–89, 248

ethnic differences, 16, 83, 135–36, 170–71, 201–2, 221, 261–62; and Hardy's policies, 19, 71, 75–77, 89, 91, 94, 126, 146–48, 227. *See also* ethnology

ethnography, 16–17, 19, 72–75, 77, 118, 123, 201–2; as scientific endeavor, 145–46. *See also* ethnology

ethnology, 79, 207, 249; of Berbers and Arabs, 47–49, 137–38, 142–44; and colonial education policy, 16–21, 59–60, 89–90, 113; dissemination of, 34, 59; Hardy's reliance on, 19–20, 73–74, 84, 89–91, 113, 115–17, 121–34, 136–37, 142–49, 170, 227, 232–33, 240; Maurice Delafosse's, 72–74; and the "Moroccan soul," 20, 30–31, 87, 98, 117, 124–37, 142–43, 170–71, 197–200, 223; and nationalism, 224, 227; and pedagogy, 19, 101, 117–23, 127–28, 134–37, 143, 149, 233, 260–61; as scien-

INDEX | 313

tific endeavor, 145–46; and the Vichy regime, 240. *See also* psychology
European businesses. *See* business community, European
European settlers, 34, 53, 54–55, 56, 112–13, 152, 173, 188–89, 251; number of, 270n53
évolués, 68–70, 83–84, 135, 214. *See also* resistance

Fanon, Franz, 213–14
Fasi, Alal al-, 210, 216, 217, 234, 241
Fasi, Mohammed al-, 210, 219, 248, 250–53, 259, 285n26
female education, 50, 95, 218, 222, 227, 239, 245; and enrollment, 52–53, 110, 174–75, 242–43; in French West Africa, 109–10; and vocational training, 51–53, 108–9
Ferry laws, 9, 24
Fez, 3, 6, 34, 39, 40, 52, 58, 109, 126, 167, 191–92; nationalism in, 204
field schools, 243
First Republic, 27
Four Communes, 27, 68–70, 83–85. *See also* French West Africa
Fourth Republic, 171, 222, 248, 251, 257
France: and citizenship, 36, 68–70, 84, 224, 235; educational discourse in, 93–98, 121; educational reform in, 98–101; ethnological institutions in, 17–18, 262; First Republic, 27; Fourth Republic, 171, 222, 248, 251, 257; July Monarchy, 68; and the Popular Front, 237–40; and postcolonial identity, 262–63; republican values in, 10–11, 12, 70, 219; Second Republic, 24, 27, 68; Third Republic, 9, 11, 24–25, 27, 36, 56, 68, 94–96, 198; and the Vichy regime, 240–41, 242, 259n59. *See also* colonial administration; French West Africa
"free schools" (Salafi schools), 189–90, 191, 216, 227, 239, 247–48. *See also* Salafiyya
French language instruction, 35–36, 111, 134–35, 164, 183–85; in Berber schools, 140, 141; in *collèges*, 40–42, 43, 45, 102–3, 180, 183–85; and female education, 109, 175; in French West Africa, 66–67, 77–78; in postcolonial Morocco, 250–51, 257; and vocational vocabulary, 91–92, 104–5, 156. *See also* language instruction
French Mission schools, 251–52
French Revolution, 36, 244
French West Africa, 17, 26–27, 72–74, 129, 131; colonial education system in, 26–28, 62–68, 71–72, 74–87, 91; economy of, 76; and female education, 109–10; resistance in, 61–62, 68–71, 74, 79, 83–84, 85–87, 101, 214, 235

Gallieni, Joseph, 11, 14, 62, 113, 153–54, 228
Gaudefroy-Demombynes, Roger, 151, 162, 171, 196
gender. *See* female education; masculinity
Géographie de l'Afrique occidentale française (Hardy), 59, 64
girls' schools. *See* female education
Glaoui, Thami al-, 246
Gorée, 27, 68, 69, 83–84, 85
Gotteland, Jean, 168, 172, 173, 195, 211
Gramsci, Antonio, 8
Les grandes étapes de l'histoire du Maroc (Hardy), 124, 138–39, 233
Great Britain, 4–5, 12, 19–20, 23
Great Depression, 154, 176
Guérin, Daniel, 219

Hajoui, Mohammed al-, 33, 37–38, 41
"handicrafts schools," 51–53. *See also* craft industry
Hardy, Georges, 152, 175–76, 188, 203, 220; appointment of, as Morocco's director of Public Instruction, 28, 59–60, 61, 89; and Associations des Anciens Élèves, 191–94; and Berber-Arab differentiation, 50, 137–43; and *collèges*, 101–2, 178–83, 188; and craft guilds, 159–60; and curricula, 67, 76, 91–92, 94, 96, 101, 102–3, 105, 107–8, 122–23, 134–35, 180–81, 196, 222–23; departure of, from Morocco, 172, 195; dismissal of, by de Gaulle, 242; and ethnology, 19–20, 73–74, 84, 89–91,

Hardy, Georges (cont.)
113, 115–17, 121–34, 136–37, 142–49, 170, 227, 232–33, 240, 260–61; and female education, 53, 108–10, 174–75; as French West Africa educational director, 26, 28, 59, 64–68, 71, 73–86, 92–93, 109–10; and general education emphasis, 64–65, 87, 103, 156–57, 164, 167, 185; influences of, 62, 71–72, 73–74, 75–76, 87, 92–93, 98, 144, 224; and Islamic education, 105–8, 225; and Jewish school administration, 54, 110–12; legacy of, 262; and mission of colonial education, 93–94, 108, 115–17, 121, 144; and "moral" instruction emphasis, 64–65, 67, 81–83, 105, 156; and "Moroccan" (archetype), 98, 116–17, 124–37, 143, 148, 154, 170, 190–91, 196, 233; and pedagogy, 59–60, 90, 94, 101–3, 112–13, 123–24, 134–36, 143, 154, 182–84, 233, 238, 260–61; service dates of, 2, 18, 86, 242; and Vichy regime, 240–41, 242, 259n59; and vocational education, 103–5, 156–57, 164, 167
— Works: *L'âme marocaine d'après la littérature française*, 124–25, 130–31, 142, 233; *Les deux routes*, 82–83, 84–85, 86; "L'education française au Maroc," 126; *L'enfant marocain*, 124, 127, 132, 142, 233; *Géographie de l'Afrique occidentale française*, 59, 64; *Les grandes étapes de l'histoire du Maroc*, 124, 138–39, 233; *Mon frère le loup*, 144–48; *Une conquête morale*, 59, 77–78, 82, 86
Hassan, Moulay (sultan), 3–4
Hassan II, 253–55
Henrys, Paul, 48
Hespéris, 118, 121, 122, 127
Huot, Charles, 159–60
hybridization, 213–15, 237, 258. *See also* colonialism theories

independence, Moroccan, 246–60, 262–64. *See also* nationalism
India, 258–59
Indigenous Affairs, 42, 46, 50, 72, 108, 117, 141, 179, 186
Indochina, 23, 85, 101, 247
Indochinese University, 23

Institut des hautes études marocaines (IHEM), 17, 90, 119–24, 128–29, 141, 148–49, 245, 247, 261; post-secondary program for Muslims in, 181–82, 186
Institut d'ethnologie, 18
Institut d'études et recherches pour l'arabisation, 257
Intelligence Service. *See* Indigenous Affairs
Islam, 15, 140–41; and Salafiyya reformism, 38; as unifying cultural factor, 30, 138, 139–40, 143, 208, 218–19, 233–34, 279n59. *See also* Islamic schools
Islamic law (*sharia*), 49, 143, 189–90, 229, 279n59
Islamic schools, 38, 44, 56–57, 105–7, 109, 225–27; in Algeria, 24; in French West Africa, 27; *madaris*, 3, 24; under *makhzan* control, 7, 34, 45, 247–48; Qarawiyyin (mosque-university), 3, 34–35, 37–38, 45, 179, 180–81, 189, 210, 218, 247–48; Yusufiyya (mosque-university), 3; *zawaya*, 3
Islamism. *See* pan-Islamism
Istiqlal, 217, 246, 250, 254–55. *See also* independence, Moroccan; nationalism

James, William, 99
Jews. *See* Alliance israélite universelle (AIU); Moroccan Jews
job placement, 156, 158–59, 163–66, 180–82, 186. *See also* vocational education
Jules Ferry education laws, 9, 24
July Monarchy, 68

Kabyle Berbers, 15, 47, 49, 118, 140. *See also* Berbers
Kholti, Mohammed al-, 210, 215, 217, 219, 285n26
Kittani, Abdelhay al-, 38, 218, 246

Labonne, Erik, 243
Lakhdar-Ghazal, Ahmed, 257
language instruction, 98, 107–8, 132–33, 138, 191–92, 196, 289n57; in Algeria, 24; in the *collèges*, 40–42, 43, 44–47, 102; for colonial administrators, 23; and female education, 52; in France, 98; in French West Africa, 66–67,

77–78; and pedagogy, 67, 77–78; in postcolonial Morocco, 250–51, 253–54, 256–60. *See also* Arabic language instruction; French language instruction
Laraki, Azeddine, 255
Laval, Pierre, 212
League of Nations, 144, 145–46
Lebovics, Herman, 237
LeClerc, René, 34
Le Glay, Maurice, 139–40, 141, 142, 143, 279n59
Léguillette, André, 64
Lévy-Bruhl, Lucien, 18
linguistic pluralism, 258–59. *See also* language instruction
Longuet, Robert-Jean, 219
Loth, Gaston, 18–19, 33, 34, 36, 53, 78, 101, 116, 117; appointment of, as director of education, 26; and Berber schools, 49–50; and *collèges* commission, 42–43, 44–45, 46–47; and curriculum, 35–36; dismissal of, by Lyautey, 57–58, 101, 102; and enrollment expansion, 55–56; and Moroccan Jews, 54
Loti, Pierre, 83; *Au Maroc*, 126
Lyautey, Louis-Hubert, 1, 17, 23, 93, 220, 276n11; anti-assimilationism of, 15, 25, 27, 36–37, 183–85, 188, 228, 230; and anti-intellectualism, 13, 19, 90, 145; appointment of Hardy by, 28, 58–60, 61; and collaboration with Morocco's elites, 13–14, 33–34, 37–39, 41–44, 89, 182, 206–9; colonial philosophy of, 11–15, 29, 36–37, 52, 90, 95, 112–13, 120, 153–54, 213, 230, 261–62; conservatism of, 12, 13, 14, 25, 106; and Gaston Loth, 26, 57–58, 101, 102; and Institut des hautes études marocaines (IHEM), 17, 119–20; and mission of colonial education, 14, 15, 35, 45, 57–58, 116; and "new colonial man" ideal, 12, 13, 50–51, 111, 116, 240; resignation of, 172
Lyautism, 11–15, 29, 36–37, 41–45, 221–23, 228, 243, 263. *See also* colonialism theories; Lyautey, Louis-Hubert
Lyazidi, Mohamed, 217, 285n26
lycées, 41, 43, 95, 188, 201, 222, 224–25, 245–46. See also *collèges*

Macheul, Louis, 26
Madagascar, 23, 62
Maghreb, 211–12, 217, 219, 225, 226, 232
makhzan, 38–39, 48, 57, 153, 187, 217, 229; and Berbers, 139–40; and conflict with the French, 37, 41–44; and craft guilds, 159–60; decline of, 4–7; education of future members of, 178–79, 181–82; and Islamic education, 7, 34, 45, 247–48; and supervision of *collèges*, 40, 41–45, 46. *See also* colonial administration
manual education. *See* vocational education
Marc, Raoul, 42, 179
Marrakesh, 3, 40
Marty, Paul, 158, 185, 190, 193, 215, 230; and assimilationism, 183–84; and Associations des Anciens Élèves, 203, 219; and Berber schools, 140–42, 143
masculinity, x–xi, 12, 50–51, 262, 263
Mattieu, Camille, 170–71
Mauss, Marcel, 18, 278n44
Meknes, 6, 39, 40, 41, 48, 57, 117
memorization, 46, 93, 131–32, 198
métissage, 15
Middle Atlas, 230, 231; arabization of, 47; pacification of, 28, 43, 48–49, 117–18; schools in, 50, 140–41, 143
military academies, 39, 41
Ministry of Culture, 262
miscegenation, 15, 223
Mission scientifique du Maroc, 16
Mission Universitaire Culturelle Française, 251–52
modernization, 21, 28, 38–39, 102, 178; of Moroccan economy, 19, 34, 76, 130, 151–53, 158, 172–73, 176, 244
Mohammed, Sidi (sultan), 3–4, 212
Mohammed V (Mohammed ben Youssef), 30, 245, 253
Mokri. *See* El Mokri (grand vizier)
Mon frère le loup (Hardy), 144–48
De Monzie, Anatole, 145
"moral" instruction, 64–65, 67, 81–83, 105, 156
"Moroccan baccalaureate," 245–46. *See also* baccalaureate

316 | INDEX

Moroccan Jews, 221, 224; education of, 3, 4, 53–54, 110–12, 188, 241; and stereotypes, 126
"Moroccan soul," 20, 30–31, 117, 136–37, 142–43, 223; Hardy's description of, 124–35; and pedagogy, 87, 98, 170–71, 197–200. *See also* ethnology
Moroccan state. *See* makhzan
Muslim elites. *See* elites (Muslim Moroccan)

Naciri, Mekki, 219
Nasserism, 253
nationalism, 2, 28, 29, 30, 48, 87, 144, 189, 204–10; and arabization, 257–59; and Berbers, 227–34, 259; and end of protectorate, 246–47; and independence, 246–57, 263–64; origins of, in French-run schools, 217–19, 232–33, 235; origins of, in Morocco, 212–16, 220; platform of, 220–27, 230–31, 234–35; and Popular Front, 237–39; and secret societies, 210–12. *See also* resistance
National Revolution, 240–41
naturalization. *See* citizenship, French
Nehlil, Mohamed, 117
Neigel, J., 40, 42, 43, 46
"new colonial man" ideal, 12, 13, 50–51, 111, 116, 240. *See also* Lyautey, Louis-Hubert
New Right, 263–64
Noguès, Charles, 238, 241, 242
non-attendance. *See* enrollment

"oil stain" colonialism metaphor, 14, 187, 221–22. *See also* colonialism theories
orientalism, 16, 22, 207; and Edward Saïd, 125; and ethnology, 18, 19, 20; and Georges Hardy, 90, 125
originaires, 27, 68–70. *See also* resistance
Ottoman Empire, 4, 5, 25, 44
Ouazzani, Mohamed Hassan, 217, 219, 221, 229, 234, 239
Oufkir, Mohammed, 254
Oujda, 5, 189

Palestine, 215, 216
pan-Arabism, 138, 212, 215, 218, 250. *See also* nationalism

pan-Islamism, 138, 144, 215, 218, 219, 253
Parry, Benita, 233
Paye, Lucien, 171, 241, 242
pedagogy, 8, 75, 77, 199; and "adolescence," 97; and assimilationism, 9–10, 55, 92, 103, 191, 218, 235; and Berber-Arab dichotomy, 50, 100; and colonial goals, 153–54, 182–84; and education reform in France, 99–101; and ethnic groups, 97–98, 113; and ethnography, 74–75; and ethnology, 19, 101, 117–23, 127–28, 134–37, 143, 149, 233, 260–61; and female education, 108–9; foreign-language, 67, 77–78, 102–3, 255; Hardy's theories of, 59–60, 90, 94, 101–3, 112–13, 123–24, 134–36, 143, 154, 182–84, 233, 238; and Moroccan Jews, 111–12; and nationalism, 217–18; postwar, 242–46, 247; and reculturation, 248–49, 255–60. *See also* curriculum
Pérès, A., 64
Pétain, Henri-Philippe, 59, 93, 98, 172, 185, 240
physical education, 100, 111
Plan de réformes, 220–24, 226–27, 230–31, 247. *See also* nationalism
political dissent. *See* resistance
Ponsot, Henri, 212
Ponty, William, 27–28, 62–68, 70, 73, 75, 78, 92; death of, 70–71. *See also* French West Africa
Popular Front, 237–40
postwar education expansion, 241–45
pre-apprenticeship training, 156, 157. *See also* apprenticeships
Premiers conseils (Brunot), 197, 242
primary schools, 103–5, 107–8, 155, 156–58, 171, 188, 195; and arabization, 252, 253, 254–56; for Berbers, 141; and curriculum, 95–96, 108, 164; enrollment in, 34, 152, 153, 174, 188–89, 248; in French West Africa, 72, 83, 85; postwar reform, 245. *See also* professional schools
professional schools, 103–4, 155–59, 161–63, 171–72, 181, 226; enrollment in, 152, 153, 174, 188–89; reform of, 163–69. *See also* primary schools; vocational education

psychology: and "adolescence," 97; and "Moroccan soul," 20, 30–31, 87, 98, 117, 124–37, 142–43, 170–71, 197–200, 223; and recapitulation theory, 97–98, 198. *See also* ethnology

Qarawiyyin (mosque-university), 3, 34–35, 45, 179, 180–81, 189, 210, 218, 247–48; attempted reform of, 37–38. *See also* Islamic schools
Quranic instruction, 105–6, 107, 109, 132, 143–44, 175, 225. *See also* Islamic schools

Rabat, 6, 39, 40, 52, 53, 57, 161, 167, 192, 238
racial traits. *See* ethnic differences
recapitulation theory, 97–98, 198. *See also* psychology
reculturation, 248–49, 255–60. *See also* arabization
reform, educational: and Associations des Anciens Élèves, 193–96, 200–201, 210, 226, 238–39, 245; elite demands for, 178–82, 185–92, 200, 237–39, 245–46; in France, 98–101; under Noguès, 238; postwar, 242–46; of professional schools, 163–69. *See also* arabization
resistance, 260–61; in Algeria, 214, 218, 226, 235, 247, 262–63; and Associations des Anciens Élèves, 191–98, 200–201, 203–4, 207, 210, 211, 216, 217, 218–19, 226; and Berber *dahir*, 229–30; to educational age restrictions, 254; to French colonial education, 8, 28–30, 37–38, 41–45, 56, 136–37, 149, 172, 185–90; in French West Africa, 61–62, 69–71, 74, 85, 87, 101; of Middle Atlas Berbers, 118; and 1911 rebellion, 6; to Qarawiyyin mosque-university reform, 37–38; and Rif rebellion, 172, 191, 231; and secret societies, 210–12; in Senegal, 61–62, 66, 68–71, 79, 80, 83–84, 85–86, 92. *See also* nationalism
Revolution of 1789, 11
Ricard, Prosper, 160–61
Rif rebellion, 172, 191, 231
Rivet, Paul, 18
Roorda, Henri, 100, 198

Roume, Ernest, 26, 27
Rousseau, Gabriel, 161
Roux, A., 242
Rufisque, 27, 68, 69
rural schools, 104–5, 155, 156, 165–67, 168, 173, 222, 238, 244; in French West Africa, 64, 65, 67, 86–87; language instruction in, 105–6, 108, 134–35, 138, 226. *See also* primary schools; urban schools

Saïd, Edward, 125
Saint-Louis, 27, 68, 69
Salafi schools ("free schools"), 189–90, 191, 216
Salafiyya, 38, 189–90, 212–13, 216, 218–19, 222, 228, 234
Salé, 40, 51–52, 53
Sallefranques, Charles, 184–85, 215, 245
Schools for the Sons of Notables. *See écoles des fils de notables*
Second Republic, 24, 27, 68
secret societies, 210–12. *See also* Associations des Anciens Élèves; nationalism
secularism, 9, 27, 95, 197, 219
segregation, educational, 15, 23, 26, 39–40, 66, 94, 188–89, 222, 224. *See also* elites (Muslim Moroccan)
Senegal, 28, 63; political agitation in, 61–62, 68–71, 83–84, 85–87, 214, 235. *See also* French West Africa
Senghor, Leopold, 87
Service de l'enseignement public. *See* Direction de l'instruction public (DIP)
Service des antiquités préislamiques, 89
Service des arts indigènes, 89, 160–63, 223
Service des monuments historiques, 89
Service des renseignements. *See* Indigenous Affairs
Service économiques, 34
Service of Higher Islamic Education, 250
Simon, Henri, 85, 117–18
social hierarchy, 36, 38–39, 44, 95, 113, 206–7, 222. *See also* elites (Muslim Moroccan)
social mobility, 29, 96, 165–66, 167, 176
Société d'ethnographie de Paris, 16, 17
Sonolet, Louis, 64
Steeg, Théodore, 172, 195

stereotypes, ethnic, 20, 75–76, 126, 129, 131. *See also* ethnic differences
Syria, 46, 215, 216

Taifa, 211
Tamazight (Berber dialect), 2
Tangiers, 3, 4
Tarifat (Berber dialect), 2
Tashlehait (Berber dialect), 2
Tazi, Abdelqader, 203–6, 207–10, 215, 219, 220, 222; letter of, to General Decherf, 204–6, 207, 208–9. *See also* Associations des Anciens Élèves
Tazi, Mohammed, 210, 215
teachers: from Algeria, Egypt, and Tunisia, 102, 138; and colonial education policy, 196–99, 214; and crafts courses, 162; European, in Morocco, 4; Muslim, 34, 106–7; in postcolonial Morocco, 247, 250–53, 254, 255; recruitment of, 35, 123, 252–53; as "salesmen of empire," 8; shortages of, 45–46; training of, 122–23, 124, 127–28, 141, 163, 222, 238, 242, 243; *ulema* (Muslim professors), 5–6, 37–38, 44; West African, 80, 82–83, 86
Terasse, Henri, 130–31
Tetuan, 4
Thabault, Roger, 242, 243–45
theater, 216
Third Republic, 9, 11, 24–25, 27, 36, 56, 68, 198; and public education, 94–96
Tonkin, 23
traditional crafts. *See* craft industry
Treaty of Algeciras, 7
Treaty of Fez, 6, 33, 36–37, 56, 178, 211–12, 230
Treaty of Madrid, 7, 36
Tunisi, Khair al-Din al-, 25
Tunisia, 25–26, 46
Turkey, 216

ulema, 5–6, 37–38, 44. *See also* Islamic schools
Une conquête morale, 59, 77–78, 82, 86
universalism, 10, 27, 61–62, 72, 146–48, 244, 263

Université Mohammed V, 247
University of Algiers, 16
urban crafts. *See* craft industry
urban planning, 14–15
urban schools, 103–4, 105, 155–57, 165–66, 173, 222, 244; in French West Africa, 64, 65–66, 86–87; language instruction in, 107–8. *See also* primary schools; rural schools

Van Vollenhoven, Joost, 71, 72, 76
verbalism, 77–78, 91–93, 135. *See also* language instruction
Verne, Jules, 78
Vichy regime, 240–41, 242, 259n59. *See also* Pétain, Henri-Philippe
Vietnam, colonial education in, 23
Vignon, Louis, 184, 245
vocational education, 58, 104, 109, 111, 153, 156–59, 167–72; and European business community, 154–55, 157, 159, 164, 165, 168, 176; in France, 96–97; in French West Africa, 72, 79; and "handicrafts schools," 51–53; and job placement, 156, 158–59, 163–66. *See also* professional schools
Vogue, E. M. de (Vicompte), 12–13

wars of pacification, 28, 43, 48–49, 117–18
West Africa. *See* French West Africa
Whorf-Sapir hypothesis, 258. *See also* language instruction
Wilson, Woodrow, 99, 216
World War I, 35, 36, 38, 49, 54, 61, 70, 79–80, 93, 118, 144, 172
World War II, 10, 239–40

Young Algerians, 25, 62, 68, 218. *See also* Algeria
Young Senegalese, 62, 69–70, 79, 80, 85–86
Youssef, Mohammed ben (Mohammed V), 30, 245, 253
Youssef, Moulay, 6, 37, 247
Yusufiyya (mosque-university), 3

Zawiya, 211

IN THE FRANCE OVERSEAS SERIES

*Regeneration through Empire:
French Pronatalists and Colonial
Settlement in the Third Republic*
Margaret Cook Andersen

*To Hell and Back:
The Life of Samira Bellil*
Samira Bellil
Translated by Lucy R. McNair
Introduction by Alec G. Hargreaves

*Colonial Metropolis: The Urban
Grounds of Anti-Imperialism and
Feminism in Interwar Paris*
Jennifer Anne Boittin

*Paradise Destroyed: Catastrophe and
Citizenship in the French Caribbean*
Christopher M. Church

*The French Navy and the
Seven Years' War*
Jonathan R. Dull

I, Nadia, Wife of a Terrorist
Baya Gacemi

*Transnational Spaces and Identities
in the Francophone World*
Edited by Hafid Gafaïti, Patricia M.
E. Lorcin, and David G. Troyansky

*Contesting French West Africa: Battles
over Schools and the Colonial Order,
1900–1950*
Harry Gamble

*The French Army and Its African
Soldiers: The Years of Decolonization*
Ruth Ginio

*French Colonialism Unmasked: The
Vichy Years in French West Africa*
Ruth Ginio

*Bourdieu in Algeria: Colonial
Politics, Ethnographic Practices,
Theoretical Developments*
Edited and with an introduction by
Jane E. Goodman and Paul A. Silverstein

*Franco America in the Making:
The Creole Nation Within*
Jonathan K. Gosnell

*Endgame 1758: The Promise, the
Glory, and the Despair of
Louisbourg's Last Decade*
A. J. B. Johnston

*Colonial Suspects: Suspicion, Imperial
Rule, and Colonial Society in Interwar
French West Africa*
Kathleen Keller

French Mediterraneans:
Transnational and
Imperial Histories
Edited and with an introduction
by Patricia M. E. Lorcin and
Todd Shepard

The Cult of the Modern: Trans-
Mediterranean France and the
Construction of French Modernity
Gavin Murray-Miller

Cinema in an Age of Terror:
North Africa, Victimization,
and Colonial History
Michael F. O'Riley

Medical Imperialism in French North
Africa: Regenerating the Jewish
Community of Colonial Tunis
Richard C. Parks

Making the Voyageur World:
Travelers and Traders in the
North American Fur Trade
Carolyn Podruchny

A Workman Is Worthy of His Meat:
Food and Colonialism in Gabon
Jeremy Rich

The Moroccan Soul: French
Education, Colonial Ethnology,
and Muslim Resistance, 1912–1956
Spencer D. Segalla

Silence Is Death: The Life and
Work of Tahar Djaout
Julija Šukys

The French Colonial Mind,
Volume 1: Mental Maps of
Empire and Colonial Encounters
Edited and with an introduction by
Martin Thomas

The French Colonial Mind,
Volume 2: Violence, Military
Encounters, and Colonialism
Edited and with an introduction by
Martin Thomas

Beyond Papillon: The French
Overseas Penal Colonies, 1854–1952
Stephen A. Toth

Madah-Sartre: The Kidnapping, T
rial, and Conver(sat/s)ion of Jean-
Paul Sartre and Simone de Beauvoir
Written and translated by
Alek Baylee Toumi
With an introduction by
James D. Le Sueur

To order or obtain more information on these or other University of Nebraska Press titles, visit nebraskapress.unl.edu.

www.ingramcontent.com/pod-product-compliance
Lightning Source LLC
Chambersburg PA
CBHW021832220426
43663CB00005B/213